RUBBLE

THE SEARCH FOR A HAITIAN BOY

Sandra Marquez Stathis

LYONS PRESS
GUILFORD, CONNECTICUT
An imprint of Globe Pequot Press

Lyons Press is an imprint of Globe Pequot Press.

Some material from "Initiation to the Violence" and "Paradox Island" previously appeared in *Tropic* magazine and is re-published with permission of *The Miami Herald*.

All illustrations by Junior Louis Davilma

Text design: Sheryl P. Kober
Layout: Mary Ballachino
Project editor: Ellen Urban
Map: © Footprint Handbooks Ltd.; re-design by Melissa Baker © Morris Book Publishing, LLC

Library of Congress Cataloging-in-Publication Data is available on file.

ISBN 978-0-7627-7265-0

Printed in the United States of America

10 9 8 7 6 5 4 3 2 1

For Alexander Joaquin Stathis and
Christopher Junior Davilma.
May *Bondye* always shine his light upon your paths
and illuminate the wonders of this world.

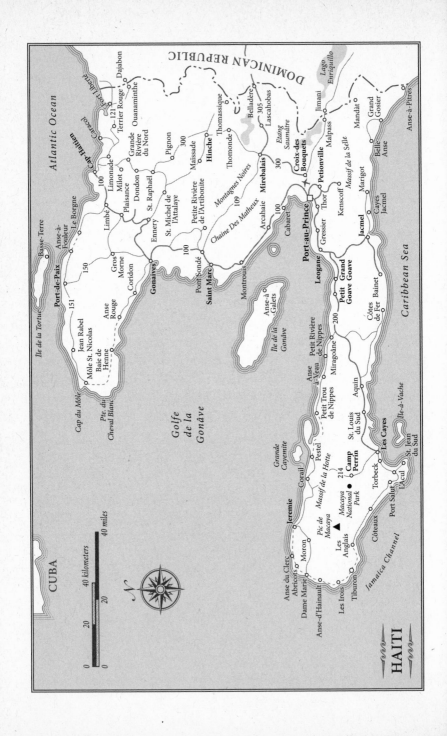

CONTENTS

Prologue. vii

PART I: JE (EYES)

CHAPTER 1: Meeting Junior. 2
CHAPTER 2: Becoming an Observer 7
CHAPTER 3: Initiation to the Violence 21
CHAPTER 4: Dark Days 32
CHAPTER 5: Democracy and the Almost Adoption 42
CHAPTER 6: Paradox Island. 52
CHAPTER 7: Breakfast at the Montana 63

Part II: Ké (Heart)

CHAPTER 8: Cathedral in the Sky. 70
CHAPTER 9: Return 76
CHAPTER 10: The "New" Haiti 83
CHAPTER 11: Finding Junior 94
CHAPTER 12: Reunion. 104
CHAPTER 13: Dimanche. 113
CHAPTER 14: Sunday Dinner 134
CHAPTER 15: Hotel Montana 139
CHAPTER 16: Junior's Journey 147
CHAPTER 17: Nature and Art 159
CHAPTER 18: Return II 172
CHAPTER 19: Zwazo 189
CHAPTER 20: Anniversary. 203
CHAPTER 21: The English Teacher 230
CHAPTER 22: New Beginning. 258
Acknowledgments 293
About the Author 294

He had seen everything, had experienced all emotions, from exaltation to despair, had been granted a vision into the great mystery, the secret places, the primeval days before the Flood. He had journeyed to the edge of the world and made his way back, exhausted but whole.

—STEPHEN MITCHELL,
GILGAMESH: A NEW ENGLISH VERSION

PROLOGUE

It goes on and on for as far as the eye can see. Rubble, a mass grave of final breaths and buried dreams. Rubble, a newly formed tundra of boulders, concrete slab, mangled metal rods, detritus of daily life, and cinder blocks returned to their natural state of cement ash. Rubble, a shifting archipelago forever altering the topography of land and memory.

I am navigating through the debris field that is Delmas, a major north-south artery dissecting Port-au-Prince, in my quest to find Junior Louis, a young homeless boy who was like a son to me when I lived and worked in Haiti during the 1990s. When I last saw Junior, ten years ago, he told me he was staying with an aunt in this crushed corridor of the capital. He would now be twenty-three years old.

The scorching heat is searing a fine layer of silt onto my skin and tightening my face like a mask as I sit in the passenger seat of a Nissan Pathfinder with a broken air-conditioner. It has been two months since the earthquake. I am clutching a photo of Junior and me from happier times. We are sitting on a porch swing on the veranda of the home where I once lived, basking in the shade of a mango tree. Now, I stare out into the sea of survivors trudging through the heat and rubble all around me, hoping to find a glimpse of Junior. There is just one question burning inside me. *Is Junior still alive?*

Accompanying me on my search is Pierre, a quick-witted and enigmatic television cameraman who moonlights as a guide and driver for foreign journalists and aid workers. Pierre attended a funeral early this morning for a young female relative who died from a poorly treated leg injury sustained during the quake. This leads us to discuss Haitian beliefs about death and the afterlife as we carve a zigzagging course through the capital in search of Junior. I know the basic assumption that after death Haitians believe souls travel to the bottom of the sea where they pass through a portal to their ancestral homeland of Guinea, in Africa, ground zero of the slave trade that launched them to Haiti. Without a proper burial, Pierre explains, it is feared that a soul will be trapped and unable to complete its final journey home. I think about all those souls vying for entry into the portal right now, and I worry that the improper burials at the capital's mass gravesite could clog the gateway to the afterlife.

I ask Pierre about the controversy surrounding the government's decision to dump hundreds of thousands of unidentified quake victims in the mass gravesite of Titanyen. Missing from the discussion in the United States, I say, is the terrible irony that this was the killing field of choice used by the military in the early 1990s to exterminate the country's grassroots democracy movement. Back then, the mere word "Titanyen" evoked the imagery of a slow and torturous death. How cruel to survive a military dictatorship, I think, only to have the subsequent democratic government bury you in the mass grave. I do my best to convey this thought in Creole.

Pierre's response reminds me that reality has many layers in Haiti. "When I was a boy, Titanyen had another meaning," says the father of two, now in his late forties. He speaks in a low, tinny voice that keeps me on the edge of my seat, goading me to catch his every word. Before its more modern association as a mass gravesite, he tells me, this was a place of spiritual rebirth. If someone was having financial or romantic woes, an *hougan*, or vodou priest, would bring them here and bathe them in the pungent spring waters of this desolate copper-mining hillside. Something about the sulfuric plunge bath would give them a new chance at life, he explains. I am somewhat comforted by this new imagery. Perhaps the souls who ended up here will find some peace after all. My thoughts immediately revert to Junior.

Throughout the day we have been trying to locate people who knew Junior—knowing that the powerful Haitian network of "telediol," or word of mouth, known as "mouth television" in Creole, will be far more resourceful than any database or search engine in pinpointing his fate. We've had mixed findings so far. Some people have told us they have not seen him since before the quake, an ominous sign. Others say he is alive and living in the hills above the capital. And one person told us he heard that Junior had died in the rubble.

Pierre has closely scrutinized my photograph of young Junior. He has not registered any hint of recognition. In fact, he shook his head remorsefully, his eyes never straying from the photo, and said he was certain he did not know Junior. And then, inexplicably and unpredictably following a round of inquiries with a group of young cell-phone repairmen on a busy street corner, he shouts: "I am certain Junior is alive!" I look at Pierre in bewilderment—and yet I know better than to dismiss his premonition. My four years living here taught me that Haiti is an exacting and unorthodox teacher. Together with her assistants Love, Fear, Beauty, Humor, and Death, she teaches you to see duality, embrace contradiction, and to surrender to pain and hardship in life. Because she saw that I was young and inexperienced when I first arrived on her soil, she sent a special young guide to help me learn these lessons. He was a seven-year-old homeless boy and his name was Junior Louis. And now, Haiti seemed to be leading me back to him once again.

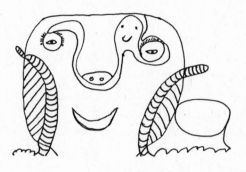

Part I: Je (Eyes)

. . . she grasped the idea that one could study culture, one's own or that of others, truly attending to it rather than using the stance of an observer as a way to dominate.

—Mary Catherine Bateson,
Composing a Life

CHAPTER 1

Meeting Junior

I first remember seeing him as I was stepping outside the glass doors of Public's supermarket in Petionville. He was there in the pack of homeless boys waiting for me to come out. His big brown eyes stood out in the bouquet of young faces. There was something gentle and wise in his gaze. I was drawn to him from the moment I saw him. And then the chaos began. The flock encircled me as I walked the one-block distance to my apartment after work, tugging at my bags and crying out in a frenzied cacophony, each boy pleading his case for "yon ti kob," some pocket change that would give him a chance to eat that day. I looked through the swirl of dust and tattered clothing and saw something that amazed me. The little orphan with the big brown eyes was not begging. He walked alongside the crowd, his arms reaching out, trying to keep the other boys from trampling me.

Junior Louis and I found each other. And from his earliest days he has always been trying to save *me*. This story is my attempt to finally assume my parental privilege and show him my gratitude.

During my first days in Port-au-Prince, I soon realized I needed to go to the supermarket each night. I was a twenty-four-year-old recent college grad and I was getting used to so much.

Coming home to purple-colored turkey slices in the fridge one night opened my eyes to the futility of stocking up on groceries in a country besieged by constant power outages. After a few dizzying outings, I came up with a plan. I decided that each night I would select a different child to be my porter, paying him a wage for the favor of helping me with my bags. Then I would pull two baguettes from my groceries and tear the bread into thick pieces, making sure each child had something to eat. The chaotic frenzy soon gave way to a playful ritual. The children knew they would each get a turn to help and I came to know them as individuals. I watched out for and cared about each Haitian child I saw living on the street. But Junior was the one with whom I shared an unspoken bond and understanding.

After several trips to the market, I noticed that Junior's tennis shoes were frayed. They looked like they were about to fall apart. One Saturday morning we went on our first outing together, a foray deep into the marché to buy new shoes. I held Junior's hand, as if he were my son, as we carved our way through the narrow streets. We were competing for space with crowded tap-tap buses, women carrying baskets of chickens on their heads, and vendors peddling everything from stalks of sugarcane to imported Chinese watches. Each time a fast-moving vehicle careened in our direction, Junior's arm instinctively shot out, pushing me deep into the fold and away from the hazards of street life. Once we were safely inside the pedestrian area of the market, we strolled past the market women with their neatly tended piles of avocados, soaps, and homemade charcoal—Junior politely greeting the women and exchanging pleasantries, seeming so proud to have me by his side. When at last we found the tennis shoe vendor and had settled on a bright new pair, I suggested we throw away the old ones. Junior looked at me as if I were proposing we throw away food or money. "I will give these to one of the boys who needs shoes," he said plainly. Walking back from the marché, Junior held my hand and clutched the old shoes with his other hand, intently focused until we came upon one of the homeless boys in the street and he tenderly offered his gift. We capped our outing that day with a visit to the ice-cream parlor on the street level of my apartment building. And this became one of our favorite outings: going shopping on Saturday mornings and sharing an ice-cream cone together, like mother and son.

It wasn't long before Junior told me he was sleeping underneath the stairwell of my apartment. Ever the conscientious little boy, he had gotten permission to do so from the building's night watchman. This posed a terrible moral dilemma for me. I agonized over how it was possible that I was in Haiti as a human rights observer and yet I was unable to protect a child who needed my help. Our human rights mission, a joint undertaking of the Organization of American States and the United Nations, had strict rules intended to create a delicate firewall and shield our unarmed personnel from attack by the Haitian military. It had been drilled into us during our training that we could not provide safe haven to anyone. In fact, we were even forbidden from transporting Haitians, unless they were staff, in our cars. This dilemma would peak for me much later on when I would be jolted awake one night to the sound of machine-gun fire on the street below my bedroom window, my heart pounding, knowing that Junior was steps away from this deadly fire.

But I am getting ahead of my story.

One day, as I was still getting to know Junior, I invited him upstairs to my apartment for lunch. I felt as if I was crossing an invisible line by having him enter my home, but the thought that returned was, *He is a child,* and I squelched any concerns I had about possibly breaking a fuzzy rule.

As I prepared a sandwich in the kitchen, Junior sat in my living room surrounded by books, stationery, and pens. When I stepped back into the room, I was startled to see him fully concentrating on writing his name over and over again on some blank postcards on the coffee table. I knew he attended school with the help of a UNICEF program, but it hadn't occurred to me that he didn't have an outlet to express himself. This launched a new tradition: I began buying him notebooks, sketchbooks, pens, and colored pencils—and he became a regular visitor to my home. In no time I realized he had an innate artistic ability. Several members of the mission were dismayed to learn I was allowing a homeless child to come into my home. But soon, they too began to befriend Junior and he developed an impressive network of friends.

Three years after my arrival in Haiti, my bond with Junior was as intricate as seagrass on the ocean floor. I still remember the potted plant he brought me for Mother's Day, my first time being honored as a mom. I felt an overriding desire to adopt him. By then, democracy had been restored and with the euphoric taste of freedom, the old "rules" about not providing safe haven had become obsolete. I was now engaged to be married to an Argentine observer, Marcelo Garcia. But my desire to adopt Junior threatened to uproot my relationship even before I was married. Although Marcelo admired Junior and had a nice camaraderie with him, at age twenty-five he didn't feel ready to become a father, and he worried that Junior's years on the streets might have consequences we could not anticipate. I argued that we would do our best for Junior and at least we would provide him with a loving home. My dream was eventually to return to the United States with him and give him a chance at a college education. After much negotiation, we settled on a compromise. Junior could move his meager belongings into our home and he would be allowed to sleep at our home for up to a week at a time. After that, he would have to go to someone else's house.

At first the arrangement seemed to work. International aid workers from a host of organizations followed our lead. But with time I wondered if we were doing Junior more harm than good. At the end of the day, he was still a homeless boy and it was left to him to straddle the steep precipice between wealth and poverty.

I left Haiti in November 1996 to begin a new life in South Florida as a newlywed and a reporter for the *Miami Herald*. I felt guilty and tormented about agreeing not to adopt Junior, and I settled this moral dilemma by detaching emotionally. Several of my colleagues remained in Haiti and I knew that there would be a support network that would remain in place for Junior. I would stay connected to my network, and I knew I would be able to get periodic updates on how he was doing. I also knew that our network would be a lifeline by which Junior could reach me if ever he was in trouble. This was before the age of widespread Internet access and cell phones in Haiti. I felt this was the best I could do. I had lived overseas in Saudi Arabia for four years in my youth, and I remembered the pillar of sadness I felt before moving back to California, when I contemplated that I would probably never again see most of the friends and classmates with whom I had attended middle school and junior high. I learned then the lesson of letting go.

Although I left Haiti, I never forgot Junior.

CHAPTER 2

Becoming an Observer

I got the job almost on a dare. It was a dreary January day in Washington, D.C., and I was staring at the view of the parking lot from my reporter's desk at a small weekly newsletter chronicling the U.S. Latino community, where cockroaches sometimes made unwelcome appearances from the woodwork. The phone rang and it was my friend Anni on the line. We were part of a network of twenty-something recent college grads working our first jobs and internships in the nation's capital. It was January 1993, in the giddy euphoria as the Clinton administration was first coming to office. As this was in the days before Facebook, our network would check in by phone several afternoons a week to see what was going on around town. Most of us were working in public policy circles and we could collectively pinpoint receptions taking place almost any night of the week. This gave us a chance to network—and more important, to have access to free food and drinks. On this night we would be attending a gathering at the Carnegie Endowment for International Peace, where my longtime friend Paula worked as an intern and a new report on Latin America was to be unveiled. Anni, who was completing an internship at the Organization of American States (OAS), was calling with a proposition. "I have the perfect job for us," she announced enticingly.

Anni and I had developed a bond based on our mutual love of writing and running and our shared heritage. Her parents were from Ecuador; mine were from neighboring Colombia. And yet, I was wary of her plan even before she revealed the details. Anni had just returned from a stint as an OAS electoral observer in Peru's rebel-threatened elections—a gig I had feared would be doomed to violence. The international community had pressured President Fujimori to stage the balloting, following his suspension of parliament months earlier. The country's Maoist Shining Path rebels responded by vowing to thwart the election. Anni had been assigned to monitor voting in the rebel-held "zona roja" or *red zone,* being flown in by helicopter to remote villages, and had managed to emerge unscathed. Luckily, the bomb that went off at her Lima hotel did not harm anyone. Even if it was good politics on the part of the international community to pressure for the election, I had thought it too dangerous to be a foot soldier for democracy. And yet, I had admired her pioneering spirit. After tallying the ballots, Anni traveled to the Incan ruins of Machu Picchu and Cuzco, returning to Washington with a suitcase full of herbal remedies from the Amazon. I sensed she was gearing up for more adventure. "What is it this time?" I asked hesitantly.

The OAS was laying the foundation for a new human rights mission to Haiti. It would be the first of its kind. As the world's oldest regional organization, the OAS, headquartered in Washington, D.C., had been dismissed by some as a country club for retired Latin American diplomats willing to turn a blind eye to illegal power grabs and corrupt governments. But change was coming. The organization was in the midst of revitalizing its image. A key element in its improved public persona was a newly minted doctrine declaring the organization would no longer tolerate government overthrows in the American hemisphere. With President Jean-Bertrand Aristide's violent ouster, in which the military hunted down and murdered an estimated three thousand of his supporters, Haiti posed the first test case to this new policy.

The OAS responded by slapping an economic embargo on the military junta in power and approving Aristide's request to deploy a human rights observer team to document what was happening on the ground in Haiti—to monitor conditions for his eventual return to power. For this ambitious enterprise, the OAS would team up with a seasoned partner: the United Nations. The two organizations would work together under a single leadership structure, the first joint operation of its kind.

"The OAS and the UN will each recruit one hundred observers," Anni informed me. She laid out the job requirements as she knew them: You had to have a college degree, speak French, and have some past international experience. It sounded like an incredible opportunity, perhaps even too good to be true. And yet, I tried not to be swayed by the adrenaline-inducing details. My dream was to go into journalism and one day to become a foreign correspondent. I had just a couple of months left to complete my yearlong reporting internship, after which I hoped to get hired by a daily newspaper. I had heard the admonishments of many who warned how hard it was to break into the field. In fact, the founder of the small, family-owned newsletter where I worked, who took credit for launching an entire cadre of Latino journalists to some of the nation's most vaunted newsrooms through his apprentice program, had made me promise I would not follow the example of one previous fellow intern who had "squandered" her opportunity by accepting a job in corporate communications. From what I could tell, journalism wasn't like other professions. It was more like going into the priesthood. Journalists seemed to have a "holier than thou" status, peering down on their subjects and disapproving of would-be scribes distracted by worldly pursuits, such as commerce, public relations, or activism. I wasn't sure if going to Haiti would help or hurt my chances of getting closer to my dream. I tried to protect that elusive and temperamental bubble from escaping my grasp by pretending not to be interested in the opportunity. "Don't even try to tempt me," I said to Anni, rather unconvincingly.

Anni had saved two important considerations for last. "The contracts are for only six months. And the salary is $6,000 a month. You can do anything you want to after that." The thought of AIDS and paramilitary thugs immediately flashed through my head. I wondered what good it would do to earn 6K a month if you couldn't live long enough to spend it. We agreed that we would take up the discussion with Paula that evening over drinks, courtesy of the Carnegie Endowment.

A few hours later, we were sitting in an intimate audience of foreign policy luminaries and journalists. It felt as if we had crashed a party at a think tank—and the Ivory Tower police weren't yet on to us. I heard a familiar voice posing a question and I looked up to realize it was longtime National Public Radio commentator Daniel Schorr. Hearing his voice and careful reflection helped me distill my thoughts. The very reason I was drawn to journalism was to follow current events as they happened. To bear witness to history with my own eyes. It occurred to me that it was worth forging my own path to my dream, even if it wasn't necessarily the safe or prescribed course. I was starting to see how living through a political crisis in Haiti as a novice journalist could be a rare opportunity. This was an assignment I would otherwise have to wait years to get—and meanwhile, I would get a behind-the-scenes look at how international organizations like the UN and the OAS mediated a crisis.

By the time Anni, Paula, and I gathered over gin and tonics, I was pretty certain I would apply for the Haiti mission. But I was keen to hear Paula's opinion. Paula was the first friend I made when my family moved to Irvine, California, following our return from Saudi Arabia. We forged a connection as two teenage transplants settling in Southern California by way of the Middle East. Paula was born in Iran to Armenian parents. She moved to Southern California in junior high, following time spent in Spain. We studied French together in high school and carpooled to the University of California, Irvine, together where we were both political science majors. During our junior year of college, I transferred to UC Berkeley and she spent a year abroad in France. After graduating, we both landed our internships in Washington, D.C., on the same day and we had joked that the next time either of us made a career move we would first discuss it. Now it was time for that talk. Paula was a good appraiser who could step back and evaluate a situation with a clear and critical eye. I knew I could trust her take on the Haiti mission. Anni and I still hadn't had a chance to discuss any of the details with her. She listened carefully now, not revealing her opinion with her expression. "What if the army turns on General Cedras and stages another coup?" she asked. Anni and I didn't have an answer for her question. Perhaps it was youthful optimism, the effects of a sweet cocktail on empty stomachs, or a chance to connect our international backgrounds with our college degrees and experience an adventure in the world. But in that moment we all agreed that the OAS wouldn't deploy an observer mission without some kind of security plan. And we all three agreed to apply. Within two months of that toast, Anni, Paula, and I were all living in Haiti.

When I arrived at the stately OAS headquarters on the day of my job interview, a group of us were called into a room together. I assumed we would be asked to fill out paperwork. Instead, the elegant Argentine chief of staff, whom I had earlier seen enter the building wearing a fur coat, went around the table and asked each of us if we were prepared to leave for Haiti that Sunday. I asked to see a copy of the job description of an observer. "It hasn't been written yet," she said.

⚬━━⬥━━⚬

As our group gathered in the VIP lounge at the Port-au-Prince airport, where military officials inspected our newly printed OAS passports, I exchanged my first words with an Argentine observer I had seen on the plane. Marcelo Garcia Pojmaevich was of Spanish and Croatian heritage. He was dashing and handsome and had a splash of salt and pepper in his brown hair that added some depth and a hint of knowingness to his twenty-three years. He had graduated from university in Buenos Aires with a degree in international relations and had been working as an aide to a member of the chamber of deputies who held a seat on the foreign relations committee. I immediately sized him up as someone who lived by his wits and I was charmed by him. We exchanged brief introductions and looked around, acknowledging that we were about to enter a whole new world.

Outside, we boarded the bus that would take us into town and I got my first chance to survey the landscape. The streets looked dusty and chaotic, with no obvious traffic lanes. Cows shared the road with brightly colored tap-tap buses. People walked on the side of the road, and market vendors carried bundles of merchandise on their heads. The bus dropped us off at the Hotel El Rancho in Petionville, which soon revealed itself to be a curious choice of accommodation for a human rights observer team. The hotel was decorated in an ornate, over-the-top style mirroring the excesses of the Duvalier family. And it had a casino that attracted a thuggish crowd at night. From the moment our group first checked in, it was apparent the front desk staff was apprehensive about our presence. I wondered if this was how most Haitians would perceive us—or if this was simply the brush-off we could anticipate from those in the elite class who had supported the military coup.

Our observer group was composed of almost twenty people, primarily recent grads from college and graduate school culled from the United States, Latin America, and the Caribbean island of St. Lucia. We joined a core team already on the ground that included human rights experts, lawyers, diplomats, former Peace Corps volunteers, and teachers. In the months to come, the human rights mission, otherwise known as the International Civilian Mission, or MICIVIH (pronounced Mee-See-Vee) for its French acronym, would take on a truly international identity as UN colleagues began to arrive from around the globe.

On that first night, some of the members of our newly arrived team ventured out for dinner, led by one of our more seasoned colleagues. We were traveling on foot to a nearby restaurant housed on the grounds of an art gallery. As we stepped away from the hotel, we were completely engulfed in darkness and had to feel our way in the dark. I was afraid I might fall into a pothole. I kept waiting to see if our experienced colleague was going to suggest we turn back, or if he commented that this was an unusual situation. Apparently it was not. At that moment I knew I was in a very different reality—and I was going to have to learn how to find my way in the shadows.

During the next three weeks, we spent our days at the Hotel Montana, a one-time family home perched high on a hill with sweeping views of the capital and the site of mission headquarters. Each day, we listened to lectures, learning about Haiti's history, culture, and legal system. After lunch, we had a daily Creole lesson. And some afternoons, we role played, enacting textbook interactions with human rights victims who would be coming to see us at our offices around the country.

Our teacher on the Haitian constitution was a visionary lawyer named Guy Malary. When he spoke, it was like he could see something that was invisible to others. Like Harold with the Purple Crayon, he helped me recognize that Haiti's highest law could provide a framework for shelter and protection, even though it was still only make-believe.

Malary would soon be appointed Haiti's justice minister, charged with overseeing the separation of the police from the army and helping to lay the groundwork for President Aristide's return to office. I noticed how his wife waited for him after class and they held hands together as they walked through the hotel lobby.

By now, Marcelo and I had started dating tentatively. The tentative part was based on the fact that he had a girlfriend back in Argentina whom he referred to as his "fiancée." He gave me an early insight into his impassioned character when he looked me in the eye and told me he wasn't dating anyone else. His fiancée was back in Argentina and he wasn't seeing her because he was in Haiti. I held my ground on this one and told him he was going to have to choose. I also discovered his caring side. He was the most down-to-earth Argentine I had ever met. He was a complete natural with no airs or pretense, something I would later attribute to his experience of growing up on an apple farm. And he had an incredible knack for making things with his hands. He once ingeniously wired a VCR to a car battery so we could watch a movie during a blackout.

Our dating began innocently enough, after a game of footsie during Creole class at the Montana. Marcelo was one of the people who picked up Creole effortlessly; the idiomatic expressions just rolled off his lips and he would laugh a deep-bellied laugh at the cleverness of the language. My experience with learning Creole was completely different. After a week of classes, it was clear some observers were getting it and some were not. I knew I was in trouble when I kept stumbling on "Ki jan ou ye?" one of the most basic greetings in Creole. This frustrated me. I liked to think I had a knack for languages. The timing of the class wasn't helping my cause. I had to struggle to keep my eyelids open during the two-hour session that began immediately after our lunch break. I soon grew distracted during the vocabulary drills as I felt my body drooping into digestion mode in the afternoon heat. It didn't help that the instructor's natural, conversation-based teaching method did not allow for writing phrases on the blackboard. I wanted to see how the words looked. I had gleaned from a local Creole newspaper that the clunky French word for water, *de l'eau,* was reduced to its core essence, *dlo,* in Creole. And the

French word for church, *l'eglise,* was made simpler by *legliz.* I soon realized another factor was also inhibiting my progress. I had to overcome my own resistance to the language. I was afraid that by forming phrases in Creole I would somehow permanently mutate my French and lay waste to years of careful study. Once I was left to fend for myself, I realized how mistaken my thinking had been.

At the end of the three-week training period, each observer received a formal letter detailing his or her base assignment. Word soon got around that the seaside colonial towns of Jacmel and Cap Haitian offered a picturesque work setting. Hinche, a landlocked rural town in the center of the country dominated by the notorious Colonel Zed, was a dreaded destination, where electricity, telephones, and running water were virtually unavailable. Gonaives, a drab port city renowned for its political activism, was dubbed the mosquito capital of the world. I didn't know what to expect. I was tempted to step forward and request a tough posting. We had all heard the horrors about the human rights situation in the country and I wanted to see for myself what was happening. In the end, I decided to wait quietly and see what my fate delivered. The assignment letters arrived one day before lunch. Our team ripped them open in nervous anticipation. Anni was elated. She was on her way to Jacmel, a town with a rich cultural tradition and historic architecture, where Latin American independence hero Simón Bolívar found haven and support for his quest to liberate Venezuela from Spain. Marcelo was on his way to Gonaives, where Paula had arrived about a month earlier. My letter said I was being deployed to Port-au-Prince. The news required a slight mental adjustment. Besides the mission directors and administrative staff at the Hotel Montana, I hadn't realized there was an actual observer team assigned to the capital. Port-au-Prince, the site of military headquarters, was the most populated part of the country. Much of the terror campaign was being launched from its corridors. It would soon make sense why we had a team of observers stationed there.

Once I got to the base, though, I realized that no matter how thorough our training, nothing could have prepared us for what awaited us. Each day, frightened and worn-out-looking faces came to our office, located in a former language institute in the busy Bois Verna section of the capital. People took the risk of coming to our office to report abuses committed against themselves or a family member. There were accounts of arbitrary arrests, beatings by soldiers, disappearances, relatives killed or missing since the coup, and a lot of displaced persons. Nearly everyone we interviewed told us they were "an mawonaj," which I deciphered into French as "en marronage," or *in hiding*. It was a complicated and somewhat abstract concept. The term—and state of mind—was a holdover from the country's violent slave history. Runaway slaves or "maroons" were subject to the harshest of penalties in the French colony of St. Domingue. Colonial-era maroons could face such severe punishment as castration or being burnt alive. The *marrons* I encountered in our office wore no disguise and walked around in broad daylight. Some went into hiding after an armed attaché, or paramilitary, gave them a dirty look. Others after having been tortured in prison.

The violence was so widespread that it was easy to see how so many people could feel targeted. It didn't take much to end up in the military's line of fire. Anyone perceived to be a supporter of the exiled president—either because they campaigned for Aristide; kept a photograph of him in their wallet or home;

or had the misfortune of being among the poorest of the poor, making them a potential beneficiary of Aristide's campaign to lift people from misery to poverty—was at risk of being arrested, tortured, or killed. Conversely, we observers existed in an orb of a false sense of protection. So absolute was the military's power that there was virtually no common crime at this time. Soldiers needed direct orders from a superior to kill someone—or so we convinced ourselves. It didn't seem to be in the army's interest to provoke the ire of the international community. We felt shielded from the bullets.

My first interview was a painfully drawn-out experience, made almost unbearable by my infantile Creole ability. After a series of circular questions and answers, I finally understood that the man sitting before me had fled his home and plot of rice in the countryside after a paramilitary told him he would have him arrested. I knew that the threat of an illegal arrest was not the most serious of human rights abuses on our checklist; certainly it was not on par with EJE, or extrajudicial execution. But nonetheless, here was a man who was a refugee in his own country and he had no money or place to go. Surely there must be something we could do to help him. By some form of divine intervention, I managed to reach Colin Granderson, the head of our mission, via the decrepit phone system at his office at mission headquarters. I explained the situation to him. Colin was a skilled diplomat and meticulous planner who possessed an excellent sense of brinks-manship and a warm human side. He had worked as an English teacher in West Africa early in his career, before beginning his ascent up the ranks of Trinidad and Tobago's foreign service. He relied on that schoolmaster instinct now, bringing me back in check. Certainly, I had read over the mission's legal mandate during our training course and remembered that we were not able to protect anyone. "Yes, of course," I replied. But that was training. This was reality, I thought. I felt both disappointed and embarrassed. We had the banners of both the OAS and the UN outside our office. People came to us seeking some form of help. Couldn't the international community do more than this? And yet, I also suddenly felt quite naïve. "We cannot do anything to help him. Just write down what he tells you and ask him to come back if anything changes." Colin did not make any effort to soften the blow. He needed me to understand.

From the moment I first began to imagine myself becoming an observer, there was no question in my mind that I would be part of a safety net to help rescue people who were in danger. Even if that was not to be my primary duty, I imagined that was the underlying objective of our presence. Letting go of that ideal was painful. Our reports would be the basis for the UN General Assembly Situation Reports on Haiti, which would inform the world community of the atrocities taking place. In this regard, it was crucial to mission leadership that we not be seen as a fount of money, food, or other material aid to victims, as this could motivate some to tell tall tales and jeopardize the accuracy of our reports. In very serious cases, our mission did intervene to make recommendations for some persecuted individuals to receive asylum in the United States and Canada. And a medical unit was added to treat injuries that victims suffered at the hands of the military. But it would take a while before this big picture view would become clear to me.

Being confronted by the desperate pleas of Haitians fearing for their lives and having the Creole ability of a five-year-old was stressful. I imagined how I would feel if I lived in a country under a military dictatorship and I reported my persecution to a human rights observer who spoke English as poorly as I spoke Creole. That weekend I met Paula, Marcelo, and some other colleagues at a beach resort halfway between Gonaives and the capital to unwind. Paula and I spent the better half of an afternoon floating on a yellow raft tethered out at sea, staring at the expansive sky and sharing stories from the trenches. Those getaways—and the deep ties that forged our mission into a true family—became a critical way to decompress and were how we persevered.

CHAPTER 3

Initiation to the Violence

One afternoon I was driving with a group of colleagues in the late afternoon sunlight when I looked up and noticed the dazzling beauty of the flamboyant tree, with its bursting red blooms. I was transported by the vibrant energy and life force of this tree, when I shifted my gaze onto another unexpected sight. A procession was moving toward us in a snakelike formation. At first glance I mistook it for a raucous carnival celebration, or *ra-ra*. But something was amiss. At the head of the crowd, a man with a long rifle was parading a bruised and battered man through the streets in his underpants. The National Palace stood in the foreground. Our driver stopped in the middle of the road as we watched the unraveling situation. The victim's crimson face, stained with fresh blood, pricked with dread as his captor, clad in blue jeans and black army boots, hauled him by his bound wrists. Each time the man's lagging body fell out of sync, the gunman gave him a sharp poke with the butt of his rifle. The crowd of onlookers registered each blow as they shimmied behind in dutiful formation. It was an utterly surreal sight, at once violent and celebratory.

The armed man clutched his prisoner and bobbed his head around spastically, glaring at the crowd to make sure no one interfered. The four of us in the car hesitated. We had been on the job for about a month and we were uncertain of how to proceed.

As if on cue, Guy Malary, who had instructed us on the Haitian constitution, pulled up in his white BMW. He got out of his car and ran over to our vehicle.

"Go right now and ask the attaché where he is taking the prisoner. Ask for his name and the name of the detainee. Nothing else. Do not challenge him."

We did as instructed and reported back to Malary. "The prisoner is being taken to the fire department," we reported, perplexed by this finding.

"Follow him there," he advised.

Malary joined us in our vigil outside this unlikely detention center. His courage was not lost on any of us. The Haitian military barely tolerated the presence of our human rights mission. Haitian whistleblowers had none of our protections and were subject to much greater risks, including torture, imprisonment, and sometimes death.

Our long wait outside the fire department was just beginning. The captain in charge had gone home, we were told, and it would be impossible to obtain any information until the following morning. Malary went home once it started to get dark. The rest of us were soon embroiled in debate. I was tired and hungry and thought it futile to wait outside in the dark, as the soldiers inside were completely ignoring us. Elio, an Uruguayan observer who formerly worked for Amnesty International in London, made the case in favor of staying. The debate went on for a while—and just as we were about to leave, a man in uniform came out and told us the fire captain, whom we had been told was not there, was now ready to meet with us.

The soldier led us to a dimly lit back room where we found the captain seated at his desk. I was expecting a beastly tyrant, but the captain surprised me with his neat and well-mannered demeanor. "Please have a seat," he said in crisp French. "How may I be of service?"

We described the scene we witnessed outside the palace and asked if he could explain what had happened.

The gunman we saw on the road was a soldier who had just been released from prison, the captain explained. He had been jailed several months for losing his weapon. When he was released, the soldier immediately went to confront the person he suspected of stealing his gun. "After the soldier confronted the man, an angry crowd formed and began to attack the suspect," the captain said. "The soldier had to lead him back to the station in order to protect him. The man is now a suspect in the case of the stolen weapon."

The captain's telling of events had Kafkaesque embellishments, delivered with a reasonable and civilized sensibility. I felt my brain being twisted and I understood how reality could become warped in a country without basic democratic protections. Elio and I exchanged a subtle glance, signaling our disbelief. The crowd had seemed more curious than angry. The soldier was the only one who acted violently and vengefully.

We proceeded cautiously, questioning the legality of the arrest. Was there a warrant? What evidence was there against the man? Had he received medical attention for his injuries? The fire department was not a legal detention center, we pleaded. The man would need to be transferred and formally charged within forty-eight hours, as called for by the Haitian constitution. We asked to see the prisoner. The captain granted our request. About fifteen minutes later, a soldier led the prisoner into the office. The man's injuries had been cleaned up and he was now dressed in a clean pair of shorts and a tank top. I was relieved to see he was still standing and he was no longer bleeding. The man kept his gaze firmly fixed on the floor. He seemed scared. We asked his name and address and asked him if he needed medical attention. "Wi," *Yes,* he mumbled quietly. Our short discussion did not permit us to find out his side of the story, but we were satisfied that he could still walk and talk, despite his injuries, and we hoped our brief intervention would prevent the soldiers from beating him any more. The captain agreed to transfer the prisoner to the police station the next morning, and we let him know we would follow the case.

It was 10:00 p.m. when we returned to our rooms at the Hotel Kinam, where a group of observers were now living. I was exhausted, but elated that we were able to make a difference. As I fell asleep, I remembered the explosive beauty of the flamboyant tree that captured my imagination just as we stumbled upon the macabre procession that afternoon. It was the first time I noticed the singular grace of this tree, and from then on, it would remain branded in my mind as a symbol of the beauty and pathos of Haiti.

⚬━━◆━━⚬

Given all the fear and chaos, it was nice to have a bond with a special young boy who had magically managed to survive in this environment and emerge with a kind heart. I first met Junior about three months after my arrival, when I moved into an apartment at the corner of Rue Gregoire and Rue Darguin in Petionville, and those constant power outages sent me foraging for groceries each night. During those first months, Junior was the little boy I looked for whenever I headed out to do my errands or set out on foot to go and explore my new surroundings. As soon as we found each other, we would walk together, sometimes holding hands, and through our simple conversations he helped teach me Creole. Our visits usually ended by sharing a snack and a cold drink on the street— sometimes a piece of warm *pain epice,* or spice bread, a banana, or a refreshing ice-cream cone—and I always made sure to give him pocket money, so he could buy a plate of warm food from the street vendors. I also made a point of asking Junior where he was sleeping, hoping he was out of harm's way. One day he surprised me, smiling somewhat sheepishly and telling me he was sleeping "anba," or *underneath,* my apartment. I didn't understand what he meant. He explained that he was sleeping under the stairwell that led to the building's front entrance. "M senti pi pre ou," *I feel closer to you,* he said. He must have recognized the look of shock on my face, because he quickly told me not to worry, he had gotten permission to do so from Inor, the building's guardian. Before that moment, Junior had been one of Haiti's many homeless children, with whom I shared a special bond. Now suddenly, he was my responsibility. I felt terrible anguish that I would not be able to protect him.

The situation in the country was starting to heat up as the groundwork was being laid for President Aristide's return to the country through the Governor's Island Accord, which was being brokered on the island located off lower Manhattan. The agreement called for the head of Haiti's army, Lieutenant General Raoul

Cedras, to step down, for Aristide to return to power, for the military and police force to be separated, and for amnesty to be granted to the coup leaders.

It all sounded promising, but there was still much to be negotiated on the ground. We started seeing dead bodies left on the side of the road on our way into the office in the morning, as if the military was displaying its victims like bargaining chips. By age twenty-four, I had never seen a dead body before. Whenever we happened upon a victim, we would immediately pull over, get out of the car, and do what we could to identify the person and try to determine the cause of death. A bullet wound was usually visible at the temple or forehead. At first, I would discreetly avoid looking at the victim's face. Instead, I would fix my gaze on the feet. I did this out of respect. By staring at the victim's final pained expression, I felt I was somehow perpetuating his or her torture, participating in this indignity. Eventually, I forced myself to look death in the face, to fully confront the terror gripping the country.

Although I worked in the Port-au-Prince base, I was assigned to monitor the towns of Leogane and Petit Goave for human rights abuses. I divided my time between the capital and the countryside. It was an incredible education and I soon fell in love with the timelessness and pastoral beauty of Haiti's provincial towns.

I developed a fierce loyalty to these two communities, which had quite different characters. Leogane was a thriving town with period architecture dating back to the French colony, skilled tradesmen, and a relatively prosperous local economy bolstered by the emerald-green fields of sugarcane, a cash crop cultivated to produce the region's signature *clairin,* or moonshine.

Every week, I checked in with members of the local journalist association, a group of lanky young men who rode around town on bicycles with notebooks in their back pockets and phoned in reports to radio stations in the capital. I admired their dedication and detailed reporting on the antics of the military in town—and I often found myself wondering how they pulled off their work. The Port-au-Prince stations couldn't have been paying them much, if anything at all. These skinny journalists were true masters of the medium. Every week I would seek them out, drawn to their spark. I aspired to be a journalist—and here were these reporters literally putting their lives on the line to report what was happening in their town. It was an inspiring example that would stay with me.

Also on these visits, our team would call upon the democratically elected mayor of the town, who had been pushed aside by the military. A farmer who lived in a small wooden house located off the main road into town, he didn't have much to offer, but he always chopped a coconut or a stalk of sugarcane from his garden to welcome us. With his machete, he would slice off the top of the hard fruit and prepare the cane stalks. We would sit on a fallen tree trunk in his front yard, sipping the tropical juice and talk about the situation in town. He was a man of deep intelligence and I always looked forward to our visits.

Petit Goave had the same style of vintage architecture, but it had fresher paint—and an overall tougher veneer. Located about two hours west of the capital, the town housed a bustling port and a thuggish bureaucracy that controlled profits from the contraband that flowed into town. One of the most notable buildings, the Relais de l'Empereur hotel, was an homage to local icon Faustin Soulouque, a freed slave turned army general who in 1849 declared himself emperor of Haiti. Soulouque and his bride were crowned in a grand coronation ceremony in Port-au-Prince modeled after the accession of Napoleon Bonaparte. He was later exiled to Jamaica and eventually returned to Petit Goave, where he died at his home. The Relais de l'Empereur hotel, a once lavish and hedonistic retreat complete with roaming pet leopard cubs, was part of Haiti's sexual tourism circuit in the 1970s, attracting American celebrities and later Baby Doc Duvalier and his wife Michele Bennett. By the time our team arrived in town, the hotel was a shuttered relic overseen by a dutiful custodian who allowed visitors to read the faded *Paris Match* and *Vogue* magazine clips on the wall, describing the hotel's glory days. Like a haunted house, the hotel's shadowy silhouette lorded over the town's main street, hinting at Petit Goave's lawless and ruthless power structure. Democracy activists in this town had to tread very carefully, not least because of the notorious military chief in town, known simply as "Ti Rach," or *Little Ax*.

On one visit, I had gone with two colleagues to the local hospital in Petit Goave to follow up on a report that a teenage boy, the son of a pair of democracy activists, had been brutally attacked. A man who operated a Catholic charity in town had rescued the boy from the marché, where he had been dumped and left for dead. Our contact ran a feeding program for the town's neglected and diseased prison population, giving him unique access to jailed activists. He bravely reported on their plight, until he too was brutally beaten and jailed. He was later released and went into hiding, but not before letting us know that the boy he had rescued bore the marks of an ax or machete wound to his forehead, the calling card of Ti Rach.

We found the boy, Felix Esperance, whose last name meant "Hope," in a nearly vegetative state. He was lying on a seedy mattress in an outdoor patio at the back of the hospital, a festering wound crowning the top of his scalp. Hospital staff told us the boy had not spoken in weeks and that no one ever came to visit him. We knew from our contact that the boy's parents had either been killed or were in hiding, and Felix's injuries had occurred in prison as punishment for his parents' activism. This was part of the military's practice of arresting family members if their intended target could not be found. I crouched down on the floor and spoke quietly to Felix. Standing there close to him, I thought his punishment was worse than death. I told him we were there to help him. I could tell by his eyes that he understood, and it occurred to me that his lack of speech wasn't necessarily from a brain injury, but could also be the effect of fear, trauma, and abandonment. I leaned in and asked him if Ti Rach had done this to him. He nodded yes. That night, I was so troubled that someone could intentionally harm a child in such a way, that I couldn't even bring myself to talk to my roommate, Vivian, a genial observer from Argentina who worked at mission head-quarters and whose conversation and insights I normally relished in the evenings. The pain this wounded child stirred in me was just too deep.

Our team made several more visits to see Felix until one day he simply vanished. The hospital staff had no explanation for his whereabouts. We went straight to the military headquarters and asked to speak with Ti Rach. I didn't try to be diplomatic. I told him Felix had gone missing and that we had reports he had personally scalped the child with his ax. "You should be very careful when you come to Petit Goave," Ti Rach told me. "People here drive very dangerously." This confrontation unsettled me, but what truly gnawed at me was the fear that our intervention in Felix's case may have placed him in greater harm.

On September 11, 1993, armed gunmen dragged Haitian busi-
nessman Antoine Izmery, a prominent member of Haiti's Middle
Eastern merchant class, from a church pew and assassinated him
in broad daylight in the presence of observers from our human
rights mission. Izmery, who was of Palestinian descent, had been
carefully testing the military's commitment to Aristide's return
by posting photos of the exiled president in public places. I had
greeted Izmery on the eve of his death, when he came to our
office to carefully review plans to mobilize an observer team to
a memorial mass and photo-posting campaign he was organizing the next day. I was not Izmery's primary point of contact in
the bureau, but I captured glimpses of him as he came and went
for appointments. He struck me as a slightly disheveled professor
type who was ingeniously crafting a Gandhi-like movement of
nonviolent change. Later, I came to know one of his nieces—a
gentle and wise artist who was also my aerobics instructor. The
military's decision to execute Izmery was a devastating blow to
our observer mission, shattering morale and sending a clear signal that the military had no intention of ceding power. We understood our human rights mission would not be able to protect
anyone.

Days later, Elio and I were heading out to the countryside,
where he had been named coordinator, and I his deputy, to open
a satellite office in Petit Goave. As we reached the outskirts of the
capital, we received a radio call asking us to turn around due to
security concerns. As we entered the office, the secretary came
running to us, fear visible in her eyes. What was the shooting
she had just heard outside? It had sounded like machine-gun fire,

she said. Elio and I shook our heads. We hadn't heard anything. We had been driving with the windows rolled up and the air-conditioner blasting. Frustrated by all the starts and stops in trying to open our new base, a project that had been stalled over the course of several weeks, we decided to head to lunch at the Hotel Montana. The outdoor Panorama restaurant was filled with its usual crowd of power brokers. We took a table next to UN negotiator Dante Caputo and we eyed CNN correspondent Jim Clancy at a table across from us. I was just biting into my chicken and pineapple salad when Caputo's bodyguard made a beeline toward his boss and leaned in to deliver his message: "Ils ont tué Monsieur Malary." Elio and I stared at each other speechless. Guy Malary, the brave new justice minister who had held vigil with us outside the fire department and taught us about the Haitian constitution, was dead.

The two hundred members of our mission would gather the next day at the Hotel Christopher in Port-au-Prince—after many of the regional offices manned bonfires late into the night to destroy hard copies of their notes and case reports, in an effort to protect the identities of all those who had entrusted us with their stories.

We left Haiti on a charter flight bound for the Dominican Republic where we would spend four months holed up in a faded resort in Santo Domingo. I couldn't forget the remarkable little boy who had touched my heart, and I worried that Junior would be in even greater danger without the thin veil of our presence. But the truth was that I no longer felt safe to live and work in Haiti, and if we had not been evacuated, I probably would have left at that moment, missing the opportunity to have a deeper connection with both Haiti and Junior.

CHAPTER 4
Dark Days

The faceless trio greeted passersby on the main road into Cite Soleil, a vast village of cardboard and corrugated metal shacks surrounded by emerald-green cesspools and mounds of discarded plastic bags on the edge of the capital. The first man's face had been peeled with a knife, revealing patches of bone below. Further up the road, two more bodies lay nestled in a heap of trash. Their faces, ears, and fingers had been gnawed away by scavenger pigs. But lest the killers give the false impression that they were trying to erase the men's identities, they had carefully laid their identification cards and other personal belongings on their chests. The jarring scene had elicited a slow-moving procession of residents, with schoolchildren in neatly pressed uniforms casting expressionless glances as they walked by clutching their parents' hands.

The scene revisited me in my sleep a few days later in the form of a stress dream, where something from my daily life triggered a deeper anxiety, like showing up for an exam for which I hadn't prepared. It was the night before the one-year anniversary of my arrival in Haiti. Earlier that day I had crammed three dresses onto a single hanger in my closet. In my dream I had the nonsensical thought that I was going to "stuff" an identity onto the cadavers, just as I had "stuffed" three dresses onto one hanger in my closet that afternoon. My subconscious seemed desperately to need to know who the three dead young men were whose faces had been disfigured—and it searched my memory bank, superimposing the faces of the many victims with whom I had come in contact during the past year, like a flickering slideshow.

Two months earlier, in January 1994, Marcelo and I had returned to Haiti as part of a small group of observers to test the waters. Our mission contracts were now being automatically extended every six months, and the time had come to resume our work, even if it meant entering into an unknown. The military had solidified its control of the country, and we knew we would have to tread carefully. But after four months of lounging at all-inclusive beach resorts and sightseeing with our colleagues—as the Dominican government had provided us a safe haven on the strict condition that we not work in their country—we were willing to take on more meaningful, if precarious, challenges.

The mood in Port-au-Prince was somber. It would soon become apparent that I was entering into the darkest days I would experience in Haiti. Bodies were again being dumped on the streets, but the military's modus operandi was changing. Rather than simple gunshot wounds to the head, some victims were starting to appear with skinned faces, shaved heads, and wrists bound with wire coil.

The mission leadership took preventative measures, imposing an evening curfew and initially requiring us to live in hotels. For the first two months, Marcelo and I lived in a small inn where the only other guests were a group we believed to be a Colombian drug cartel. Each night we would nod politely to our fellow guests at dinner and avoid making small talk.

As soon as we were given the all-clear to move into private homes, we returned to my old apartment. Junior had survived the tempest, and he was again sleeping under the stairwell to the building. I worried about his safety, and I held to the small comfort that he was removed from the worst violence in the city center and in the so-called "popular" neighborhoods. I felt reassured knowing he wasn't seeing the dead bodies that our teams were systematically cataloging and recording. I looked forward to our weekend outings when we could go on walks and sit and talk. I hoped my friendship with Junior might somehow bolster his young sense of self and I found comfort seeing Haiti through his eyes.

One Saturday afternoon, I returned from the market with Junior. We were saying our goodbyes on the steps leading up to the front gate when it occurred to me how absurd it was that I had been keeping Junior at arm's length, accepting Haiti's rigid social lines that relegated a young homeless child to pariah status. There was no mission rule that prohibited us from inviting Haitians into our homes. But it had been so drilled into us that we couldn't protect anyone that I feared I would be crossing a slippery slope if I allowed Junior into my home, potentially putting us both at risk. At that moment, I decided I could no longer accept the contradiction. Junior was a child, now almost eight years old. His presence posed no danger to anyone. "Eske ou grangou?" *Are you hungry?* I asked Junior. He nodded yes. I asked him if he wanted to come upstairs. I would make him a sandwich with some of the fixings I had just bought.

Marcelo and I had just returned from a week's getaway to Cuba, where I had reported a freelance article for *The Dallas Morning News* about Cuban professionals moonlighting as cab drivers. The trip had been intended as a break from the intensity of Haiti, but I hadn't let go of my dream of becoming a foreign correspondent and every conversation in Cuba had been so illuminating that I soon had a notebook filled with fodder for a news feature. When I stepped into the living room with Junior's turkey sandwich, I let out a little gasp when I saw him hunched over the coffee table, writing his name, Junior Louis, over and over again on the back of one of my souvenir Cuban postcards. "Wait, not my postcards," was my immediate thought, before I stepped back and gave in to the beauty of the moment. Of course, I realized, like any child, Junior needed a way to express himself. How come I had never thought of that? From that moment on, I had no more qualms about having Junior upstairs in our apartment. I kept a collection of notebooks, sketchbooks, pens, and colored pencils for him to draw, color, and dream. This was just as important as making sure he had sufficient air to breathe.

One night, I was awakened by the sound of machine-gun fire on the street below. It was a terrifying popping sound and I immediately rolled off the mattress and onto the cool tile floor below. Marcelo and I ran into the hallway and hovered with Elio, who was staying with us and had been jolted awake in the guest room by the sound. My heart was pounding and I was filled with fear, even though I knew I was at a safe distance from the danger outside. And then my thoughts immediately flashed to Junior, who was mere feet away from this violence, barely concealed under the stairway. I was filled with dread, guilt, and remorse. Part of me wanted to run downstairs to open the gate and bring him upstairs, but I was too frightened to leave the apartment and venture into the darkness outside. The round of machine-gun fire was followed by the sound of a car rounding a corner with screeching brakes, and I imagined that soldiers from the army outpost in Petionville might be on a joyride, celebrating a late-night conquest. We waited a while and when the sound of the darkness outside returned to silence we felt reasonably satisfied the dangerous episode had passed. We all went back to bed, knowing that the next morning, Junior would share his eyewitness account.

I soon found myself questioning whether my presence in Haiti could possibly make a difference, and I quietly began to resent how the international community guidelines under which we operated gave the greatest importance to cases where someone had been killed or severely tortured in prison. Why couldn't the principles of preventative medicine apply to human rights work, I wondered? One day a colleague and I interviewed someone who had created a phony press release about his supposed arrest during a raid on a downtown church. We had already interviewed many of the victims of this attack and it was obvious this man was fabricating his account. It was sad to see someone resorting to this behavior—and yet on another level, I also understood his action. Why sit around waiting until you ended up tortured in prison? The political violence was becoming so widespread it was becoming harder to know if someone was in imminent danger until sometimes it was too late. I found myself starting to ignore outright the rule of not giving money to victims. I wasn't lavishing cash on people, but when someone came and reported a case that genuinely made me fear for his or her safety, I simply gave them enough money so they could eat a meal and get a ride out of the capital. I could no longer sit passively listening to people's accounts of their suffering.

What got me through this existential conundrum was the growing sense of family I felt with Junior and the camaraderie of my mission colleagues. By the summer of 1994, Marcelo and I had moved into a duplex in a residential area tucked away from busy streets. Our small house had a balcony overlooking a pool and Junior was a regular visitor to our home in the afternoons and on weekends. We would sit together on the patio, and Junior would color and draw while I read a book. Sometimes he brought another little homeless boy, Ti Richard, and the boys would play together while I fixed them a meal.

Our new home was within walking distance to several of our colleagues' homes. One night, feeling stifled by the early curfew, a group of us gathered at the home of Ettore, an Italian observer who was a keen political watcher and who regaled everyone with his impeccable impersonations of both public figures and our peers. Our covert gathering, which occurred after curfew, was planned by discreet calls on our handheld radios. We all trekked on foot to Ettore's house, carrying staples from our cupboards for the impromptu potluck, which Ettore crafted into an improbable savory meal, shared over flickering candlelight. The laughter and storytelling of these spontaneous gatherings sustained me through the darkness.

It was during this time that I came to work on the case of Sylvie, a neighborhood democracy activist whose husband was murdered, his body later dumped and gnawed by scavenger pigs. Sylvie came to see me almost every day in our downtown office. She was from a working-class neighborhood of the capital where mechanics, tap-tap bus drivers, and market vendors had joined forces to fight for democracy by posting photos of their exiled president and organizing clandestine meetings in churches. So many of her neighbors and relatives had died or gone into hiding. I feared for her life. There was so little I could do for her, but still, we managed to devise a ritual. Each morning that she came to see me, we stepped into one of the small classrooms that served as our office space and closed the door. Sitting in old-fashioned school chairs, we faced each other and held hands. Sylvie would describe how she had survived the previous day, telling me where she slept. In a market stall, a church courtyard, or on a stranger's floor. Sometimes I gave Sylvie money, but I knew that was not why she came to see me. Holding hands, we cried together each day and celebrated her survival. This was our form of praying. Sylvie knew there was at least one person holding out hope for her and this helped her make it to another day. Over the course of several weeks, I saw Sylvie's large frame shrink and her spirit grow stronger.

One afternoon, I was feeling the scratchiness signaling the beginning of a sore throat and I went to see my doctor, Marco Percque. He was the U.S. Embassy doctor and kept his own private practice on the side. During my first days in Haiti, Dr. Percque administered the rounds of vaccines—for hepatitis, typhoid, and cholera—that were required to adapt successfully to life in the tropics. Born in Haiti to a Belgian father and a Canadian mother, Dr. Percque was raised primarily in Rome. He was a true world citizen and I was immediately drawn to his warmth. Seeing how he had mastered life in Haiti both fascinated me and put me at ease. Married with two beautiful young sons, he made me feel safe to live and work in Haiti. As he placed the compressor on my tongue, I could see a worried look on his face. He put the instrument down and I realized it wasn't my health that was troubling him. "The military has ordered the mission to leave the country in forty-eight hours. It was just announced on the radio," he said. He paused before continuing. "They have declared the MICIVIH *persona non grata* and said they won't be able to guarantee your security after forty-eight hours. Please be very careful."

Later that afternoon, Marcelo and I rushed home to pack our belongings. Junior came by to visit us and color in his sketchbook, and I struggled to find the words to tell him that we were leaving once again. His large brown eyes filled with sadness, but he did not cry. Instead, he turned to a blank page to express his emotion. In previous days, Junior's drawings had been scenes of "la kai nou," *our house,* a place where he felt safe, secure, and free-spirited. He would use bright colors and add flowers to the drawings, and in the center, he would write the names of his chosen family: Junior Louis, Maselo, Sandra. For this day's drawing, he again gave full concentration to his work, completely uninterested in offers of a Coca-Cola or a sandwich. This time he drew a Toyota truck as a foundation, the car driven by most observers with the UN logo branded on the doors, with his name on it. As if to fortify his sense of self, he then wrote his name on all four corners of the drawing. He understood he would be on his own, with no one to take care of him.

A couple of hours later, the phone rang. It was Junior. He had memorized our phone number and was calling from Elio's house up the hill. He had gone to find Ti Richard, so his friend could say goodbye to us, but the guard at the entrance to the private road had turned them away. The double blow of our leaving and Junior's being rejected by a figure of Haiti's establishment saddened and upset me, but I downplayed the matter in an effort to try protect his young self-esteem. I told him to wait for me at Elio's, where I would come to say goodbye to them. As I was leaving, our new landlady came by to deliver her own ultimatum. Apparently unaware that we were being expelled from the country, she came to inform me that she could no longer tolerate Junior and Ti Richard's presence on her property.

"Ils sont des amis a nous." *They are our friends,* I said tersely.

"First it will be these two, and then all the others will follow," she said. "I understand that it is a nice humanitarian gesture and that you have good hearts. But I can't allow it any longer."

The next day, July 13, 1994, our mission staff gathered at the Hotel Villa Creole, a hotel that attracted a regular clientele of American embassy officials and where I instinctively felt safe. It was not possible to leave in time for the forty-eight-hour deadline. We spent the day huddled together for safety, camped out underneath the hotel's signature almond tree, a day our mission leader, Colin Granderson, called a day of reflection. My thoughts were with Junior, who was outside the hotel's protected gates, now left to fend for himself. I wanted to run out and find him one more time. To hug him and to let him know that I would not forget him. I felt powerless to resist the situation.

That afternoon, our convoy of UN vehicles snaked down the busy corridor of Delmas Boulevard in a formidable procession of jeeps and buses to the airport. The military's threat of implied violence was not lost on anyone. What saddened me the most was that no single Haitian walking down this busy thoroughfare in broad daylight dared look up at us out of fear that even a single glance would connote support for our mission. We were invisible. Men, women, and children stared down at their shuffling feet, afraid of being the next dead body on the side of the road.

As I stepped out of the bus at the airport past an intimidating column of soldiers clad in mustard-colored military uniforms, a familiar voice called my name. It was Sylvie. Standing on the curb outside the terminal, Sylvie stood out in a flowing white shirt and skirt, a startling counterpoint to the soldiers in mustard fatigues. "I heard the news on the radio and I couldn't let you leave without saying goodbye," she said. I hugged her fiercely before begging her to flee. "Fok ou ale kounye a." *You must leave right now.* I watched as Sylvie climbed into a crowded tap-tap and faded away into the late afternoon sunlight. It was the last time I ever saw her.

Inside the nearly empty departures terminal another shocking sight awaited us. Once we filed past the area that normally served as passport control, members of the diplomatic corps—including U.S. Ambassador William Lacy Swing and the ambassadors from France, Canada, and Venezuela—had come to witness our departure. I thought of the column of soldiers we had walked past to get into the terminal and at that moment I had a sickening feeling in my stomach. I realized just how seriously the international community took the threat against us.

We left Haiti on an Air France jet bound for the Caribbean island of Guadeloupe, the last flight out before international flights were suspended and Haiti's fate was left to be determined by an armed intervention. Once I boarded the plane, one more surprise awaited me. Sitting in the row in front of me was a Haitian radio journalist whose claim for asylum I had lobbied the mission to support. He was on his way to start a new life in Wichita, Kansas. Such was the nature of our work, that we often couldn't tell who we were helping—or if our efforts made a difference at all. How I wished Junior could be sitting in the seat next to him.

CHAPTER 5

Democracy and
the Almost Adoption

The young man in the rainbow-colored wig was dancing a giddy jig. The euphoria in the air was palpable, as if the ominous smudge of clouds had parted after a threatening storm and the atmosphere contracted to reveal a dazzling panorama. A few weeks had passed since American Marines had descended on the runway at Port-au-Prince's airport and taken control of the country without firing a single gunshot, the coup leaders having hastily accepted a last-minute offer of gilded exile in Panama. Our mission was driving in a convoy across the border from the Dominican Republic when a flat tire sidelined one of our vehicles after crossing the border into Haiti. American soldiers driving by in an army tank stopped to give us an assist—and the young reveler in the rainbow wig, a Haitian passerby, couldn't contain his joy that the coup was over and President Aristide was back in power in the National Palace. I had only been back in the country for about half an hour and already it was clear that a major sea change had occurred. After patching up the tire, the soldiers offered to escort our convoy into town—a dutiful gesture that seemed unnecessary given the pressing threat was now gone—and we drove behind the armored personnel tank with a mounted gun turret into a newly liberated Haiti.

The sights and sensations on the drive into the new Haiti were so vivid. My eye was drawn to the freshly painted murals in bright colors where artists gave thanks for their newfound freedom and expressed adroit political commentary, like the image of General Cedras clutched in the claws of a chicken, the symbol of the movement that brought Aristide to power. And I noticed how people moved and talked more openly and freely.

Once back in Petionville, I scanned the streets for the one survivor over whose fate I had most agonized during our three-month absence. I found Junior near my old apartment, where he had continued seeking shelter under the stairwell. I embraced his small frame and I felt as if I was holding a bright light in my arms.

Back in the office, our human rights mission was trying to figure out its new role in a now democratic Haiti. Would our files be used to try to prosecute human rights violators? Would our old questionnaire, with the checked boxes indicating varying rungs of inhumanity, now be obsolete? Perhaps we could carve out a new niche, educating the Haitian people about the rights and responsibilities of life in a democracy. And there would be important work to be done training the new police department on the proper use of force.

One day, an activist from Petit Goave made the trip into the capital to come see me. When I spotted him in our waiting room, wearing a white T-shirt with a life-size image of Aristide's face, I did an immediate double take. I still couldn't believe this was safe. Just a few months before, this simple action would have resulted in an instant death sentence. A tall man with engraved features that made his face resemble an elegant sculpture, he was a deeply committed activist who had once dressed as a peasant and traveled by donkey to small villages during the height of the repression to keep the flame burning for Aristide's *Lavalas* party, educating rural villagers about the party's vision for the future. He was a fascinating figure who during our many interviews had struck me as a melancholy intellectual. Standing in our waiting room on this day he was euphoric. Beaming. I had never seen him this radiant before. We stood for a moment in silence, words seeming insufficient to capture the trancendence of the moment.

The sense of newfound freedom was starting to affect me, too. I was keen to break out of my box. With democracy restored, the shackles had been broken and I felt I no longer needed to keep Junior at a safe distance. For the first time since we arrived in Haiti, mission members were allowed to live downtown. Marcelo and I moved into a historic gingerbread-style home in the neighborhood of Pacot. I was excited to experience life in Haiti through a closer lens. Pacot was a graceful neighborhood of French colonial homes with wood lattice work, turrets, and shady porches. Our home, tucked behind a tall mango tree, was like a large yellow birdhouse with an inviting porch swing, upstairs veranda, period furniture, and a dining room that looked out over a sparkling pool. The Hotel Oloffson, the inspirational setting of Graham Greene's timeless novel *The Comedians,* was just a short walk away.

This was an idyllic period during my time in Haiti. Marcelo and I were now engaged and I had left the mission to begin working as a correspondent for Reuters—accepting a $4,000 monthly pay cut for the chance to live my dream. Each day, I would report to my office at the Plaza Holiday Inn, where I would team up with my colleague, French photographer Carole Devillers, a regular contributor to *National Geographic*. Together we would monitor Haitian radio reports for breaking news and attend news conferences at the National Palace. On slow days, we sometimes drove into Cite Soleil, home to the capital's most dispossessed and resourceful residents, who were finally savoring a small taste of freedom. As we stepped from our parked cars, children would emerge from the shanties, taking us by the hand and leading us deep into the labyrinth of their world.

As Haiti's first democratically elected president, Aristide—a former Catholic priest who rose to prominence by challenging the injustices of the Duvalier dictatorship from the pulpit of his impoverished parish—was determined to invite a wide cross-section of Haitian society to the National Palace as his personal guests. The delegations included rural farmers, teachers, and vodou priests and priestesses. I attended these gatherings and watched as he performed for each group in populist, revival-style celebrations. Later that year, I was standing by with my reporter's notebook in hand when President Clinton, Vice President Gore, Secretary of State Madeleine Albright, and National Security Advisor Anthony Lake each visited the National Palace. I had secured my front-row seat to history. I felt it was my job to wake up each day and interpret Haitian reality for an audience of readers in another country who were wearing blindfolds and couldn't see, touch, or feel what I was witnessing. It was my task to bring it to life.

My life felt whole and full of purpose. I wanted to complete the picture with Marcelo by adopting Junior, and become a true family. I soon realized my dream was not his own. At age twenty-five, Marcelo did not feel prepared to adopt an eight-year-old boy. We broached the subject over a series of conversations and tearful negotiations during which I quietly questioned our compatibility. I understood Marcelo's fear that a child who had spent three years on the street could manifest future behavior problems, and unforeseen violent reactions, in response to the trauma. I worried about that, too. But I held to the deeper belief that there are never any guarantees in life—and all we had to do was love Junior. Finally, Marcelo broke the stalemate by proposing a compromise: Junior could stay at our home for up to a week at a time; after that, another international staffer would have to host him.

Junior soon moved in with his meager belongings, adding his stash of T-shirts, cut-off shorts, and a prized black vest to the collection of notebooks, crayons, and colored pencils we already kept in a dresser for him. He soon settled into a routine, bathing each morning, dressing in freshly washed clothes, eating meals at the dining room table overlooking the pool, and coloring and painting in my upstairs study. While Marcelo and I were at work, Junior was in the company of Suzette, the cook, and Sever, the houseboy, whom the house's owners—a Haitian doctor and his wife who lived up the street—had required us to hire as a condition for renting their home. In the evenings, Marcelo, Junior, and I ate dinner together and talked about our day. When it was time for bed, Junior would tuck into the neatly piled sofa cushions, pillows, and blankets that we fashioned into a bed for him in the covered gallery off the dining room. Although we had extra beds and bedrooms, this was part of the compromise to which I had agreed. Marcelo worried that if we had Junior sleep in his own bed in his own bedroom it would be tantamount to his permanently moving in with us. Before going upstairs to my room, I would step in to check on Junior, sometimes sitting on the tile floor to watch him. Most children are at their most peaceful in their deepest slumber. That was not the case with Junior. At his most relaxed, he was his most tense. With clenched fists, his body would contract as hard as a rock. His face would be locked in a fighting stance. Seeing his pugilist expression, I would often wonder where he was. With what unseen danger was he facing off?

One Saturday after Junior had been at our home for almost a week, Marcelo decided we should drive him up to Petionville to drop him off. Usually, he would go next to someone else's house. But this time, there was no one lined up. I had again been making the case that day to Marcelo that we should adopt Junior, prompting his hasty decision to return him to Petionville. When we arrived, it was dusk, and Junior pretended to be asleep in the backseat of our marked UN truck. I could tell he did not want to get out. I gently stirred him awake and told him we would see him again soon. I was heartbroken, torn, and conflicted. My desire to adopt Junior was causing fissures in my relationship with Marcelo. I didn't know what to do. I was not prepared to adopt a child on my own—and I didn't have my fiancé's support.

I turned next to my former mission colleagues. I wanted to find a group home where Junior could live, and I enlisted the help of a few trusted friends in my search. After asking around, a recommendation was made for a group home off Delmas Boulevard that was run by an American. We visited the home as a team, together with Junior, and I was impressed by the living conditions, atmosphere, and overall philosophy. Every night, the boys would go around in a circle, sharing an anecdote about an act of kindness bestowed on them by one of the other children that day. I was elated. Finally, I had found the answer to my quest. My joy was soon squelched by persistent rumors that the American director running the group home was molesting the boys. One of my colleagues, who had participated in the screening process, knew a close friend who had been molested as a child. My colleague laid down an ultimatum: We would not place Junior in the group home—and we couldn't trust that any such home would be a safe place for him.

I was stumped. I didn't know what else I could do for Junior. So we continued with our imperfect solution. Junior stayed at our home for up to a week at a time. And he kept going to the homes of other international staffers—until one day an observer accused him of stealing. I also noticed that a brand new camera I purchased during a weekend trip to Miami had gone missing. I sat down to talk with Junior. I told him I understood how hard it was for him to keep moving from house to house—but that no matter what, he had to always remain true. The camera reappeared.

○━━◆━━○

The panorama again darkened. Dead bodies began to reappear. But this time, they were not being dumped at night. Leading members of the elite who had backed the military coup were being killed in spectacular daytime ambushes. One afternoon in March 1995, I rushed to a downtown street where the military's former spokeswoman had been gunned down in the passenger seat of a white Subaru. Mireille Durocher Bertin, a telegenic thirty-five-year-old lawyer with a creamy café-au-lait complexion, was a polarizing figure who had channeled her beauty and sophistication to whitewash the military's atrocities on the international airwaves of CNN. Haitian justice had caught up with her, leaving her slumped and bullet-ridden without any special protections. On the street, word soon traveled that Aristide and his forces killed "for good," acting swiftly and precisely in daylight.

The lawlessness and retribution were not limited to the powerful. Petty thieves were being hunted down and lynched in acts of "jistis popilè," *popular justice.* Following a radio report one morning on a case of an alleged thief being nearly stoned to death by a crowd, I headed to the capital's General Hospital to try to find the victim and report on the phenomenon for Reuters. The hospital staff led me to the man's bedside. His head was swollen and inflated beyond belief, resembling an elephant. At a press conference, I asked Aristide to clarify his stance. His public statements seemed to condone the vigilante justice. His response was a classic Aristide double entendre: His position on the matter, he said, had been "as clear as coconut milk"—an opaque and hazy substance.

I was starting to crash. I had put all of my hopes into Aristide, seeing him as a Nelson Mandela–like figure in the making, and I was beginning to have serious doubts about his motives and agenda. Having to interpret his actions—and report on them in real time for a wire service—while exciting, grew to be exasperating. I came to see Aristide as a blank screen onto which the Haitian people had projected all of their hope and suffering. He had risen from humble roots and was a master orator who spoke six languages and who decoded the aspirations of the masses with brilliant and often cryptic messaging that sometimes bordered on demagoguery. His greatest accomplishment would be to dismantle the Haitian military, a violent institution that had served only to persecute its own people. In doing so, he would unwittingly create a power vacuum that would prompt Aristide to extend his influence with the help of criminal gangs, reminiscent of the *Tonton Macoutes* militia of Francois "Papa Doc" Duvalier.

◦═◆═◦

Marcelo and I traveled to Argentina for a fairy-tale wedding in Bariloche, a southern town of crystalline lakes nestled in the Andes with a distinct Alpine feel. We were married on December 31, 1995, in a small wooden chapel, and we celebrated our wedding reception at a stunning lakeside resort that would later play host to gatherings of world leaders, including Bill and Hillary Clinton, who traveled there to tailor global warming policy in preparation for the Kyoto climate change conference in 1997. Several of our mission colleagues were in attendance.

Upon my return to Haiti, I attended Aristide's wedding, on assignment for Reuters, at the president's private residence. It was a dour affair, strangely void of any romance. In my dispatch, I noted that there was no bridal gown, bouquet, or wedding cake. The event felt like a political ceremony. Aristide made a vow to his wife, Haitian-American lawyer Mildred Trouillot, and a mock vow to the Haitian people.

In my own private life, I was a happy new bride—and yet I was slipping into what I termed in my journal as "my crisis of meaning." My job was to make sense of Haiti's complex political reality and I was starting to understand that the extraordinary life and death sacrifices people had made for freedom and democracy would likely not be delivered upon. Contributing to my downward spiral was my sadness over Junior. Now more than ever I was ready to establish a family and yet I knew I was going to have to let go.

Marcelo and I were buying a home in Florida. After a year working for Reuters, I decided it was time to start laying the groundwork for our move. I accepted a position working on an electoral project at the *Miami Herald* for a few months, where I would begin figuring out how to heal my heartbreak over Haiti.

Chapter 6

Paradox Island

Waking up, the first sounds were of the gardener sweeping with the handmade broom gathering falling leaves outside. It's hard to explain the sense of comfort evoked by this gentle, repetitive, lulling sound in the early morning light. The *woosh-woosh-woosh* sound of the reeds on the bare concrete floor was a sound I associated with being in a womb. The next sounds came from animals outside. They came unfiltered into my awareness because there were no glass windowpanes separating me from the world outside—just wrought iron and wooden shutters. The bird song and the rooster crows blended with the dull thud of falling mangoes and the jostling of schoolchildren who were arriving at the little school across from our home. The sounds elicited a feeling of connection between me and the natural world around me. Of course, the lack of windowpanes also meant that the sounds of gunfire would stream into my consciousness at night. I sometimes awoke to this harbinger of violence in the shantytown in the ravine that abutted our backyard. Holding my breath, I would count the gunshots. Who was being terrorized, I wondered? Whose life hung in the balance? With democracy restored, common crime was on the rise. The armed gunmen who roamed at night favored the dispossessed and vulnerable over those with a UN truck parked in the driveway for their prey. And that was my conflict. I knew I was safe. I had protections not available to the population at large. A shiny plane could whisk me away if ever the danger got too close. I could go back to sleep.

After a few months in Miami, I was again back in Haiti working with the human rights mission, this time as a press officer. The experiment in organizing town hall meetings, backgrounding candidates, and writing a front-page story on a mayoral contender had gone well, but the *Herald* was dragging its feet in offering me a full-time position, sensing they had a captive employee. Marcelo had remained behind in Haiti and we didn't want to have a long-distance marriage. So one day I picked up the phone and called Colin Granderson. He offered me my new post on the spot. It was nice to return to the fold of family and friends.

Gone was the idyllic gingerbread home. Marcelo and I had moved out, spurred by the constant meddling of the landlords up the street. I had eventually figured out that by stationing their longtime domestic staff in the home, they maintained a constant foothold in our lives. Every day, the landlady called in orders, and Suzette and Sever cooked dishes, did laundry, and disappeared for periods of time, all at her behest. It felt as if there had been a constant flurry of activity going on in our home, which we were unable to deflect.

We were now back in Petionville, living in a charming 1920s Spanish-style home with an inviting garden. A Haitian engineer who resided in Berkeley, California, owned the home, his longtime family residence. In our brief interaction with the new landlord, he struck me as a laidback and progressive member of

Haiti's educated professional class. He posed little chance of interfering in our lives, although he too had insisted that we retain his esteemed gardener, Hilaire. The old man resided in the basement with his grandson, Remy, whom he claimed was possessed by the devil because the boy was prone to acts of mischief. It was Hilaire's gentle sweeping motion at dawn that would first dabble brushstrokes of awareness to my imagination.

The home on Rue Chavannes—located just around the corner from la *Place Boyer*, a leafy public plaza surrounded by historic estates—would be our home of memorable dance parties and barbecues. Junior would come and go freely from this home. Both our new cook and gardener knew him and would let him in, and the cook, Roselaine, a gifted and kindhearted woman who could transform a pile of forlorn vegetables into delicious homemade watercress soup and spinach tarts, would fix him a meal in case we weren't home. Junior was also a regular guest at our barbecues—but he was no longer sleeping in our home. The accusations of theft had shattered Marcelo's trust and he no longer wanted Junior staying overnight. And after the heartache of not being able to adopt him or find him a group home, I had let go of the expectation that Junior would live with us. But our bond remained unspoken and constant. And Junior remained a constant presence in our home. In my own heart, I had accepted that I would not be able to save Junior. All I could do was love him.

Haiti had more lessons in store for me, lessons that would jolt me awake from the dream I had been spinning of living life fully, experiencing each moment by the senses, and believing that I was making a meaningful contribution. My newfound awareness came in the form of an assignment to monitor parliamentary elections in the town of Mirebalais. It was something that made me nervous from the start.

In my new job as press officer, I had been starting my day at 5:00 a.m., waking up early to monitor radio broadcasts in Creole and French, which formed the basis of my daily news summary that the mission circulated among its leadership and e-mailed to officials at the UN in New York. I knew Mirebalais, a town in central Haiti, was heating up. A group of young thugs loyal to Aristide that went by the moniker *Òganizasyon Mete Lòd Nan Dezòd*, the Organization to Put Order in Disorder, had been instigating violent protests. I had never worked in the Central Plateau and I didn't have any contacts there. I would have felt more comfortable monitoring elections in Petit Goave, but I wanted to be a team player and I accepted the weekend assignment, seeing it as a chance to reconnect with the Haitian countryside.

In preparation for my trip, I baked a batch of blueberry muffins at home and I picked up a copy of the international edition of the *Miami Herald* at the Public's supermarket in Petionville before heading out with a driver on the bumpy road to Mirebalais. When I arrived in town, my teammate for the assignment, Marie, an American lawyer from Pennsylvania who was based in the nearby town of Hinche, had not yet arrived at our lodgings, the Hotel St. Nicolas Papa. It was a grand name for an unfinished cinder-block building with cots for beds on a remote dirt strip outside of town. The place had a slightly abandoned feel and I sensed the absentee owners were waiting to raise additional revenue from stray visitors like myself before completing the project. There didn't seem to be any point in sticking around, so I asked the driver to take me to the local UN Police outpost. I had already decided before embarking on this assignment that I would make a point of introducing myself to the officers on duty and exchange call signs for the handheld radios we all carried. My visit went better than planned. When I arrived, I found out the officer on duty was a Haitian American who was a former detective for the Los Angeles Police Department. Over a beer at a small outdoor restaurant across the street, he entertained me with stories of Los Angeles lore. He was a close friend of O.J. Simpson's, and he had been called to the witness stand in the Rodney King beating trial. My new pal confided that prosecutors thought he might have been the guy who taught O.J. that committing a murder in the rain was a foolproof way to wash away evidence. He demurred on whether he had shared his technical expertise.

"O.J." became my buddy. The next day, as Marie and I were conducting our dawn-to-dusk visits to rural polling places throughout the region—going from 6:00 a.m. to 6:00 p.m.—he continually called me on my radio to make sure I was okay. There wasn't much going on. Voting was reduced to a trickle of voters who turned out, a sad indicator that many Haitians had already given up hope that democracy could change their lives. Marie and I made the most of our mundane assignment with a thermos of fresh coffee we had brewed that morning on Marie's trusty cof-feemaker and my stash of home-baked muffins.

I found inspiration looking at the lush scenery, as we skirted the site of the sacred *Saut d'Eau* waterfalls, home to an annual pilgrimage where both Catholic and vodou supplicants bathe in the cascading waters to seek healing from Our Lady of Mount Carmel. According to local legend, the Virgin Mary appeared on a palm tree here in 1847 and began curing the sick. As we drove,

I reflected on the contrast between Haiti's exquisite beauty and its enduring poverty and violence. Haiti paid a hefty price for her freedom, forced to pay France an independence tax of 150 million gold francs, a sum estimated at $24 billion in modern terms, leaving the descendants of the nation's slave revolt to vanquish each other in the struggle for limited resources.

It was not until our last polling place, at a schoolhouse located near our remote inn where we observed the official vote count, that we unwittingly stumbled upon drama. The voting log reflected the signatures of thirty-six voters—an impressive and somewhat suspect figure, given that turnout had ranged from four to ten voters at the other polling places we had visited during the day. When the ballot box was opened, we uncovered another surprise. There were forty-six ballots inside—ten more votes than voters. The discrepancy certainly wasn't enough to sway the outcome of the election, but it was a troubling precedent for a new democracy. The votes were overwhelmingly in support of Aristide's party. It seemed so unnecessary. The Lavalas Family party could win without ballot rigging. I looked at the two independent political party observers in the room to see if they would speak out in protest. They looked at their feet and avoided my glance. I got the distinct impression they were hoping I would pretend not to notice the extra ballots. In a small Haitian town like Mirebalais, the locals knew it was best not to challenge the power structure directly. Marie and I exchanged glances. It was our job to observe and report, not scold poll workers or to try to fix a problem on the spot. But we certainly weren't going to look the other way and ignore fraud.

The group of young male poll workers looked nervous. They became embroiled in an inexplicably complex counting process that only served to confuse everyone in the room. Ballots were strewn all over the floor. I carefully wrote down the vote tallies for each party, and we waited until everyone had signed the final paperwork.

Back at the hotel, the driver dropped us off. I was exhausted and contemplated taking a shower, but I decided against it because I didn't feel comfortable heading to the outhouse in the dark. I was lying in my cot, wearing just a T-shirt and reading the newspaper, when I thought I heard a voice calling my name. It was pitch black outside and I was sure I had imagined it.

"Sandra, Sandra, Sandra, m'bezwen ouuuuuuuu," *I need you,* the voice hissed. Now I was sure I hadn't imagined it. The voice grew shriller and my stomach tightened. I began to panic. Who was this outside my room and what did they want? My mind immediately flashed to the memory of a French gendarme who had recently been shot in the face as he had undressed in his room in Petit Goave. He had been airlifted to Miami with a severe brain injury.

Instinctively, I rolled under my bed. The voice was getting louder, but I could no longer make out what it was saying. I felt like a trapped animal. My neck stiffened to the point that I thought I might become unable to move.

I wondered if this intruder was alone and whether he was armed. There was no glass window to shield me. My room faced the front porch and metal bars were all that separated me from the outside. I grabbed my radio and called Marie in her room down the hall, but she did not respond. I began shouting her name. That was when I heard her voice from outside. She was in the backyard, taking a shower in the outhouse. I shouted at her to come back immediately. "We are in danger," I yelled. I was paralyzed by fear but I knew I had to act or I would not be able to overcome the situation. It took all of my concentration to bolt from under the bed, grabbing a nightshirt and my room key as I fled. As I stepped into the hallway, someone began pounding on the front door of the hotel. The door shook with the force. I met Marie at the back door, pulled her inside, and slammed and bolted it shut. I told her we were going to have to hide in her room with the lights off. We lay underneath Marie's cot hoping the intruders just wanted to scare us and would soon go away. I repeatedly tried reaching "O.J." and the other UN Police in town by radio, but there was no response. Within minutes, we could hear people scaling the wall around the back of the compound. Marie looked at me in silent terror. I thought they would have no way to figure out which room we were in, but I was wrong. Somehow, one of the bunch hoisted up the wall, almost to the small open space that served as her window, and said, "Nou konnai nou-la," *We know you are in there,* in a ghoulish voice.

Marie and I clung to each other, frantically making radio calls for help. We were out of range from mission headquarters in Port-au-Prince, and the UN Police remained strangely unresponsive. By chance, our colleagues stationed in the town of Hinche, two hours away, heard our distress calls. Andrea Loi, a Chilean observer and lawyer, figured out what was going on and immediately devised an ingenious rescue plan. Andrea managed to call the telephone company in Mirebalais and convinced them to send a bicycle messenger to the local Haitian police station, who in turn alerted the UN Police to our plight. When the Haitian police mistakenly drove past our hotel, which was shrouded in darkness, the whole exercise had to be repeated a second time. It was an utterly improbable chain of events and it worked.

As our rescue was being coordinated, the intruders managed to penetrate the hotel. They pounded on our door continuously and demanded that we come out. It was only when we believed that they might succeed in breaking down the door that we spoke, asking them who they were. They identified themselves as the Organization to Put Order in Disorder. I felt nauseous. When we asked what they wanted, they demanded my notes. In that moment, handing over my notebook didn't even seem to be an option. For starters, it was back in my room and I had no intention of opening the door and unleashing the floodgate of their terror. I also feared that handing them the proof of their transgressions might further inflame their rage—and a small voice inside me held onto the belief that journalists don't hand over their notes.

Commotion in the hallway followed and we heard more voices outside. The Haitian Police had arrived. We asked them to slide their badges under the door to prove their identity, but still we did not open the door to our room—fearing that despite their best intentions they still might not be able to control the crowd outside. It was not until the UN Police had arrived that Marie and I finally agreed to open the door. "O.J." was standing there and I was so relieved to see a familiar face. He apologized and looked embarrassed over having his radio turned off, later explaining his team had been locked in a mini-UN power struggle. When his African colleagues had been appointed to lead the unit, he and his American colleague grew tired of handling the lion's share of the responsibility. They settled the score by turning off their radios at night—and he had been reasonably assured that I was safe as the day had been so uneventful.

"O.J." took nine of the instigators aside and grilled them. He returned with the news that the group was still insisting on having my notes. "It's too dangerous for you to stay here," he said. Within an hour, the comforting clatter of a UN helicopter broke the nighttime silence. It landed on an empty soccer field and men in spacesuit-like uniforms descended from the aircraft to fly us back to safety in Port-au-Prince. When I finally made it home that night after midnight, Marcelo told me my back looked as if it had been scratched with sharp nails. It was covered in red hives.

Back in the office, Marie and I were tasked with writing an official report about the incident. A week later, as soon as we handed in our completed draft, I felt immediately queasy. I requested a driver take me home. There, huddled on the bathroom floor, I was unable to stop the flickering images of being trapped in that room in Mirebalais. Someone was pushing the fast-forward button in my brain and the images just kept coming. I vomited again and again. I ended up at a MASH-like tent at the American military hospital where a soldier doctor took notes about my ordeal and prescribed me some sleeping pills.

In the months ahead, Marcelo and I found ourselves awaking to the sound of gunfire several times a week. The armed robbers were terrorizing the residents in the shanty in the ravine below our home. Marcelo would get up with a flashlight, making sure every door was locked. He wanted to get a gun for our protection, but I was adamantly against it. We settled the argument by hiring an armed security guard to stand watch outside our home at night. I had never wanted to live like that. Our life was increasingly mirroring a neocolonial existence. I questioned how I could choose to live in a world of sensory pleasure and tradition when I knew that I was becoming part of a privileged class. Now I knew that regardless of my good intentions I would be tallied up with the elites. I had become part of the problem, at least in the eyes of some. The chasm between the haves and have-nots had grown ever wider and it risked engulfing me.

In November 1997, I made a conscious decision to return to the United States from Haiti after four soul-etching and life-altering years. I was twenty-eight years old. I had decided to make my life in a country where I had a stake, where I could vote, pay taxes, and feel that, good or bad, I had to bear the responsibility of being part of a society. It was no easy choice.

CHAPTER 7

Breakfast at the Montana

The telephone rang about 8:30 a.m. It was the front desk at the Hotel Montana, where I had arrived the day before, and I was still getting used to being back in Haiti for the first time in just over two years. "There is someone here to see you," the voice on the other end announced in French. I was just about to protest. Certainly they had called the wrong room. I hadn't made any appointments and nobody was expecting me. And then I stopped. I knew exactly who was waiting for me. "J'arrive tout suite," I said before hastily jumping in the shower and running downstairs.

Junior sat patiently in the lobby, wearing his Sunday best and clutching a small photo album. It was clear he had won the approval of the hotel staff, one of whom winked at him when I arrived. It was one of the qualities I had always admired about him. As a street child he had an extraordinary resourcefulness and an amazing ability to cultivate allies across all social lines. It was nothing less than grace. He was now thirteen years old and he had not lost that unique ability to create a protective web of goodwill around him. We walked arm-in-arm to breakfast at the outdoor Panorama restaurant with its sweeping views of the port and historic downtown below. We were family once again.

I marveled at Junior's seemingly telepathic ability. "How did you know I was here?" I asked him incredulously. He did not need a cell phone or a computer to tap his network. Junior explained that Regine Estimé, the daughter of former Haitian president Dumarsais Estimé, who served from 1946 to '50, had seen me arrive on the American Airlines flight from Miami the previous afternoon. Regine, who was a close friend to Elio, had come to know Junior through our network. As an artist and architect, she developed a natural kinship with Junior and paid for him to have art lessons. Later, when she moved to France, where she would serve as Haiti's cultural attaché in Paris, she looked out for Junior whenever she returned home to Haiti. The previous day, she had run into Junior outside of Public's supermarket and she mentioned that I had been on her flight. That Junior found me at the Hotel Montana was a lucky guess.

Over breakfast, Junior updated me on his life, narrating the snapshots in his album. He was now part of a government-backed soccer league comprised of street children. A drummer for Boukman Eksperyans, the country's most famous roots band that performs internationally, saw Junior playing soccer one day in Petionville and tapped him for the league. I was astonished to learn that Junior had traveled to Puerto Rico, Cuba, and the Dominican Republic to compete in matches. Junior also told me that he was now living with an aunt in Delmas. I was equally surprised to hear this. I had never heard him mention relatives before.

I was so happy to see that Junior's life was taking a positive turn. It would have been so easy for Junior to succumb to the pressures of drugs and violence in Haiti—either in a purely defensive form of survival or as a victim of its ravages. But Junior was composing his own unique arc. It was just as I expected.

After breakfast, I was off and running on assignment for the *Miami Herald*. I had flown into Port-au-Prince on short notice to cover the repatriation of a mass exodus of Haitian boat people. The refugees had endured slave-era ship conditions to try to slip into Miami harbor under the cover of millennium firework celebrations. At least ten people suffocated to death or jumped overboard to escape the grueling conditions.

My colleague for this assignment was Carl Juste, a photographer with the soul of a poet whose evocative images of Haiti are informed by his own Haitian-American roots. Carl and I were on the harbor docks when the 413 survivors were repatriated by the U.S. Coast Guard. I debriefed as many of the passengers as I could to try to piece together the story of their New Year's voyage. I learned that passengers paid as much as $5,000 for the trip—an astronomical sum in Haiti—and many would have to continue paying off their debt as indentured servants in Miami. Some passengers believed they were going on a trip of a lifetime. One young woman wore a ball gown and carried a fake pearl necklace in a clear plastic purse.

I stumbled on a key fount of information when I interviewed a twenty-six-year-old nicknamed Babou who had been paid by the smuggler to round up passengers. On board the ship, Babou had assumed godlike powers. It was his job to decide who got to come up for air from the crammed lower hold of the ship—and when they had to be forced back below. The trip took months to plan, he said, and had been organized around the delivery of two VIP passengers from China who wanted to enter the United

States. The passengers all congregated on remote Tortue Island in northwestern Haiti and the departure was carefully planned to arrive in Biscayne Harbor on the night of December 31, 1999. Organizers believed the handmade boat would cruise past undetected in the revelry of worldwide celebration and if they were intercepted, they believed they would be granted amnesty in honor of the new century.

Carl and I embarked on a week-long odyssey that took us to the northern towns of Cap Haitien, Port-de-Paix, and Tortue Island. In Cap Haitien, Carl knocked at my door at the historic Roi Christophe Hotel during a blackout and asked if I wanted to join him for dinner. We had driven in the darkness through rural towns on the final stretch of our trip from the capital. "The hotel restaurant is already closed," I told him. "I know, let's go find some place to eat," he said. I was exhausted but I did not want to stifle Carl's sense of adventure. I again found myself walking in Haiti's pitch darkness to dinner, Carl illuminating the path with a small flashlight. We found a seemingly nondescript restaurant at the edge of the water run by a French-Haitian couple. In Carl's dazzling presence, the sleepy space was transformed. Rounds of Haitian rum were served to the few lingering diners and waitstaff. Music enveloped the room. And the dancing began. It was one of my most entertaining evenings ever on assignment.

The next morning, we set out early for Tortue Island. To get there, we drove to Port-de-Paix where we hired a small fishing boat ominously named the *Titanic*. With just Carl and me and a crew of two transporting us on a small, rickety boat, I worried that

Carl's expensive photo gear, which I ballparked at about $5,000, could make us easy targets. I imagined us being pushed off the *Titanic* at sea, dumped in exchange for some fancy equipment. Carl seemed to have the same thought. Just as we were about to leave shore, he unexpectedly grabbed the two men by the collar and slammed them together. We had been speaking with them in Creole but now he switched to English. "I don't want any bullshit from you guys. You hear me?" he said in a commanding voice. He had established his alpha male status and I breathed a sigh of relief.

Back in Port-au-Prince, I didn't have a way to contact Junior. Delmas, where he was now living, was a labyrinth-like district. He didn't give me an exact address for his aunt and he didn't have a phone or e-mail address. I was saddened that I didn't have a way to say goodbye to Junior, and I imagined he would continue searching for me after I was gone. I accepted that as the reality of our lives on distant shores and I held to the belief that events still unknown to us—or another news story—would propel me back to Haiti, and we would see each other once again.

I continued following the thread of my assignment. I again met with Babou, the smuggler's assistant. At a café in Petionville, he showed me one of the Chinese passports that was still in his possession. It was an essential corroborating detail for the story.

On the eve of my departure from Haiti, I went to the U.S. Embassy for an interview with the political and economic advisors. We were talking about the conditions that led some passengers to pay such high sums for their ill-fated journey. One of the advisors glanced at his watch and noticed the date.

"Wow, today is the one-year anniversary of Marco's accident," he said to his colleague.

"Marco?" I asked. I knew of only one in Haiti. "Do you mean Marco Percque?"

"You didn't know?" the men replied in unison.

The next morning I was at Dr. Percque's office by 8:30 a.m. I remembered he kept early hours before going to the U.S. Embassy. His secretary ushered me into his office. I was shocked by the sight of him. The once trim and dashing European doctor was hobbling and walking with a cane. For the next hour I sat sobbing as he told me the story of what happened one year before, the last time he saw his seven-year-old son, Jean Marc. It began with a Saturday morning outing to Kaliko Beach where the boys loved to go fishing. The last thing he remembered was the bus that careened straight into his green Grand Cherokee jeep, the driver wanting to avoid a pothole. Dr. Percque's oldest son was killed instantly. Marco was seriously injured and unconscious. Mayhem ensued. A crowd encircled the car, stripping its radio communications and valuables. Marco's wife had to load the body of her dead son, comatose husband, and surviving child onto a passing tap-tap bus serving as an ambulance. They drove north to the city of Saint Marc where Marco was brought onto a squalid operating table. His wife panicked and ordered his body loaded back onto the bus. It delivered them to the nearby Club Med. Marco was airlifted to Miami, where he would be in a coma for days—hovering near death—and confined to his hospital bed for months.

As Dr. Percque related his story, he directed all of his emotion into a tight fist strewn anchor-like on his desk. "I can't even cry about it anymore," he told me, acknowledging my tears. The next day, his wife delivered their third child, an angelic baby girl.

PART II: KÉ (HEART)

I offer you that kernel of myself that I have saved,
Somehow—the central heart that deals not
in words, traffics not with dreams, and is
untouched by time, by joy, by adversities.

—JORGE LUIS BORGES

CHAPTER 8

Cathedral in the Sky

January 15, 2010, San Clemente, California. It has been three days since Port-au-Prince collapsed into a state of prehistoric rubble and I cannot sleep. Already I've settled into a troubling routine. I wait for my son and husband to go to sleep, and once the house is quiet I begin bingeing on online news. Tonight I am on a hunt for amateur video of the Hotel Montana, where two hundred people are trapped. I always considered this to be Haiti's international cathedral. Perched high up on a hill, with breathtaking views of the port and the historic city center below, it was the gathering place that brought together diplomats, relief workers, journalists, and so many others seeking to make a difference in Haiti. Many of the Montana's employees had worked all of their adult lives at the ninety-eight-year-old property. I remember the front-desk staff and their impeccable professionalism and warmth. And I remember the small-framed waiter at the outdoor restaurant who often sang as he made blender drinks.

I need to do this at night because I don't want to expose my two-year-old son, Alexander, to the mass human suffering on the streets of Haiti. But there is another reason why I have sacrificed my usual 10:00 p.m. bedtime and am now nightly staying up until 4:00 or 5:00 a.m. I want to sit and digest this information quietly on my own. I feel like I am watching a dear friend on her deathbed, and I want to afford her some dignity in her darkest moments.

It has been a stressful day. While I was on the phone this morning, I watched as my son slipped into our pantry to play. I was standing next to his limber figure when, in a flash, he grabbed for a can of black beans that went spiraling through the air. I just barely missed breaking the can's fall when it bounced down on Alexander's big right toe. I cursed myself for being so preoccupied with Haiti that it was affecting my normally focused parenting style. Within an hour we were having Alexander's right foot x-rayed to make sure the big toe wasn't broken. And then twenty minutes later the joyful verdict came in: The toe was intact. As we drove home I couldn't shake the thought that thousands of children were walking the streets of Port-au-Prince with serious head injuries from falling cinder blocks and collapsed concrete walls, and there were no X-rays, antibiotics, or pain medications to ease their suffering. I struggled to contain the contradictory feelings welling up inside me. I was relieved and grateful that my son was healthy and had access to excellent, modern healthcare. And yet the thought of Haitian children being buried alive and wincing in pain was starting to build a fury inside me. I couldn't help feeling guilty about that contradiction. This was my first clue that I was thinking of Junior.

The truth is that I have no way to contact Junior and I have no way of knowing whether he has survived the earthquake. I consider him Haiti's consummate survivor, so I don't even allow myself to imagine the possibility that something terrible may have happened to him. Tucked somewhere on the blurry edge of thought I can sense denial's presence and I allow it to linger there unexplored.

Feeding my anxiety today is the knowledge that the clock will soon time out. I was acutely aware this afternoon when the seventy-two-hour mark after the earthquake struck. I felt as if the crushing bag of cement on my chest had just pressed a little more air from my lungs. With each miraculous rescue that I have watched on television—like a startling reverse-birth, first the placenta breaks, then the legs emerge, followed by the torso and head—I am filled with contradictory feelings of euphoria and hope mixed with dread and anger. I believe thousands of others remain buried alive in the rubble, a feeling reinforced by the relatively unscathed and elegant appearance of some of the survivors. The efforts of Haiti's extraordinary survivors combined with the well-intentioned, but so far inadequate, response of international search and rescue teams will not be enough to save those who are clinging to life.

I am reminded of my phone call the morning after the quake with a former *Miami Herald* colleague now living in San Francisco with her husband and baby daughter who is not yet a month old. Leslie is part of a small contingent of leading Haitian-American journalists in the United States. In recent days we have had an easy dialogue by phone and e-mail talking about breastfeeding, the disintegration of American journalism, and balancing motherhood with our love of writing. I'm sitting outside Peet's coffee near my home after dropping Alexander off at his Montessori preschool, trying to pinpoint my anguish.

Me: "It's like 9/11, but imagine if no one responded to the towers."

Leslie: "I hate to break the news to you, but this is worse than 9/11."

I've been surprised that the media coverage is not providing aerial shots of the Hotel Montana wreckage. I've heard it described as if the hotel has been bombed off the hillside. I cannot imagine this—cannot get my mind to bend in that direction. I am hoping to find some amateur footage to help me understand. A winding YouTube search leads me to a video montage juxtaposing the Haiti quake with the Indonesian tsunami. It's oddly moving. Next my browser stumbles on an online broadcast by a journalist out of his home in Canada. The host—who has clearly lived and worked in Haiti before—is conducting interviews with survivors in Port-au-Prince and friends in Paris. I find myself captivated by the international scope of his homegrown newscast. The Canadian fellow's demeanor is very calm and yet he looks as exhausted as I feel. As he tries to overcome technical difficulties, viewers from Mexico City, Brooklyn, and Australia are posting messages in real time, trying to find out if friends and loved ones are alive in Haiti. People aren't so much talking to each other as they are shouting past one another in an online echo chamber. Sitting at my kitchen table, I feel as if I have entered a brave new world. This is the first time I've experienced a major disaster played out on my computer screen together with kindred strangers from around the globe.

I can find no footage of the Montana—although I find it eerie and heartbreaking that the Montana's own site is still up and running, channeling the sophisticated and tropical chic of the hotel's bright orange and green gauzy lobby. And that's when it hits me. As I am reading a description of the hotel's outdoor Panorama restaurant, I am blindsided by the memory of my last meeting with Junior in January 2000—exactly ten years ago. I remember how we walked arm-in-arm to breakfast. Junior had again amazed me with his sensitivity and sense of wonder, narrating the snapshots in his album. How was it that I had completely lost touch with him?

All of this is now crushed to dust. As I stare at my computer screen, glimpsing a fragment of my past, I suddenly realize that my urgent need to see the Montana, now a cathedral in the sky, is in fact a longing to see Junior one more time and to reconnect with my past. It immediately seems so obvious what I must do. Countless lives have been lost and there is nothing I can do to protect them. But if Junior is still alive, that is who I can help. That is what I can do.

Junior would be twenty-three years old now. During that last meeting, he told me he was living with an aunt on Delmas, a corridor of Port-au-Prince that was heavily destroyed in the quake. I'm not exactly sure how I would go about finding him and yet I know I must go. Still, something is holding me back. I feel as if I am being pulled in opposite directions from my core. I am a mommy now. I have never been away from my son—not even for one night. This is one of the hardest things I have ever had to do.

⚬━✦━⚬

Post Script
March 10, 2010

As we prepare to leave for the airport, I make a drawing with a blue crayon to make sure Alexander understands what is about to happen. "Mommy will take an airplane to help the children far away," I explain. This is both comforting and familiar to him. A few weeks ago he helped me pack up some of his outgrown baby clothes for a Haiti relief drive. Learning that his things were going to help children in a distant place captivated him. Waking up from a nap that day, he had looked at me dreamy-eyed and announced: "I want to help the children far away again." I continue with my illustration. "In a few days, you will ride an airplane with daddy. We will all meet in Florida and go to Nana's house." He stares quietly at the two blue jets in my drawing, trying to see the future.

I am going to find Junior, who was once a child who needed my help. I hope that my shorthand explanation to Alexander is as simple and emotionally honest as I can make it. As much as I worry about my own separation anxiety, I worry about how Alexander will cope for ten days in my absence. He still cries sometimes when I go outside alone to walk our dog, Humphrey, before bed.

Now in the car as we approach the airport where I will catch my red-eye flight to Florida, Alexander listens carefully as I again whisper, "Mommy is going to help the children far away." I am sitting in the backseat, my face pressed against his tender cheeks. "Mommy is always with you. And you are always in my heart. I love you." I can see that he is being very brave. He does not cry.

As I walk into the terminal, I make a wish that this trip will set an example for Alexander to follow his heart and to do what he believes. That it will help him find his place in the world. And I make a wish that this trip will give me a second chance to make a real difference in Junior's life.

CHAPTER 9

Return

It's been almost seventeen years to the day since I first landed in Haiti. For a bit of poetic symmetry, I am again about to board American Airlines flight 1291 from Miami. On that first flight, I sat in seat 16F. This time I will sit in seat 36H. That first boarding pass is still glued to the inside of an old journal. It's also the two-month anniversary of the quake. None of this is by design. After all the sleeplessness, soul-searching, and Facebook chatter with former Haiti colleagues, this was the first available opening in my husband's babysitting calendar and the first flight I was able to book.

Once on the plane, I review the scant biographical data I have on Junior. I know he left home when he was just five years old—although I have never fully understood the circumstances surrounding his flight. When he was just a child it didn't seem right or reasonable to really press him on it. I sensed it would be too painful for him to express, and he might have to rely on his childhood imagination to help me understand. All that really mattered to me was that he was sleeping on the street and he had nowhere to go. When I last saw him at age thirteen, and he told me he was living with the aunt in Delmas, the first time I had ever heard mention of a relative. Here are the scenarios as I see them: Junior's impeccable survival instinct has helped him elude the quake. Or, and I shudder to think this, he is alive but has had to have one or more limbs amputated. Or he died. Or he died and he is now survived by an infant. The last bit of information I have about his whereabouts is what most looms over me. I keep imagining the clunky '70s-era construction on Delmas and I cringe at the thought of it caving in on Junior. Still, I can't help but cling to hope. At 4:53 p.m.—the time of the quake—it's possible he was on the street. The street, his longtime shadow, could have saved him.

In the seven years since leaving Haiti, I have remarried. My husband, Tom, an Associated Press photo editor, is a big fan of the mystery writing of Raymond Chandler and esoteric French and Japanese film noir from the 1940s to '60s. He has devised some theories of his own about Junior's whereabouts. Based on what I have told him about Junior, he believes my young sidekick will either be waiting for me upon my arrival at the airport in Port-au-Prince—or he is now living in New York City and getting by as a cab driver. He has even come up with a story arc to guide me on my journey. Tom has decided that my inspiration should come from a Graham Greene novel, but not the obvious choice of *The Comedians*, which is set in Haiti. Rather, *The Third Man*, set in post–World War II Vienna, provides a better model, he assures me. "You are the detective and you are sifting through the rubble of this bombed-out landscape for a trace of your long-lost friend. Each person you meet provides you with one more clue and slowly you come to realize that your friend is not the person you once knew." In this narrative, I am Rollo Martins, author of cowboy novels under the nom de plume Buck Dexter. Junior is the elusive Harry Lime, who is brilliantly played by Orson Welles in the film version of the story. Ultimately, Tom is offering this to me as a cautionary tale. Junior's story is Haiti's story, he tells me. "Don't be surprised if you find out he is now a drug dealer or a member of an armed gang. Just be prepared that you might not find what you are expecting." I find Tom's theory an amusing diversion. But it has nothing to do with Junior. How can Tom possibly know this? He has never met my extraordinary young friend.

My thoughts shift now to someone else with a unique connection to Haiti, my ex-husband Marcelo. Marcelo and I first walked into each other's lives on this very flight, before exchanging our first hellos in the VIP hall of the Port-au-Prince airport.

I remember how he had wooed me with stories about his days as an Argentine congressional aide, sitting in on complex and arcane hearings as the foreign relations committee tried to delineate Argentina's southern border with Chile, an ever-shifting mass of glacial ice that required new boundaries to be drawn every few years. The golden years of our ten-year relationship occurred on Haitian soil. The simple explanation for why our marriage ended is that we were unable to successfully negotiate the transition to American suburban life. The complicated answer is, well, more complicated. Ours is also a story marred by tragedy. In April 2008, six years after we parted ways, Marcelo died suddenly and unexpectedly from a rare form of leukemia. There was no time for a final goodbye. He was just shy of his thirty-eighth birthday.

I am also thinking of our former colleague, Andrea Loi, forty-four, the human rights lawyer from Chile who acted so decisively to help rescue me when I was in danger in Mirebalais. In the days after the Haiti earthquake, I felt numb with anguish, knowing that there was nothing I could do to help her. Andrea died in the wreckage of UN headquarters in Port-au-Prince. Five days after the earthquake, with her brothers standing by her side to accompany her, she was removed from the wreckage and flown home to Chile.

Andrea was a rare breed in that she possessed both a free spirit and a feisty old-world work ethic. Her heritage was Romanian Jewish and she was firmly agnostic, in reverence to her grandmother's relatives who were murdered in the Holocaust. With her bright smile and long, curly blonde hair, she was a luminous presence. I never met her father, Chilean architect and former newspaper columnist Isidoro Loi, but anyone who knew Andrea was aware of the kinetic bond they shared. Weeks after I learned of her death, I came across an online edition of a heartbreaking interview he granted a Chilean newspaper. On the night that Port-au-Prince erupted into calamitous ruin, Isidoro Loi was autographing copies of his sixth book of reflections on humor and culture, *El Cuerpo y sus Miembros* ("The Body and its Parts"), at a book launch party attended by fans and members of Chile's literary establishment. Andrea had called her father just thirty minutes before the quake to wish him well. She asked him to call after the event. She wanted to hear every detail.

The last time Marcelo, Andrea, and I were all together was on an Easter Sunday after we left Haiti. Andrea had come to stay with us at our home outside Miami during a layover on her way back to Haiti. We all had breakfast in the morning and then said goodbye. Marcelo and I went to the beach; Andrea was heading to the airport. Later that afternoon, Andrea surprised us by reappearing. She had missed her flight. This was extremely out of character for her—and yet she seemed unfazed by it. I sensed that she wanted to be with family. And we were. Marcelo made a wonderful Argentine *asado* and we dined outside. It's hard to imagine them not here for this. I picture them together now, having an *asado* in heaven and together resolving their countries' intractable border dispute over good laughs, before the disputed territory dissolves into slush.

And I am also thinking of my doctor and friend, Marco Percque. The image that will always stay with me from our last meeting was how he clutched his fist like an anchor on his desk as he told me the story of the last time he saw his first-born son. Haiti had exacted too high a price for the privilege of living on her bloodstained soil. Dr. Percque was the person who always made me feel safe to live and work in Haiti. In the event that cholera, malaria, or a bullet ever found its way to me, I held on to the belief that he would be there as my invisible safety net. The loss of his son forced my eyes open, made it painfully clear there never was a safety net.

As the 767 transporting me through the clouds comes in for landing, I see white tents dotting the perimeter of the airport. This is my first glimpse of the "new Haiti." Once on the ground, we share runway space with a C-130 American military cargo plane and we park near a curiously named Planet Airways plane, harbingers that we have arrived in Disasterland.

Inside the old airport terminal I notice deep-fissured cracks in the walls and kaleidoscope gashes of broken glass doors. A band playing traditional Compa music is making a nice attempt at establishing a sense of normalcy, but it's not terribly convincing. Dressed in matching black Western Union T-shirts, the emaciated musicians have the glum expressions of a graveyard band. They keep their eyes fixed closely on the tip jar. I wonder if any of them still have homes left to return to at night.

We step outside to board a bus to an open-air hangar now operating as the customs and baggage claim area, and I feel as if someone is scorching me with a blowtorch. The intensity of the heat is overpowering. It's much hotter than I remember—an observation I hear echoed by other return travelers. I can't help thinking that several thousand metric tons of crushed cement hovering in the atmosphere are wreaking havoc with the elements.

My first astonishing glimpse of how Haitians are coping with this humanitarian calamity comes in the form of an elegantly dressed airport official named Gattine, who is helping my seat-mate recover her lost passport from the plane. As my seatmate disappears to meet a ground agent, Gattine begins to confide to me in Creole. She speaks to me with the intimacy of an old friend. On the day of the earthquake, she was in the original air-port building—the one with the Compa singers and all the deep cracks. One person was injured by a falling wall, but no one died. It wasn't until nightfall that she knew whether her four-year-old son had survived. Her home had collapsed on him and together with her neighbors she dug for over two hours to rescue him from the rubble. Home, Gattine explains softly, is now under a piece of plastic sheeting on a friend's empty lot, shared by her extended family. I look at her in shock. "How do you manage to look so calm and byen abiyé, *well dressed?*" I ask. "Do you hang your blue dress from a tree?" She smiles sweetly. "Nou pa ka fait ayen." *There is nothing we can do.* This is not defeatism talking. Rather, it is acceptance of a terrible situation and managing to rise above it and move on, which so quintessentially captures the Haitian spirit. "I don't know how long we will live like this," Gattine won-ders nervously. Already, her son has diarrhea and she is worried about epidemics breaking out. I am moved by her story and yet

I know that in many ways she is one of the lucky ones. She is educated and has a good job, although she is not from Haiti's elite class, and her entire immediate family survived the quake. She has a shot at a future. What will happen to Gattine, I wonder? And what will happen to Haiti and her long-suffering people?

Outside, I make it past the gauntlet of porters and beggars who jam the airport exit. Making it through this crush is always Haiti's first test upon arrival. I see my name on a sign and feel a rush of relief. The hotel where I will be staying has followed through on its promise to send a trusted driver. Pierre wears gold-rimmed glasses and is holding a brightly colored umbrella over his head as protection against the heat. He stands out from the crowd. In the days ahead, he will prove to be an unexpected ally in my quest to find Junior.

CHAPTER 10

The "New" Haiti

Pierre and I walk over to his green Nissan Pathfinder, which I easily identify by the bold-faced "PRESSE" signs posted on the back window. I'm uncertain whether this kind of self-disclosure serves more as a protection or a risk. The road from the airport into town is one of the most notorious targets of roving criminal gangs. Haitian Americans returning from years of life in the "diaspora" chock full of new appliances and knowledge gleaned abroad are the most frequent targets, but anyone with perceived wealth is vulnerable to a speedy execution upon arrival. Still, I have to assume that under the circumstances even the bandits have suffered immense losses and have probably declared a temporary cease-fire. As we curve past a newly created tent city on the perimeter of the airport, I ask Pierre where he was when *it,* the *tranbleman,* happened.

"I almost died sitting down," Pierre tells me. As he waited in his parked car for five American aid workers to emerge from a meeting in a downtown building not far from the National Palace, a concrete wall collapsed on his car. He thought a bomb had gone off and he wondered why he hadn't heard the explosion.

The concrete rubble entombing his car pinned him to the driver's seat. Luckily for him, the aging SUV he was driving had rickety fixtures and his seat instantly released to a reclining position, buckling under the pressure. Had he been driving a newer car, Pierre tells me, he probably would have died instantly. Instead, Pierre felt a crushing pain coming from his forehead. And he felt a loss of feeling in his right arm, which was crushed by debris. Slowly and steadily he managed to wiggle his way out of the vehicle. When he finally emerged, he looked as if someone had dumped a sack of flour on him. When he reached up to touch the throbbing pain on his forehead, the white powder became stained by fresh blood.

Standing amid the stunned survivors, Pierre managed to reunite with his American charges, a team of health-care experts, who had run out of the building unscathed. His car was totaled and there was no point trying to flag down a vehicle or to wait for help. Together they joined the procession of thousands who roamed the streets like refugees, and within a few hours the capital was plunged into medieval darkness. They walked late into the night until they reached the U.S. Embassy on the outskirts of town, near the airport. It wasn't until the next afternoon that Pierre arrived at his home in his semi-rural neighborhood of La Pleine. Like his car, his home was a total loss. However, his wife and two teenage sons had survived, with some injuries. "We are alive," Pierre says triumphantly. "There are people with a lot more money than me who died in the quake. Their money could not save them."

Pierre is one of the few people I will meet who has not only survived the quake, but who is also in some ways thriving because of it. After a few days at "home"—in his neighborhood, camping out with no tent and recovering from his injuries—Pierre was back working with an American television network as a driver, translator, and fixer earning upwards of $150 a day. I had assumed the sturdy-looking car we are driving in was the property of the hotel where I will be staying. It is not. This is Pierre's newly upgraded car for which he paid US$4,000—cash. To be sure, Pierre is worse off today than he was on the day of the quake. He lost everything he owned; the only clothes he managed to recover were the few items he had stashed at the dry cleaner's. Two months later, he still doesn't have a tent and he hasn't had a medical check-up, X-ray, or MRI to assess the extent of his injuries. At lunch one day, I notice that liquid keeps oozing from one of his eyes, which he blots with a handkerchief he tucks in his pocket. I learn this has been happening since the day the concrete wall collapsed on him. He can probably afford a check-up at a private clinic, but he hasn't had the *time* to see a doctor. He is a true mover and shaker—an enterprising deal maker and a hustler, with all of the inherent and fascinating contradictions that implies. He has managed to seize all of the opportunities embedded in the hardships that have come his way. When I see someone like Pierre I think he would be a very wealthy man if he lived in a country with real opportunities.

We've made it past the isolated warehouse district near the airport and are now snaking our way through a maze of crowded streets where I am getting my first close look at the quake damage. The sight of the pancaked apartment buildings, homes, supermarkets, shops, and offices is chilling. The floors of a once four-story building neatly stacked to a few feet off the ground grab hold of my gaze until they vanish from view. What most surprises me is how continuous the damage is—extending beyond the frame of camera images that have shaped my perception until now. And for a reminder of how fickle nature can be, I notice perfectly intact buildings scattered about, many of which appear to have shoddier construction than their decimated neighbors. I'm reminded of a question that has been troubling me. Why is the hotel where I will be staying—the Hotel Villa Creole—still standing when its cousin up the hill—the Hotel Montana—built in roughly the same time period in a similar architectural style, disintegrated to dust? My question is motivated partly by self-interest. Will I be safe staying at the Villa Creole? And also, my heart breaks for the families who lost loved ones at the Montana and I wonder how this same question must haunt them.

I listen carefully to Pierre's answer. While not "official," I'm always interested in knowing the word on the street in Haiti. More often than not, it usually contains seeds of truth. "The Montana kept building and building on top of the same base. It couldn't support all the weight," he tells me. I shudder as he explains this, suddenly remembering all the construction crews and scaffolding during my last stay at the Montana. I remember thinking there was a veritable boom going on as the hotel arched to keep up with the ever-growing demand for a top-tier property with international standards. Certainly the Villa Creole maintained these same standards, but it always had a quieter, more discreet style.

As we pull up to the hotel I am happy to see its understated elegance remains unchanged. Its style always struck me as a kind of American retro—Palm Springs meets Port-au-Prince. And yet I know there is more than meets the eye. In the first minutes and hours after the quake, earthquake victims began stumbling into the parking lot in front of the hotel, driven by the knowledge that many foreign aid workers and diplomats frequented the hotel. American proprietor Roger Dunwell's daughter, Melissa, was at the helm that day. I had read about her impressive test under fire; she made an immediate decision authorizing the hotel furniture and linens to be stripped and converted into makeshift splints for broken limbs. Hotel guests—most with just basic first aid training—treated victims throughout the night and for days after, using car headlights to illuminate their staging area in the darkness. Melissa kept the teams going with improvised supplies, sandwiches, and sodas.

As I step into the lobby to check in, my eyes are immediately drawn to the yellow police tape cordoning off a large pile of rubble from the front desk. Glancing idly, I look up from the pile of debris and see a former room where the ground beyond the hotel door has broken off in big chunks. I imagine someone stepping outside of that room—cartoon style—and flying through the air. It is hard to believe that no one died at this hotel on the day of the earthquake.

The first room I am given is Room "U"—which I presume stands for "underground" as it is located on the hotel's very bottom level. It is dank and small and I envision myself being trapped in its dungeon-like walls should a violent aftershock strike. I know that a team from the United States Geological Survey has deemed the hotel's handful of remaining rooms safe and habitable, but it is a small consolation to my imagination. The bellboy laughs as he sees my concerned expression. Call the front desk, he advises me. "B'am yon ti chans," *Give me a chance,* I say to Robert, the front desk manager with whom I have established an e-mail rapport during two weeks of coordinating my trip and arrival. Robert understands immediately without my having to explain further. Back at the front desk, he puzzles over his computer trying to figure out how to parcel out the few remaining rooms to his competing constituents. I know many Americans on official business with the U.S. Embassy stay here, and I find myself wondering how he makes what could end up being a life and death decision. Ultimately, I am upgraded a floor to Room "T." This spacious room opens up to a wrought-iron railing, which I picture myself jumping over jackrabbit style to an open garden in the event that an emergency evacuation is needed.

I am ready—and eager—to begin my search for Junior. Pierre is waiting for me outside the hotel entrance, and together we chart a course. We'll go first to the palace. It's not that I expect to run into Junior there, but this is Haiti's most enduring national symbol. I can still feel the shock I felt when I saw that first crushed image of the destroyed neoclassical beauty—like seeing a bride turned into a corpse. This being the two-month anniversary of the quake it just feels right to begin by paying my respects by strolling there and communing with the local residents. Next, we'll head to the former UN compound where I want to light a white candle in Andrea's memory. And then we'll return to Petionville to begin searching for clues leading to Junior's whereabouts.

Outside the palace gates, I meditate on the sights of Haiti, old and new. A boy flies a homemade kite fashioned from a plastic bag and fallen branches. A mom holds one end of a jump rope in the dusty afternoon shadow of a makeshift camp directly facing the palace. Vendors sell bags of popcorn, pirated DVDs, sandals, and packets of cheese and crackers, gum, and cookies. The mood is calm and almost playful as a cluster of children approach me, eager to meet this new visitor. I buy five packs of cheese and crackers and five packs of cookies, hoping for a twofold benefit of paying the market vendor for her wares and in turn feeding her children. I ask the children how they are doing. "Kai mwen krase," a little girl with yellow bows in her hair tells me. *My house is destroyed.*

The reporter in me knows always to follow the crowd in Haiti—at least from a safe distance—as that is generally where the story is. Today is no different. I notice a steady flow of young men with shovels and picks making their way to a colonial building on the southern side of the palace. Pierre is still back at the car when I decide to follow the crowd and get a closer look. As I approach, I recognize the building as the Ministry of Finance and Economy. A sense of anticipation is palpable and I watch in amazement as groups of young men are systematically stripping the remains of this historic building with their bare hands—in some cases passing pieces of recovered materials in a chain-like formation. Although it defies expectation, most large crowds in Haiti are generally quite calm. It has to do with a society used to bearing witness and being there to support each other in the absence of a functioning state. I ask several of the people gathered outside the building what is happening, and they explain to me that people are collecting "bwa" or *wood* from the building to use for fuel and rebuilding. But this form of collective recycling is risky, and on this two-month anniversary of the quake, eight young men have newly been entrapped in the rubble. Reports are somewhat conflicting, but it appears the men have just been rescued and taken to the hospital—their condition unknown. The fate of the eight victims has not deterred other would-be wood-gatherers. A feeling of controlled frenzy abounds, and I notice that crews are not busy deconstructing other quake-damaged government buildings in the area. And that's when it dawns on me what has so far remained unspoken. Because of the nature of this building, it's only natural that people would expect to find some secret treasures buried deep in the rubble—even if that means risking one's life and possibly being buried alive a second time to achieve it.

I return to the car and tell Pierre about what I have discovered at the Ministry of Finance. He is intrigued and together we go stand vigil for a while trying to determine if there are still people who may be trapped inside. It is approaching 4:53 p.m.— the official two-month anniversary mark of the quake—and I want to get into position in front of the palace gates. It's not that I expect doves to spontaneously release from the catacombs of the crushed ruins. Nor do I expect anyone to mark the occasion outwardly. All around me life and survival are taking place. It's just that this is my only way to connect with that moment when time stopped and Haiti and her amazing people were plunged into darkness. I felt so helpless from far away. All I want to do is stand quietly in front of Haiti's shattered patrimony and show my dear friend that I am here for her. *Mwen la.*

Pierre, I soon learn, has other plans. He mumbles something about how it is time to go pick up one of his friends. I'm not quite sure what he is talking about. He never mentioned anything about this when we set out from the hotel. My first instinct is just to ignore him. I can't imagine he would ever pull this kind of stunt on an American television network or embassy delegation. But then I start to second-guess myself and I worry that perhaps Pierre needs to do a favor for a friend injured in the earthquake. I want to help. I press Pierre for more details. He is being vague but eventually I figure out he has a daily commitment to drop off and pick up a Canadian cell-phone technician from work. I am disappointed but I realize there is no point in fighting it. This other client will need to be picked up. Plus, I will need Pierre's help in finding Junior and I decide it's not worth getting things off to a rocky start. "Okay," I say. "But once we pick him up we'll continue with our plan, right?" *Men wi,* Pierre assures me.

As we pull past the guard gate to the entrance of one of Haiti's primary cell-phone providers, located on a hill in the *Canapé Vert* area of the capital, I am taken aback by a heavily armed security presence. A troop of about a dozen men dressed in black with semi-automatic weapons are standing guard on the cement steps of the headquarters. Serge, the technician, emerges and climbs into the car. He is a friendly, if slightly jaded, chain-smoking and globe-hopping contractor. I ask him what the show of force is all about. Serge explains that foreign multinationals are very nervous. Nobody knows when the general calm reigning over the capital might swell like a bloated rain cloud and erupt into torrential violence. "They are taking no chances," he tells me. I learn that curfews are in order for many aid groups and private companies.

I expect Pierre to drop Serge off at his home, but instead we go to a sports bar in Petionville that is part of what I observe to be a new high-rise and McMansion trend in the once modest neighborhood that has long housed the capital's finest shops and restaurants. Like many of these newly oversized buildings, the restaurant looks kind of lopsided, and I can't help thinking that our outdoor café table would be engulfed in concrete debris should another major trembler strike. Pierre orders a round of Presidente beers, from the neighboring Dominican Republic, for the table. Haiti's beer—Prestige—is quite good and I would love to taste it again. Pierre tells me it's almost nowhere to be found right now as the bottling company has been busily producing bottled water since the earthquake. But the truth is I'm really in no mood to sit around and drink a beer right now. There is not much I can do about it for the moment, so I decide to try to accept the situation.

Serge is launching into a story about what happened at the cell-phone company on the day of the earthquake when two ten-thousand-pound batteries slid from their bases and a fuel tank with five thousand gallons of diesel fuel spilled down the hillside to what is now a makeshift refugee camp. "If this had happened in Canada, we would have spent millions of dollars trying to clean that spill," he says as he draws deeply on a cigarette. "It's a good thing Haiti is not a green country."

A young woman with a sad face has shown up during the conversation and it's clear that Pierre has been expecting her. He stands up to greet her warmly with a kiss. She is an off-duty Haitian police officer from the city of Leogane, near the epicenter of the quake. Her fiancé—who worked for a competing cell-phone company—died at his desk. The table descends into a hushed quiet and a kind of inertia sets in with everyone, except myself, scrolling on their phones and checking messages. I am thinking of the candle that I am carrying for Andrea in my purse and I am anxious to begin looking for Junior.

It's clear this trio wants to go out to dinner and Pierre doesn't know how to break the news to me that his workday is over. Turning to Pierre I say, "I think I will go back to my hotel now." He lights up. "Okay. Let's go!" I concede this loss, but I don't roll entirely. Once we are in the car alone I ask Pierre to drive me past the nearby Place St. Pierre, which has morphed into one of the main camps for displaced quake survivors. As we approach, I can barely recognize the once open plaza. In the smudged light of dusk it looks like a scene out of Dickens. Smoke from fires hovers in the air, I can make out the silhouettes of families illuminated by kerosene lamps behind tarps, and the stench of urine permeates the air.

⚬━✦━⚬

That night I walk to dinner alone. I find a small restaurant where Haitians are having dinner and enjoying live music. It feels good to see Haitians enjoying themselves. I think of how this scene contrasts with what I have seen today at the Ministry of Finance and the camp earlier this evening. One thing is becoming clear: The scope of the humanitarian crisis is of epic proportions and so far very little international aid is reaching the people. Nonetheless, I am amazed at the calm and determined demeanor of quake survivors. After dinner I walk back to my hotel, stopping briefly to watch a bulldozer transform the remains of a former hospital into a bare concrete slab. As I turn the corner and am halfway down the private road back to my hotel I am unexpectedly caught in a total blackout. I can barely see even a few feet in front of me. I think of the flashlight I forgot to pack and wait a moment to see if the hotel switches to a generator. It does not. No matter. I do not panic. I feel strangely safe here. I am surrounded by a people who have survived so much and who are only managing to move forward by helping each other. I can barely make out the shadow of a guard gate up ahead and I call out: "Gen moun la?" *Anyone there?* I can hear two hushed voices talking and then a "Wi," is offered in response. A lone guard emerges. "Yo te prann kourant," he tells me. His words make me smile. *They took the power.* Who are they, I wonder, and why do they always do that? He has a small flashlight and together we walk to the entrance of the hotel.

CHAPTER 11

Finding Junior

I am sitting poolside having my breakfast of coffee and scrambled eggs under the shade of the Villa Creole's trademark almond tree. It's kind of a timeless scene, except for the fact that the roof of the main building still housing the reception area has caved in. It's only at this moment—gazing directly at the structure from outside—that I fully understand the extent of the hotel's damage. Relief-expert types are sitting at outdoor tables next to the boarded-up damage, working unperturbed on laptops. I always loved the coffee at the VC and this cup is just as good as I remember it. As I sip it, I recognize many of the hotel's longtime Haitian waitstaff, and I'm happy to see they have survived. It's a nice moment, and yet I'm feeling an underlying sense of unease and anxiety. I'm on the ground here in Haiti for just eight days, the longest I have ever been away from Alexander, and I'm worried. What if I don't find Junior or recover any trace of him?

My task this morning is to decide on a course of action for the day. During the four years that I lived in Haiti, from 1993 to '97, Junior was what one would call "moun" Petionville, or *a Petionville person*. But that last time I saw him he told me he was living with his aunt off Delmas. That would make him "moun" Delmas. Based on what I know about Haitian society, relationships to community are paramount. I know I need to zero in on his social fabric, no matter how frayed. So do I begin my search in Petionville or in Delmas? It's possible I am reacting to the overwhelming anomie of the camp I saw yesterday evening, but today my instincts are telling me to forge ahead with the Delmas lead. The camp felt so anonymous and dehumanizing. I imagine no one there would know Junior, at least not by name. It would be like going to the Superdome in the immediate aftermath of Katrina and trying to find someone on a first-name basis. Plus, if Junior had started to make a life for himself with a reunited relative in Delmas, why would he ever return to a life on the street? Wouldn't he have laid down roots in the area? The damage I fleetingly witnessed on Delmas yesterday as I came in from the airport is also troubling me. It was so extensive. If Junior was there on the day of the quake he could be injured and need my help.

Regardless of the neighborhood in which I decide to concentrate my search, I am clinging to one clue, which I believe offers my best hope of deciphering the what and where of Junior's life before the quake. I know it sounds a bit improbable, but I need to track down the drummer for Boukman Eksperyans, the country's most famous roots band, which regularly tours throughout Europe, the United States, Canada, and Africa. The musician, who has seen Junior playing soccer and tapped him for the government-backed soccer league, was one of his last-known mentors. If I can just get to this guy, whose name I don't actually know, I'm betting I'll have a much clearer picture of Junior's life before the earthquake. And I figure that will point me to the correct refugee camp.

That brings me to the word "refugee," which merits some discussion. I am well aware that in the world of UN-speak a person needs to have crossed an international border to qualify as a refugee. That makes Haiti's 1.5 million displaced people just that: internally displaced people, or IDPs. In telling Junior's story, I will be using both terms interchangeably, in part because it is colloquial, but also because I think one can make a strong case that Haiti's displaced quake survivors are a stateless people.

I mentioned my quest for the Boukman drummer to Pierre yesterday, and we agreed it best to start by contacting the band's front man, lead singer Lolo Beaubrun. I had heard Beaubrun give an interview on NPR in the days after the quake and I remember sitting still in my car, listening to his poetic and calming description of life after near-death, before getting out to go do some grocery shopping. Pierre told me he would make some calls and have the address to Beaubrun's home when he picks me up today. It's almost time for our 11:00 a.m. meeting, so I go to the front of the hotel. Pierre negotiated a little extra time this morning to attend the funeral of a relative. How could I possibly quibble with that?

I step outside to the front entrance of the hotel and am mortified to see Pierre pull up with Serge and the female police officer in tow. The last thing I want to do today is end up sitting at a sports bar with two of his charges as my limited time on the ground here ticks away. Pierre is wearing a dress shirt and his police officer girlfriend, dressed in yesterday's clothes, is sitting in the front passenger seat, sadly fingering the program for the morning's funeral mass. It's an amusing irony I can't help ignore. The funeral was for one of Pierre's *wife's* twenty-something female cousins, who died from a poorly treated leg injury sustained during the quake. I'm trying to imagine the scene of Pierre at the somber gathering, together with his wife and his melancholy girlfriend. Apart from a certain humor of the situation I am quickly losing patience. Pierre had assured me he would be on his own when he picked me up today, so we could get started right away on our search for Junior. I tell Pierre I will have to work with another driver, because I have a lot to do today and I don't have time for his shenanigans, which I translate as "magwi," or *schemes.* He straightens up right away and assures me he is just dropping off his two passengers. Serge sits politely in the backseat, refraining from stepping into the discussion. I take a moment to assess the situation. I will lose more time if I ask the hotel front desk to help me contract another driver. And more important, I know that Pierre is much more than just a driver. He is a true guide and a fellow journalist. I take a deep breath and step into the car. I have decided to trust Pierre, to embrace life and its contradictions.

We head first to drop off Serge. As we ascend the hill to his company headquarters, whose groundwater I imagine is now saturated with diesel fuel, I see a woman wearing a T-shirt that reads: "Why do you hate me?" I wonder if that is how Haitians sometimes feel, given the country's propensity for tragedy. I nod to the woman to acknowledge her as we pass; however, she is preoccupied with her chores at hand. The irony of her T-shirt appears to be unintentional.

Next we head downtown, passing a steady trail of debris. One collapsed building that catches my eye in particular is the crushed remains of Twins Market, which looks as if Godzilla might have picked it up and slammed it to the ground. In Haitian vodou belief, twins, or *marassa* as they are known in Creole, have a special, divine significance. They represent the ultimate duality. The twins are often depicted in paintings and popular culture as each being both male and female. They are mysterious and play-ful children who transcend the boundaries of human existence, hinting at our potential for godlike awareness. So powerful is the metaphor that when President Jean-Bertrand Aristide reluctantly prepared to step down at the end of his first mandate in 1995, he dubbed his hand-picked successor, Rene Preval, as his *marassa*. The public understood the message and elected Preval handily to office. Now, sitting here in traffic, I am surprised to see this build-ing in such shambles. If a market named Twins could not with-stand the force of nature in Haiti, who or what could, I wonder.

Our destination right now is Portail Leogane, a phalanx of clogged streets surrounding the capital's main outdoor stadium. It's from here that tap-tap buses leave for the provincial town of Leogane, epicenter of the quake and home to the sad-faced girl sitting next to me. Pierre does his best to drive his car close to the line of waiting, brightly colored buses. But when it appears that we are going to get trapped in a sea of vendors, carts, and opposing traffic, he finally pulls over and gently tells his girlfriend that she will have to walk to the bus. He has reluctantly decided to honor his commitment to working with me for the day. I am sitting in the backseat of the car, doing my best impersonation of a mosquito. After his girlfriend steps out, we drive in silence for a few min-utes until we drive past a collapsed mortuary next to the stadium. "Those people died twice," Pierre exclaims happily, slapping his leg for emphasis.

Our workday is beginning. Never mind that it is now past noon. True to his word, Pierre has gleaned the home address of Boukman frontman Lolo Beaubrun. I am happy to learn it is in Delmas. Even though what is referred to as "Delmas" is a labyrinth-like district defined by a long boulevard outlining its north-south boundary,

I'm hopeful that Lolo himself might even know Junior. As we turn off of the main thoroughfare, Pierre begins to display his detective-like skill. Without referring to any written notes, he negotiates a winding maze of twists and turns on rocky back streets. I ask him if he has been to this stretch before and he assures me he has not.

Eventually we pull up to a large *peristyle*—or vodou temple—and we both nod, realizing this must be right. The music of Boukman, which takes its name from the vodou priest who helped unify Haiti's slaves against their French masters, is defined by its soaring and energetic spiritual hymns rooted in vodou gospel. It makes sense that the band leader would live near a vodou temple. In fact, he might have even commissioned this for his neighborhood. I stop to admire a striking, yet chipped, black Madonna and child mural on the wall of the open-air temple. A thick pole stands at the center of the structure, supporting an intricate wood beam roof. The pole is the "poto mitan," or *center pole* representing the center of life. Most rituals, worship, and dancing take place around this cornerstone. But today, the temple is empty. A large pair of drums hangs from one of the roof's exposed beams. And there are remnants of candle wax on the floor. During my time living in Haiti, I never sought out the experience of attending a vodou ceremony, although I sometimes caught sight of the rituals at outdoor festivals and events. Something about going to a vodou temple struck me as voyeuristic. It didn't feel right to peer into someone else's private religious expression. And I imagined that outsiders were likely to observe a special performance for "tourists." This temple, tucked far from view and away from the hub of the city, has the energy of a low burning flame that might spark at any moment. This is one temple where I wish I could see what happens in the darkness.

A local resident has approached us to find out why we have come. He leads us to "Kai Lolo," or Lolo's House. At first glance the neighborhood strikes me as an unlikely choice for a world-traveling musician. Looking beyond the quake damage that has destroyed some of the cinder-block homes, it's clear many were in a state of semi-construction even before the devastation. As we approach the gate to Lolo's home, I have a better understanding. Now I get it. It looks like a large compound. And it's located next to a soothing stream. I realize this location is more in keeping with the band's roots to the people than a flashy mansion in the hills. A young male caretaker with dreadlocks greets us at the gate and goes inside for about fifteen minutes. He seems guarded and somewhat mysterious. Pierre becomes a bit agitated and disapproving. He tells me that in Haiti, people with dreadlocks are generally pot smokers. I tell him this is the rap of people with dreadlocks everywhere. We don't need to worry about it, I reassure him. Eventually the young man re-emerges and informs us that Lolo is not home. Come back after 3:00 p.m., he tells us. Pierre does not believe him. He thinks Lolo is inside, either sleeping or eating. I'm disappointed, but grateful we have at least found Lolo's home and are on our way to having an audience with him. I imagine we would have no greater luck had we knocked on Mick Jagger's front door and expected to meet with him immediately.

We contemplate our next move. I propose we begin canvassing the camp at the Place St. Pierre, which we drove by last night, or to the main soccer field in Petionville to try to find a soccer player who might remember Junior. Pierre counters with another idea. Let's go get some lunch. We don't have quite enough time to launch a new search before our meeting with Lolo, he reasons, and he knows of a place that has a good buffet. It will be quick, he assures me. To sweeten the deal he offers to treat me to lunch. I accept. This will help build our camaraderie. I know he had to get up very early for this morning's funeral and I can see that he looks tired. Earlier in the car, as he told me about his wife's cousin's leg injury, which morphed from seemingly minor to fatal in two months, I thought I detected a look of worry on his face. It got me thinking about how many of Haiti's quake survivors are walking around with latent time bombs.

Pierre takes me to lunch at a small, family-owned restaurant. It's a hot-pink colored building that is quite narrow and several stories high. My first impression is that it looks like a structure out of one of my son's Dr. Seuss books. As we climb three flights of stairs to the restaurant level, I fight off a heebie-jeebies sensation. The building's construction seems fairly rudimentary. I'm surprised it withstood the quake and I wonder how stable it is. Once we reach the top level, I take in the views from the open terrace restaurant and contemplate how far it would be to jump to terra firma below. Pierre introduces me to the restaurant owner, who is part of Haiti's Syrian-Lebanese merchant class, which exists in a universe of French, Creole, and Arabic. Behind him is an inviting spread. There are platters of sautéed spinach, grilled eggplant, kebobs, and rice. It soon becomes apparent that Pierre's restaurant choice was not entirely random. He has brought me here to see if I might be interested in trading my hotel for one of the building's spare rooms, which the owner sometimes rents to visiting news crews. Poor Pierre. He can't help himself. He is a deal maker. I politely decline the offer. Then we sit down to lunch and I watch in admiration as the owner's extended family arrives and gathers for a sumptuous Saturday afternoon meal on their outdoor terrace. Several generations are present, from the family matriarch to a young granddaughter. They are an elegant and sophisticated clan, maintaining their traditions and standards despite the calamity that has transformed their lives. It reminds me of my last trip to Colombia, when my aunt Alicia and uncle Tomás invited me to lunch on a weekday, and I was astonished that their three adult children and a son-in-law all made time to come from work and home to join us. We sat down to a very memorable and delicious three-course meal over great conversation. Watching this family now, I wonder, why have we lost the ability to live this way in the United States?

The restaurant where we have lunch is located on the same private road as the Villa Creole and I am aware of the fact that I have traveled in a complete circle. But I have decided to go into "Zen" mode. Anything else will be counterproductive. As we are about to turn onto one of Petionville's main streets, Route Pan Americain, Pierre pulls over to show my photo of young Junior to a group of street vendors selling brightly colored handicrafts. A lanky man without any wares who has been resting against a stone wall steps forward. "Ki jan ou ye?" he asks warmly. *How are you?* I have no idea who this man is. "You don't remember me," he says chuckling. "I am the one with the flashlight from last night." In the pitch darkness of the blackout I was unable to make out even the outline of this helpful stranger's face. Now in the bright light of day, he stares at my photo. It turns out he recognizes Junior—and me, too. "It's me, Canada," he tells me. "I was visiting my friend in the guardhouse last night and I walked you back to your hotel. Don't you remember me?" His unusual moniker jogs my memory and I can't believe the incredible coincidence. I suddenly remember the affable driver with the sky blue sedan from the early '90s who used to ferry groups of our human rights observers on weekend outings to the beach. In fact, he was the driver who drove Marcelo and me, together with some friends, to Kaliko Beach early in our courtship. I still remember that first kiss on the beach. Canada is talking rapidly, stirred by his memory. "M'songe ou. Se ou menm ki te toujou okipe Junior." *I remember you,* he tells me. *You are the one who always looked after Junior.* And then, without hesitation, he tells me that Junior had been making a living working as a cell-phone repairman. However, he has not seen him since the quake. He does not know if he has survived. But still, there is more. Canada offers one more tantalizing piece of information. He tells me that Junior's work base was directly below my first apartment, the same apartment where Junior used to sleep under the stairwell and where we used to eat ice cream on Saturdays. I can't shake the feeling of coincidence and connection. It's almost too much to take in at once. This is the magic of Haiti, where people come together using their instincts and imagination to solve almost any problem. And so it is that a kind, faceless stranger who led me in the dark last night is now pointing me toward Junior. Learning that Junior had set up shop directly below my old apartment has also triggered my instincts. Is it possible that Junior had been searching for me, too?

CHAPTER 12

Reunion

The apartment building remains unchanged, except for a new Tuscan-inspired olive-and-burgundy-colored trim. There are no cracks visible on the façade. The corner ice-cream shop retains its sleepy tempo, its cool tile floor devoid of long lines. (Apart from Junior and myself, the parlor never seemed to have much of a fervent following.) Pierre pulls up to the corner, directly below my old second-story balcony, and signals for the troupe of cell-phone vendors to approach. They advance in a pack, mistaking us for customers in need of a card to replenish our phones with more minutes. Perched behind the wheel, Pierre directs the group with precision. We are looking for one of their colleagues, a certain Junior Louis. He motions to me to hand him the photo, which is passed from vendor to vendor. "She is Junior's mother," Pierre informs the crowd. "When she finds him, she will do everything for him." I smile wanly, realizing this information must seem rather incongruous, as I am clearly a *blan*, or foreigner. And I'm nervous at the implication that I, an unemployed writer and stay-at-home mom, have shown up to snap my fingers and instantly deliver salvation, although I do believe that my finding Junior will be the first step in helping to transform his life.

I see looks of recognition on the young men's faces, followed by whoops of laughter and backslaps. Junior's chums are thrilled by the sight of him as a little boy. The laughter instantly puts me at ease. They wouldn't be laughing if he were hurt, I think. The excitement soon morphs into clamorous shouts as the young men begin offering varying accounts at once. The energy of the crowd makes me feel as if I am entering an electrical storm field. I sense that I am physically getting closer to Junior. One young man wearing a wool vest without a T-shirt underneath and a stylish cap says he has heard that Junior is alive and living in the hills. The others are less certain. They haven't seen him since the quake. And yet, out of the excited shouting emerges some happy news: Junior is now a father. He has a young son; however, his peers cannot tell me how old the boy is. I am elated at this news and for a moment I contemplate the thought that at age forty-one I might have an honorary grandson. Still, I am growing concerned. It has been two months. Why isn't Junior back at work right here alongside his peers?

Pierre gives his cell-phone number to the young men and instructs them to call him with any news about Junior. It's now past three o'clock so we decide to continue with our appointment to see Lolo Beaubrun at his house. Still riding high on the excitement of the crowd, Pierre's demeanor suddenly reminds me of a game-show host. "So, tell me, what will you do for Junior once you find him? Will you take him back to America with you?" he queries. I realize this is the "lottery" that so many Haitians dream of, the prize for which legions of villagers have risked their lives in improvised and clumsy vessels, like homemade 747s of the sea. The question instantly arouses mixed feelings in me.

Bringing Junior to the United States was exactly what I wished for him as a child. And yet, I now regard him as one of Haiti's most gifted sons. I think of how badly this broken nation needs someone with his intelligence and social graces. At the same time, I think of how travel has opened up the world to me, starting when I was just ten years old and I moved with my family to the Red Sea town of Jeddah, Saudi Arabia, where my father helped design runways for an airport project. I still remember the sensation of pressing my face against the jet window as we flew above the rice paddies of Thailand and the snakelike formation of the Nile in Egypt on family holidays. I could have been sitting on the actual wing of the plane. It felt magical.

In college I spent a summer working in Switzerland and then traveled in the Middle East, crossing the Sinai Peninsula with two other travelers in a dented Mercedes-Benz station wagon by moonlight. My post-graduate year in Washington, D.C., led me to Haiti. Four years later, I was reporting for the *Miami Herald,* where I covered local news and parlayed my travel bug into assignments in Cuba, Kosovo, and Zimbabwe. My life is more settled now—happily so. The world has become more dangerous since I was out wandering about. And I'm grateful that I've been able to be home with my son for his early formative years. Still, I can't imagine not being able to take flight should the inspiration strike. So, I am demure in my response to Pierre's question. It will depend on what Junior wants. But thinking as a parent, I quietly hope that he travels, sees the world, and then uses that knowledge for good back home. First, though, I must find him.

We drive in silence for a bit on the now familiar and bumpy road to Lolo's house, kicking up clouds of dust behind us. And then, suddenly and inexplicably, Pierre has a thousand-watt lightbulb moment. The announcement is delivered in shouts. "I know he is alive. I am certain Junior is alive." I look at Pierre in total bewilderment. "Did someone tell you something I didn't hear?" I ask him quizzically. In fact, someone did lean in and say in a hushed voice that he thought Junior was dead, Pierre tells me. But, no matter. He is now certain that Junior is alive. I am excited too, and I want to believe him. I want to trust this intuition. But I also want to understand what it is rooted in. "Don't you see?" Pierre is saying, "If Junior was dead, one of the cellphone vendors would know that for certain." In the absence of such definitive news, Junior is certain to be alive, Pierre reasons. It's an interesting theory, although one not likely to hold much validity for quake victims still buried under countless schools, homes, offices, supermarkets, and landmarks around town. "Plus, I know Junior," Pierre is saying with a grin. Now I am thoroughly confused. He told me with certainty and sincerity that he did not know Junior when he first studied my photo yesterday. He brushes off my confusion. Talking with the vendors jogged his memory, he says. "I remember that Junior once fixed my phone," he tells me.

Arriving in Lolo's neighborhood, we park next to the vodou temple, climb out, and make our way back to the Boukman compound. The caretaker's demeanor has changed. He seems less guarded and fesses up that his boss is out of town. Lolo has gone to the countryside for a few days. The young man has been authorized to give us Lolo's cell-phone number. I write it down and decide I will call him once back at my hotel.

We are driving back toward Petionville when Pierre's phone rings. It is THE call we have been waiting for. Junior is on the line. He wants to know who is searching for him. Pierre talks to him like an old friend. "Brother, go take a bath, put on some nice clothes, and make sure you smell good. Your mother is here to see you!" He does not say my name.

○━┼━○

Our meeting will take place at the Hotel Kinam, a converted villa with traditional gingerbread-style woodwork. It's a familiar place. I lived here for over a month when I first arrived in Haiti. It too has been transformed by the tragedy. The hotel sits directly across from the Place St. Pierre, the camp now housing hundreds of the displaced, which I first saw last night. Across the square sits an air-conditioned corner market, and I hastily run inside to buy provisions for Junior and his son. I am too nervous to stop and take stock of my feelings, to entertain the fear that Junior the young adult may have been pulled into the vacuum of drugs or crime, although I do not doubt for a moment that our core bond will be changed by time. I scan the aisles trying to imagine what they might need right now. I select ten-pound bags of rice and beans, powdered infant cereal, baby food jars, milk in the special juice-box-like packaging that doesn't require refrigeration, biscuits, and bananas.

My next stop is the outdoor flower stall, located directly in front of the market and across from the Eglise St. Pierre, a still-standing yellow church that is a neighborhood landmark. Many families are just starting to bury their loved ones who died in the quake. I weave past the funeral wreaths on display and opt for a bit of an extravagance: a large bouquet of tropical flowers bursting with red, yellow, and orange. This will be my gift to Junior, a symbol to celebrate his life and survival.

Junior is in front of the hotel when we pull up. His baby face has become a man's, but he has not lost his gentle expression. His large brown eyes are looking at me with both recognition and disbelief. I immediately notice that he is intact. He has no broken limbs or visible injuries. And yet, he has the weary look of a stranded traveler who has been forced to sleep in a public park or a bus terminal for weeks. We hug. He tells me that he knew it had to be me when Pierre told him his mother was searching for him. And yet, he couldn't believe it was true. "Even if it took fifty years, I knew I would see you again," he tells me. We enter the hotel, taking a seat in the dining room, overlooking the pool. Pierre joins us. He is looking at Junior as if he is a rock star. His admiration is apparent. "Listen, friend, do you have any idea of how I could get a tent?" Pierre asks. The question makes me smile. I still haven't had time to find out about Junior's situation, but I am certain that Pierre has a much stronger financial footing. I invite Pierre to sit and join us, but he happily declines. "Oh, no. I know you two have much to catch up on. I'm going to be out front, talking with some friends I just saw in the plaza."

The waiter comes to take our order and Junior orders a Presidente beer. We've never had a beer together and I feel a little funny having alcohol with him. I have to remind myself he is now twenty-three years old. I imagine he must be famished, so I order a plate of *banan pese,* fried bananas, one of my favorite treats, to make sure he doesn't drink on an empty stomach.

He begins by telling me about his life before the quake, when he had reached his pinnacle. For the first time in his life, he had a one-room, cinder-block home. He was a true self-made man, earning his living fixing and reselling used cell phones, something he had taught himself to do. He is guided by a simple purpose.

"I don't want my son ever to sleep on the street, like I did." The power of the phrase, combined with the realization that he and I are both now parents, immediately brings me to tears. It's so simple and pure. No child should ever sleep on the street. And yet, in Haiti, thousands do. So many of us who came to live and work here somehow accepted that as part of the reality of this mysterious place. I'm feeling both sadness for what he experienced as a child and admiration for his ability to persevere. "Don't cry," he says gently in English. "You know, now I am a man."

Junior tells me Christopher, now two years old, is the product of a short-lived relationship with a young woman named Stephanie, whom he nicknamed Fanfan. "If you care about someone you give them a nickname," he explains. "That's why I call you *San.*" From the beginning, the girl's family, who reside in a favela-style shantytown burrowed high in the hills, looked down on Junior as street trash. And yet the news of Fanfan's pregnancy was one of the happiest moments of his life. "I always wanted a child, especially a little boy," he tells me. "And the first child *Bondye* (God) gave me was a boy." Although he and Fanfan are no longer together, they carefully balance child-care duties. Junior watches his son every evening, dropping the little boy back at Fanfan's family home in the shanty each morning.

On the day of the quake, Junior was walking to a pizzeria in Petionville where the Italian owner often treated him to free pizza. I immediately recognize this as part of the protective shield of goodwill that Junior has created and that surrounds him always. He heard a loud rattling sound and then moments later he felt the earth shake. Thinking there had been a terrorist attack, he began to run. As he crossed a bridge, he watched as a three-story home collapsed "like a cheeseburger." Fanfan and Christopher had been at his home when he left and he raced there now like a madman. The streets were filled with chaos and people screaming out to God as if it were the end of the world. Junior made it to the collapsed remains of his home but there was no sign of life there. Some of his neighbors told him they thought they had seen Fanfan and the baby step out before the quake. Junior wasn't sure. He wandered the streets for hours, ending up at the Place St. Pierre by nightfall. In the darkness, enveloped in a chorus of people moaning in pain and others singing spiritual hymns, Junior finally spotted mother and son. Junior and Christopher lived in the refugee camp that sprouted from the public plaza for a month—until the stench and overcrowding became unbearable.

A young middle-class couple expecting their first child invited Junior to come stay with them. It's an unusual living arrangement in Haiti's caste-like social structure. The husband, Yuri, a baby-faced office worker in his late twenties, is a member of a homegrown band for which Junior is the lead singer. Junior brings Christopher to the couple's home every night to sleep with him. And while the living arrangement is far superior to the 1.5 million displaced people now residing in camps, Junior is eager to once again carve out his own space. He has not been given a key to the couple's hillside condominium, and he doesn't even feel right showering in their home. "They are helping me. I see that. But I don't feel comfortable," he tells me.

Our conversation is covering so much ground. At one point he casually asks me how Marcelo is doing and again the tears return to my eyes. Being back in Haiti. Sitting here with Junior. I'm feeling so much right now. "Marcelo died," I tell him. I don't get a chance to say anything more. Ever so tenderly, he changes topics. I can see that Junior is still so protective of me.

Still, Junior the young man bears traces of the grit he has had to scrape through in order to survive. In subtle ways, he is rougher than the adorable and wise little boy who has long lived in my heart. I see traces of it in his speech, body language, dress, and experience. He always took great pains to be well dressed and fashionable, making careful selections from the roadside secondhand vendors who sold cast-off American clothing for mere pennies. Now, understandably, he looks like a perpetual camper. Or a refugee. I think of how hard that must be for him. Junior's speech has long reflected his knack for language. It was something I first noticed when he began striking up conversations with the American soldiers who arrived in Haiti in 1994 and I started hearing English slang cropping up in his speech. Now, his slang has taken on an edgier, more urban tone. He says things like, "You feel me?" And most disturbing of all, he tells me that he worked for about a year in a brothel, before he reinvented himself as a cell-phone repairman, making US$20 a day to accompany the Dominican prostitutes on their daily outings to the supermarket and beauty salon.

And yet, none of these changes shroud the essence of Junior's spirit. His beauty and humanity cannot be repressed. He tells me: "When the earthquake happened, I knew you would come back to Haiti. When the journalists first started to arrive I went to the airport to see if I might see you. I wanted to see if you had come back."

CHAPTER 13

Dimanche

It's Sunday morning. At 10:00 a.m. the light is soft, almost hazy. The full force of the sun is not yet blazing. Junior and I have embarked on a walking tour of Petionville. We will be looking beyond the restaurants, shops, sports bars, hotels, and gigantic mini-malls that have transformed this upscale quarter of the capital. Today, Junior wants to show me *his* Haiti. The streets are still relatively quiet without the bustle of honking cars and crowded tap-tap buses. We've only been walking a few minutes together when we are approached by two young homeless boys who shyly ask us if we might have some pocket change, or *yon ti monnai*, for them. One of the boys is wearing a blue T-shirt and frayed pants. The other is wearing a purple polo shirt over a white T-shirt and long shorts, in the way that Haitian street children often wear multiple layers of clothes so as not to lose track of their meager wardrobes. Junior's response to the children immediately takes me by surprise. He asks them their names and ages, what part of Petionville they sleep in, and he advises them not to follow the pack, to stay out of trouble. Junior's tone is warm, tender, and encouraging, like that of an older brother. "You are no different from me or anyone else just because you sleep on the street," he counsels the boys. "Tout moun se moun." *All people are people.* As he speaks, he wraps one arm around the purple-clad boy's forehead and clasps the other boy's wrist in his hand, gently holding the boys in an embrace. The boys, Jean Benet, ten, and Davidson, eleven, have the appearance of wilted flowers who have just been revived with bursts of sunlight and water. Junior reaches into his pockets and gives the boys each some gold-colored coins and small bills. It's enough to make sure they will each eat today. We say goodbye and wish them well. "Kembe fem," Junior tells the boys. *Hold on tight.* He will be back again to check up on them, he adds.

The exchange has shown me a whole new dimension of grown-up Junior, and I am both moved and immensely proud of the man he has become. He didn't just stop to shoot the breeze with these boys. He was coaching them and trying to impart his hard-earned survival lessons. I ask him if this is how he normally relates to *ti moun la ri,* or homeless children, or was this perhaps an unusual exchange initiated on my behalf? "I did that with all my heart," he replies. "I came from that. When I see them in the street, I know all that they suffer. I understand their problems." Junior tells me that before the earthquake he routinely used to round up a group of homeless boys whenever he had extra money from his cell-phone sales. He would gather with the boys in La Place Boyer, a leafy public plaza in one of Petionville's historic residential neighborhoods, where he would pay a street vendor to serve them a hot meal and they would all gather around and eat together, like a family. Following the meal, they would break into an impromptu soccer match. Then he would pay another vendor for buckets of water so the boys could bathe, and hence the children would re-enter the world with stomachs full, soccer-induced endorphins flowing, and a sense of renewal. And this is when Junior first tells me about THE DREAM. He wants to make a difference for these children. For the next generation of Haiti's homeless boys. "I see and feel what they are going through and I want to change it," he tells me. His dream is as simple as it is complex. He wants to overcome the shackles of poverty and indifference that have long made homeless children—primarily boys, although girls, too, are at risk—an unquestioned reality in Haiti. He longs to build a home and school where the future Jean Benets and Davidsons can live in safety, learn to read and write, and nourish their bodies and spirits. As soon as Junior tells me about his dream, it's like he's telling me something I've known all my life, like a buried memory. It's the same feeling I have toward my son, Alexander. I feel that he has always been a part of my life, even before he was born.

Last night, as Pierre and I were dropping Junior off at the hillside apartment home of his friends, I gave Junior all the remaining cash I had left in my purse. It wasn't much, only about US$20. The truth is, I don't have a lot of money on this trip and I will be limited in how much I can actually "bail out" Junior. It's a topic that is already grating on me as I am now a stakeholder in his dream. As a stay-at-home mom right now, my husband and I are making sacrifices to live on one salary and we couldn't really afford this trip. But Tom understood how important it was to me and we made it happen. I will have to carefully monitor my expenses. With a $3,000 travel budget—financed by a serendipitous tax refund—being eaten into by airfare, hotel, and Pierre's American television network fixer fee, already I am feeling a pinch. Making matters worse, Haiti's steep inflation from the past decade has rendered local currency values into mystifying gibberish. Nothing jives with the prices of the past. As if to avoid the charade altogether, vital commodities like gas are simply quantified in dollars. It retails for US$5 a gallon, pushing up the price of so many basic services. This makes Haiti one of the most expensive poorest countries on earth. I wish I could do so much more for Junior. And yet, I can already see that the small amount of cash I have given him has made a difference. During our talk yesterday evening, Junior showed me his bank deposit booklet. I was impressed to see he had an account, that he had made this passage into the formal economy. And at the same time I was crestfallen to see that his balance was just 50 *gourdes,* which I later tabulated as just $1.25. This morning, I can see that Junior has bathed and shaved and he has proudly told me that he used some of the money to buy this "new" shirt, a black uniform-style shirt with a bright logo patch on the front. He looks like the stylish and energized boy I remember. And with the small amount of money I have given him, he has stopped to help two more boys in his likeness.

In some ways, this walk through Petionville feels like old times. And yet, some things are strikingly different. Junior has stopped to point out an ornate ivory-colored office complex, home to several foreign embassies. It's a six-story structure labeled the Hexagone building. And together with the lone European Union flag hanging from one of the upstairs suites, it looks like it would fit in perfectly on a Paris street corner—following an Allied bombing attack. The building sits noticeably empty, like an elegant patient awaiting surgery. Scaffolding has been placed around it in a kind of nervous expectation. The building is markedly crooked, buckled, and swollen. It resembles a house of cards that might collapse at any moment.

Not far from the house of cards we pass a small home with a handwritten sign posted outside in French that reads: "Ici, chaque dimanche matin vous aurez de soupe de giromon." *Here, every Sunday morning you will have pumpkin soup.* It strikes me as a kind of signpost out of *Alice in Wonderland* and Junior and I instinctively walk down the narrow alley/rabbit hole leading to the rustic feast. For me, pumpkin is one of those wonder foods in the same category as salmon and spinach that instantly elevates one's mood and sense of well-being. In Haiti, pumpkin soup has an added cultural significance. It's a traditional dish that Haitians drink on New Year's Day to cleanse and give thanks. This day is like a new beginning for Junior and me, just as Haiti, too, is undergoing a rebirth, and we sit down to savor the moment and reflect. Junior tells me that he got up early this morning to attend Catholic mass. To pray and give thanks that I had come back. I am both touched and surprised. I did not know he attended church. He is wearing a silver cross on a long chain around his neck, but I had thought it a fashion accessory that blended in perfectly with his hip-hop influenced style. I realize now it is also a reflection of his faith. He tells me he has always prayed. He has always maintained a dialogue with *Bondye,* God, and he credits this ongoing conversation with having saved his life on the streets as a child and for protecting him and Christopher on the day of the earthquake. I am trying to understand how this new information squares with the image I have of Junior, the hip twenty-three-year-old garage band singer who has made it no secret that girls tend to flock to him. He smiles and explains, in a hybrid of Creole and English: "Ou konnai, lifestyle mwen. Gotta do it." *You know my lifestyle.* In other words, he is like any other twenty-three-year-old male elsewhere in the modern world balancing his discovery of life with his emerging sense of self. Our bowls of soup arrive, two steaming, savory dishes of thick orange stew with pieces of meat, turnip, and noodles. The warmth of the dish is comforting and Junior says a little prayer before we eat, giving thanks for the meal and asking *Bondye* to protect us both and to give us courage.

As we eat, the conversation naturally shifts to "our" former colleagues from the International Civilian Mission, MICIVIH. To so many of us, Junior was an honorary member of our human rights family. It has been thirteen years since most of us left Haiti, with the two-hundred-plus members of our personnel now scattered around the globe, from Kathmandu to Kigali, with many concentrated in Geneva, London, New York, and Washington, D.C. I am astounded by how clearly Junior remembers so many, some even by last name. He is peppering me now for updates. "Have you had any news from Paige and Claudia? Where is John Bevan? Have you seen Wendy? And Farah, where is she? I remember her—and her *ménage*, her boyfriend." They are married now, I tell him, living in California with two boys. "Oh, that makes me so happy. Tell her I say hello." He continues, "What about Sandra Beidas and Anne Russell?" The list goes on. I share what I know about all of the marriages and children that have grown our extended family during this long interval. He looks genuinely happy to hear of everyone's good news. And yet his expression leads me to wonder what he might be feeling deep inside. Here he is so eagerly and earnestly remembering everyone. Yet, the truth is that so many of us have "moved on" and formed families and gotten caught up in the noise of modern life. But I want him to know we haven't forgotten him. For those of us who have wondered and worried about him over the years, there wasn't an easy or natural way to reach out. Although Junior is now incredibly, and improbably, adept at configuring mobile phones, he still doesn't have an e-mail address. (And what good would that do without a computer or Internet access?) But at least in my case, I realize now that I just wasn't being creative enough to stay in touch with him. I was too absorbed in my immediate daily life.

Junior updates me on what he knows about some former mission members who have continued to live in Haiti, or who have returned on official business, and I am heartened to hear of their outreach to him. Lizbeth, a New Hampshire transplant and UN human rights officer who first came to Haiti by way of the Peace Corps, has been a constant friend and presence in his life. John Scutts of New Zealand, a UN communications expert now in New York, bought him a motorcycle a couple of years ago, which Junior later had to sell when it broke down. And he tells me that a certain "Javiel" gave him US$200 shortly before Christopher's birth to prepare for the baby's arrival and this "Javiel" later paid for him to take computer classes. I am assuming he must be referring to Javier Hernandez of Peru, a UN human rights expert now working in Colombia. Still, I am having a hard time processing this information. With his long braid and über-intellectual manner, Javier, an esteemed member of our Latin American contingent, was kind of like a Brahmin priest or professor. I remember him once approaching me telling me there were rumors that Junior wasn't really homeless. "What do you mean?" I asked, bewildered and a bit peeved. He might actually have family, was Javier's response. I paused for a moment to contemplate how best and succinctly to respond to his assertion. "That may be," I said. "But he is homeless just the same." In his professor-like manner, he encouraged me to conduct an investigation into the matter.

Now, to learn all these years later that Javier came through for Junior during one of the most important transitions in his life, makes me smile. That is a true family.

After finishing our soup, Junior and I continue on our way. We walk past an old-fashioned white structure with columns and a wraparound terrace. Signs identify the building both as the *Ecole Nationale Republique de l'Uruguay* and the *Ecole Nationale Republique du Guatemala*. In its former life this was clearly some kind of secondary school. Now it is dotted with tents and has the external appearance of a well-organized refugee camp. Women are washing clothes and cooking in groups. We walk past tents pitched in the courtyard and make our way to a covered patio that appears to be the hub of the camp. A young man with the manner of a university student steps forward and tells us that he is one of the six members of the camp's leadership. He tells us this school-yard is now home to two hundred families. Overall, conditions are tolerable but people are worried about how long they will be living in such an improvised state. The UN has come under intense criticism following reports of women being raped in the anonymous and unprotected void of the camps at night, and I'm curious to know if that terror has reached this seemingly peaceful enclave.

The criticism peaked after Anthony Branbury, the deputy head of the UN peacekeeping mission in Haiti, awkwardly stated that the toll of only three reported rape cases in the aftermath of the quake "almost elates me," in a bungled attempt to express relief that the number was not higher. Our young leader tells us there have been no reports of rape in this camp; however, as soon as nightfall hits they are plunged into a total blackout, with nothing but the flicker of kerosene lamps to guide them. The threat of insecurity is ever present.

Of greatest concern, the leader tells us, are the latrines, which have not been emptied in weeks. Food supplies are holding, but their last water shipment was two weeks ago. And in the two months since the quake there has been only one mobile health clinic, which set up shop in the camp for one day. The young man's leadership skills are impressive. He introduces himself as Fritzner Jean, a fourth-year accounting student at the Université Americain. With his enterprising spirit and communal outlook, Jean perfectly personifies how Haitians have managed to survive and persevere for decades. "Nou tranquil paske nou oblije abité avec nou memn," he says. *We are at peace because we must live together.*

I ask Jean to lead me to someone who is injured. We traverse a dirt-paved corridor crammed with tents and tarps to the American-style camping tent of medical technology student Leon Dolande. She sits listlessly on a mattress, her left leg visibly bandaged, with her mother acting as nursemaid at her side. Dolande, twenty-four, was buried under the rubble of her four-story college for nearly twenty-four hours after the quake. Her left leg pinned under the debris and wincing in pain, she listened to the cries of other students, some of whom did not survive, as she waited for help. Rescue came in the form of her entire family who dug with bare hands until they recovered her and carried her to safety. Since the quake, Dolande has had two operations and her left foot is still in terrible pain. Her demeanor is both calm and patient and yet she seems scared and uncertain. She still can't walk and the road ahead is a complete unknown. The tent we are sitting in is now base camp for ten people. Like Jean, the camp leader, she wonders nervously how long she will be living here. The tent is not a home and is certainly not big enough for so many people. And yet, it's hard to ignore its comparative "high standard" of living. I see a Toshiba laptop and a pair of cell phones tossed on the mattress next to Dolande. A twenty-inch television propped on top of a music boom box lies next to a twenty-five-pound bag labeled "Premium Quality U.S. Rice." This was clearly a working class Haitian family on the brink of entering the middle class that lost nearly all of its possessions and who had made a great investment in their daughter's education. Looking at Dolande, I see a bright young woman who was just embarking on her life when her world literally collapsed. I want to know what she dreams of now. "I hope to walk again and one day to work in a medical laboratory," she says simply.

Junior has been at my side this whole time. He has been quiet, listening intently and at times interjecting a question to make sure I catch a point. He can tell that I am fusing my memory of Haiti with the current reality. From here we continue on foot to his crushed neighborhood, Monequil. Basically, this visit to the camp has been a practice session for what comes next. Junior begins his tour with a history lesson, telling me his quarter of rudimentary cinder-block homes is named after Charlemagne Peralte, a Haitian nationalist hero who led a band of "Caco" insurrectionists in defiance of the 1915 U.S. occupation of Haiti. This is one of Haiti's so-called "popular" neighborhoods, a label that has nothing to do with a high count of Facebook fans or Twitter posts, but rather is reflective of the teeming masses concentrated within its maze-like streets. Buried off the main road below the Petionville marché, it is a place I have certainly passed hundreds of times by car but never realized was there. The fact that Junior is familiar with the etymology of the neighborhood's name is a signal of how Junior sees the deeper meaning of things. It's not common knowledge, I later find out.

We are walking past a landscape of pancaked structures and barely standing homes. I see a once four-story building reduced to a pile of four concrete slabs. A survivor has pitched a tent on top of the new foundation. A plastic garden chair serves as a porch bench. Turning off the main road, we enter a cavernous passageway of alleys reminiscent of an underground subway system. We are entering a debris field of boulders, rocks, and twisted metal rods that once served as the flimsy spines of homes. Junior makes his way nimbly through this jumbled terrain, which is still teeming with people. He is walking with determination, and I scramble to keep up as the path grows steeper. We arrive at a clearing and he stops to face me. "This was my home," he tells me. I immediately do a double take. There is nothing here. It's then that my eyes move to the ground and I realize that his small home completely collapsed. We are standing on a mound of rubble measuring roughly 8 by 10 feet. It's at that moment that I realize how close Junior could have come to death. I am seized by a swirl of emotions. I feel so grateful that he and Christopher were not inside the house at the time of the quake. And at the same time, I feel so proud that he had managed to get off the street into his own home. Everything he had managed to achieve is now shattered below our feet. Looking down, I see a still life composed of concrete slab mixed with a shattered porcelain plate, cooking utensils, a broken red chair, and a plastic Coca-Cola can. Buried somewhere in the debris is a used, crushed computer, his most prized possession. Junior's expression is somber. But he is not looking down at the ground. His gaze is fixed on the horizon. "That is where Fritznel's house was," he says, referring to a fellow homeless boy who grew up on the streets with him and came to be his closest companion. At the time of the earthquake,

Fritznel was living with an aunt and cousin—and he and Junior were neighbors. Junior points to an empty void where a swath of terrain slid down the canyon into a sea of buckled shanties below.

Junior's pain is echoed in the expression of his surviving neighbors, the Celestin brothers, who have lost eighteen of their relatives, including their wives. One of the brothers is standing with just a red towel around his waist, his grief etched on his face. Junior walks over to greet the brothers and offer words of support. Much of the neighborhood is scattered now, with people sleeping in tent camps at night and coming back to the old neighborhood by day to bathe, try to retrieve a lost possession, and to seek the community of friends and neighbors. Mesin Celestin, fifty-one, tells me he lost his wife and two children. Brother Camille lost his wife and two daughters, aged fourteen and four. A surviving teenage daughter sits on the ground listening quietly as her father talks. Brother Lejeune Celestin also perished in the quake, together with his wife and six children. And brother Jusner Celestin died together with his wife and two children. In all, four family homes were completely destroyed. The Celestins are a family of masons, carpenters, and iron workers. They have a quiet dignity about them and it is hard to find the words to offer in the face of their loss. "We have always been close," brother Camille tells me. "We are always together now."

As we continue weaving our way through this destroyed corridor, I start to feel the sting of some of the pent-up resentment of Haitians toward foreigners, as I am apparently the first "blan" or *foreigner* who has bothered to come back into this crushed back alley. Never mind that I am here to understand Junior's story. I have suddenly been thrust into the role of international community representative. People are calling me over and giving me their two cents. One woman, Marie Solange Jean, forty-five and the mother of three children ages twenty-two, twelve, and fifteen, has returned to her shattered home to try to clean up and salvage what she can. I admire her perseverance. She has no tools and everything around her is crushed to bits. I see nothing that can be salvaged. This is a clean-up job that will require a dump truck, and yet she has returned to somehow try to change her fate. She is angry about her situation and clearly needs to vent. Her anger is very different from the quiet devastation of the Celestin brothers. Both strike me as entirely human responses to the tragedy. Junior understands the tension that my presence is causing and he works delicately to try to mitigate it. He explains that I am a journalist. I can help best by drawing attention to their situation. I make a point of writing, dictation style, as Marie Solange frets about the hardships she is facing. We are standing in the shell of her extended family's two-story home built in 1987. She has lost every material possession and like many members of the Monequil community is now living like a squatter in the camp that has sprung up in Petionville's Place Boyer. Marie Solange grows calmer as she tells her story. She obviously has not been listened to until now. Waiting in the wings is a fellow household member who does not feel a need to interject. She is Bernadette Jean, a seamstress who has lost something that can never be retrieved. On the day of the quake, Bernadette called to her three-year-old son, Ernst, who was playing downstairs when the house began to rumble. He never responded.

We bid goodbye to Junior's neighbors and begin a winding trek through the underbelly of Monequil to return to Petionville. Our path leads us to a wobbly wooden plank precariously suspended as a bridge over a sea of human waste and debris. Junior laughs as he sees me nervously eyeing a large black scavenger sow and her piglets gnawing on the trash below us. He stands on the middle of the plank and bounces up and down to show me it is sturdy enough to support our weight. "Come on, San. It's okay. We are safe," he calls to me. I cross the bridge and feel the sense of exhilaration that one feels when accomplishing a daunting challenge. I know I am getting a rare, up-close look at a pocket of Haiti that doesn't get a lot of outside visitors. There are some popular neighborhoods, like notorious Cite Soleil, the sprawling slum now rife with criminal gangs, that are more obvious and have a certain cachet for foreigners who manage to survive a visit. Monequil is notable for its quotidian quality. And yet, I admit, there is a new feeling I am having, one that I didn't experience when I went deep into Haitian reality before. It is fear. I promised Tom I wouldn't do anything risky or dangerous, and here I am far off the beaten track. The one thought that keeps hovering over me is: I must make it back to Alexander.

We continue walking and eventually re-emerge in the hustle of upper Delmas. We have done a circuit. Petionville marché–Monequil–Delmas. Up ahead of us is the Petionville cemetery. I see a large, modern billboard that catches my eye for the directness of its message, written in a hybrid of French and Creole. "Oser! Aimer Ayiti." *Dare to love Haiti.* Usually, Haiti's taunt is more subtle but I can see that she is not beyond relying on more modern tools of communication to poke and prod those of us who have registered bits of our souls for her cause.

Further up the road, a second sign catches our attention, this one for its handwritten quality. It states, in English, French, and Creole: "WE NEED HELP. Water. Food. Medicine. Clothes. *Comité de la Rue Lambert Abri Pwovizwa.*" The note is signed by the Rue Lambert Temporary Shelter Committee and lists two phone numbers with a large blue arrow pointing ahead. Although not a fancy billboard, this sign is just as noteworthy and sophisticated. The handwritten message is inscribed on a white bed sheet and is attached to a poster of a beaming Haitian schoolboy. It's the first time I have seen displaced camp residents relying on advertising to draw attention to their plight. Junior and I follow the arrow to a small, crowded camp at the end of a road, overlooking a ravine. The mood is much different from the camp we visited earlier in the day at the Ecole Guatemala/Uruguay. That camp seemed like a country club compared to this dehumanizing place. The atmosphere feels very discordant from the optimistic and unifying spirit of the sign with the happy schoolboy. A group of women are sitting around a table playing cards. They have rough and hardened expressions, some bearing scars. The scene reminds me of the gritty realism of Toulouse-Lautrec's turn-of-the-century paintings from the brothels of Montmartre. We introduce ourselves, explaining that I am a journalist. We saw the sign and want to know what life has been like in this camp since the quake. The women barely look up from their card game. It is clear that our presence is not welcome.

When I pull out my handheld tape recorder from my bag the dynamic suddenly shifts. It's no longer me they are talking to but the unseen world at large. The women begin shouting over each other, each louder than the last. It's so raucous and overwhelming, I can't even make out any distinct complaints. One thing is clear, however. This is a very neglected camp that has received very little outside assistance—despite their very effective signage. The cacophony is reaching a frenzied pitch. I click off the recorder and slip it back into my bag. The voices come down.

Junior and I repeat our promise to share their story. The women shrug. They don't begrudge us. We ask if it would be okay to walk around the camp and they wave us on.

A group of children has been waiting in the wings. One little girl, about three years old with a radiant caramel-color complexion and blue and white bows in her hair, approaches me and takes my hand. She doesn't let go throughout our walk. She is a beaming ray of light and I am astounded by her healthy appearance, even in comparison to the other children around her who appear a bit more sad and disheveled. The children lead us to see their home. We see a cluster of tents pitched around an existing tin-roof shanty. There are empty oil drums scattered about and clothes hanging from a line. Large black scavenger sows walk aimlessly around the camp, eating whatever garbage they can uproot. I am looking at this beautiful, happy little girl by my side and I am filled with wonder. How is it possible to live in this environment and emerge so joyful, healthy, and rooted? She's been tenderly holding my hand, and when we stop at the edge of the ravine to take pictures with the other children, she curls up and clasps one hand on my shoulder and begins to suck her thumb on her other hand. I feel an instant and natural bond with this little girl. It's a powerful feeling. Intuition. Love. Recognition. I'm not sure what to call it. I briefly stop to imagine the life and family I could provide for this little girl in America. And then I stop and force myself to ignore what I feel in my soul. This little girl is surrounded by her people, her culture, and her heritage. How could I possibly interfere with that?

We've arrived back at the table where the women are playing cards. "Se ki moun, sa?" I ask the women. *Who is this child?* I learn that her name is Jenny. Her grandmother sits in the group of women. She has short, cropped hair and looks emaciated, but right away I detect that the grandmother is alert and has keen judgment. Clearly, she is doing an exceptional job of raising little Jenny under dire circumstances. I'm holding Jenny in my arms now as we talk, marveling at her halter top with big yellow flowers, jean skirt, and Dora the Explorer shoes. I know there are great finds to be had from the secondhand *pepe* vendors, but Jenny's dress and the beautiful bows in her hair are testament to the loving care she is receiving. I ask Jenny's grandmother what happened to her mother. Her response crushes my heart. "She died in the earthquake."

As I am reeling from this information, a camp resident approaches and asks if I will come see a man who needs medical help. We walk over to see him. He is slumped outside a tent, sitting on a piece of cardboard, and he appears to be near death. Unable to walk, the man, in his fifties, has a leg injury that has not been treated since the quake. I give the man most of the cash I have in my purse and advise his fellow camp mates to take him by taxi in the morning to the private clinic on the Rue Lambert, which has been offering free triage medical services. A woman, presumably one of the camp leaders, promptly takes the wad of bills from the man's hands. This camp is most likely surviving by pooling its resources and I pray that this sick man will be deemed a priority for them. Jenny has not left my side. We walk back to her grandmother. I give them both fierce hugs and then Junior and I walk away.

I don't think Junior has noticed just how much this encounter has moved me. Or it's possible that he is just giving me a chance to absorb and to take it all in. All the realities that I have witnessed today are part of his daily life. This is his world.

Next on our agenda is a brief side trip down Memory Lane. I want to visit the last home I lived in here in Haiti before I moved to Florida in 1997 to begin working at the *Miami Herald*. It's not more than a fifteen-minute walk from this camp, located near the faded but still elegant public plaza, the Place Boyer. The house itself was cozy and charming, with its red-tile roof, arched entryway, inviting patio, and wooden shutters. What I most remember, and most want to see, are the towering mango tree in the front yard and the gracious lawn where Marcelo and I hosted many a barbecue. Admittedly, some of these get-togethers ended on a slightly over-the-top note. Maybe it was the beginning of the late '90s exuberance, a certain *joie de vivre* that came from the spirit of living life intensely. Our hearts and minds were in the right places. We were fully present in what we did and we shared high ideals for what we hoped Haiti would become. And in tandem with those risks came the realization that life could be fleeting. What we knew was that we had this moment and that was a good enough reason for celebration. Out of this mindset came an appreciation for Veuve Clicquot French champagne among our circle of friends. It's not like we had the stuff flowing from swan-shaped fountains at our gatherings. It was more a case of *Where's Waldo?* Inevitably, one or two of our guests brought a bottle of the good stuff, which tended to make an appearance toward the end of the gathering, and we would pour the frothy champagne into plastic cups and savor the moment with all present. The most extreme expression of this fetish came on the occasion of my going-away barbecue as I was preparing to move to Miami to start my new job. Marcelo would follow in a few months. One of our French friends from our human rights mission arrived at our get-together triumphantly waving a magnum of Veuve Clicquot in the air, like a trophy. It looked like one of those phony bottles you might see in a supermarket display. I wondered where in Haiti he had ever managed to find such a thing. (Perhaps in a hidden vault at the French embassy?) It was such an extravagance and a gesture of whimsy and love. Our colleagues had been our true family for four years. Our gatherings were how we managed to survive amidst all the hardships and horrors. Once I realized the bottle was real, I remember laughing so hard and not being able to stop.

On the flip side, we sometimes hosted no-frills, impromptu Friday night dance parties. We were limited in terms of what we could do for socializing and we knew we had to create our own fun, our own community. To this day, those memories stand out as some of my best dancing memories. The formula was simple: good friends; good music; good times. We pushed all the furniture to the sides of the living room. People came after having dinner at home. Everyone brought whatever drinks they had lingering in their fridge. We threw everything into coolers loaded with ice and complemented the selection with the best Haitian rum, Barbancourt. The lights were dim. You could barely make out individual figures. And we danced and laughed into the wee hours of the night, barefoot on the cool tile floor. I remember how Andrea was one of the most fervent supporters of our dance club. She would often encourage Marcelo and me to send the signal for a gathering, even on a Friday evening when we thought we were too tired. I can still make out traces of her wispy blonde curls dancing in the shadows.

Junior and I arrive at the gate of the house, and as is to be expected, it doesn't exactly mesh with my memory. I'm pleased to see the house is still standing and the mango tree is as resplendent as I recall. But the garden is shriveled and lackluster, and the soul of the home appears to be gone. The house has been transformed into the headquarters of a Dutch health nongovernmental organization (NGO). A metal file cabinet stands on the once graceful tile porch. As it is Sunday, the office is closed. A guard on duty allows us to tour the grounds. A tall cinder-block fence has come down, perhaps in the earthquake, revealing the ravine abutting the property. I always knew it was there. The dry riverbed led to a shantytown below, where we sometimes heard the gunshots fired at night. Standing here now on the crumbled fence, it's the first time I realize the magnitude of the ravine's pollution. It's littered with plastic bags and dumped trash. It looks like a veritable landfill. I stand and stare for a long time. Was it always this polluted when I lived here?

Yuri, the friend and fellow bandmate with whom Junior has been staying, has arrived to pick us up and take us to visit Junior's son, Christopher. When we get in the car, we immediately realize it has a flat tire. As we wait for a mobile repairman to be summoned on foot, Junior and I walk over to the nearby Place Boyer and mill about. The once tranquil plaza has been transformed into a camp. This is our third "refugee" camp of the day and it seems the most residential. There are some timeless scenes unfolding before us. People are gathered around a barber giving a man a shave, all eyes focused on a soccer match playing on a small television screen. A vendor tends to a steaming pile of chicken Creole that smells delicious. A group of young boys is playing a Sunday afternoon soccer match. I am sure the quest for meager resources is just as dire here as in the other camps, and yet the scenes we see played out here most closely resemble the fabric of Haitian daily life that I remember from the past.

As the sun begins to set we ascend to the favela-like neighborhood of Stenyo Vincent where Christopher spends his days in the company of his mother's relatives. Yuri has dropped us off on a residential street. We will continue walking from here. The transition on the street is striking. We begin walking past mansions, some resembling bank buildings, with fortress-like gates and satellite dishes. As the street rounds a corner, the architecture suddenly morphs into a shantytown built right into the hillside. To reach Christopher, we must climb a steep path of stairs, into a maze of cinder-block homes stacked like boxes, reminiscent of Adobe cliff dwellings. There is no reasonable explanation for how this neighborhood managed to emerge unscathed from the quake. When we arrive, Junior pushes open a rudimentary wooden door and my eyes struggle to adjust to the darkness. The setting can best be described as a cave, as there is no natural light or electricity. Once my eyes adjust, I see a little boy with bright eyes and tiny colored beads braided into his hair. He has been lying in the darkness, in the loving embrace of his maternal grandmother. This hardly seems an ideal environment for a toddler. Christopher is just a few months younger than my own son. I wonder how this dank, non-stimulating setting affects a child's development. And then I watch as Junior reaches for his son and they begin to chatter happily together. "Kote ou ale, jodi-a?" *Where did you go today?* I hear a sweet voice ask. Somehow, despite the crushing poverty and primeval conditions, Christopher, like so many of Haiti's children, is happy, bright-eyed, and thriving. The only explanation I can come up with for this anomaly is the love that is lavished upon him.

CHAPTER 14

Sunday Dinner

I barely have enough time to change my clothes after my day-long outing with Junior when my former colleagues, Elio, from Uruguay, and Heiner, from Germany, pick me up at my hotel for dinner. It has been thirteen years since I have seen Heiner and ten years since I have seen Elio, although I have stayed in touch with Elio over the years. The mood for our reunion is quite moving. We don't fully have the time or the words to express what we are feeling. So much has happened since we last met. Haiti has collapsed into unrecognizable ruin and countless lives have been lost. Death's presence lingers in the piles of uncleared debris on every street. We have come together and yet the feeling that prevails is one of absence. Andrea is gone. And before her, Marcelo. And Heiner's presence is a miracle of sorts. He was working in a villa on the UN compound when the quake struck. Sensing the imminent collapse of the Hotel Christopher, which served as UN headquarters, he had to make a split-second decision on which corner of his office to run to. He made the right choice. The Hotel Christopher collapsed and instantly buried part of the villa, including his desk. He was given a second chance. Nobody could have predicted this turn of events. Our tribe, that once numbered two hundred people, is now scattered around the world and connected online via Facebook and e-mail. I feel as if we are the three representatives who have been chosen to attend a special summit meeting.

It's a strange contrast to dine at a restaurant a mere hour after descending from a shantytown. This is one of the contradictions that we all learned to accept when we lived here. By day we investigated human rights killings and at night we often ran into each other at many of Petionville's fine restaurants. There isn't a good rationalization for it. It's just the reality. This will be my one fancy restaurant meal on this trip.

As we are arriving at the beautiful converted villa with a swimming pool that now serves as a French restaurant, Elio mentions that two Doctors Without Borders workers were just kidnapped in this same neighborhood and held for a week before being released for a presumed ransom. This doesn't entirely surprise me, given that Haiti went through a spate of very high-profile kidnappings and beheadings—known as Operation Baghdad—a few years ago. It does shatter my sense of safety though. In the days ahead, I too will notice the contradiction between all the fancy SUVs driven around the country by aid groups and the fact that people have yet to receive much, if any, material aid.

This conundrum has become part of Elio's daily nightmare. Now working as a political advisor at UN headquarters in New York, Elio has just arrived in Haiti for a two-month stint to assist with the humanitarian effort. He's been tasked with a Herculean assignment: to help ensure the international community is upholding the human rights of Haiti's 1.5 million quake survivors in its disaster relief efforts. Since arriving four days ago, he has been in a total pressure-cooker, sleeping in a tent near the airport and working sixteen-hour days. Each time I have managed to reach him on his cell phone he has sounded nearly breathless.

Elio and I share a special fondness for Junior. In my own mind, I have always seen the three of us as a kind of surrogate family. In the years since we left Haiti, Elio and I have crossed paths in Miami and Kosovo and stayed in touch via e-mail and occasional phone calls. Always, Junior's name has been a constant in those conversations. In recent years, when Elio had returned to Haiti on official business, he had given Junior his office number. From time to time, after Junior learned how to access an Internet phone line, he would call and leave sporadic messages on Elio's voice mail at work, offering updates on his life. In the aftermath of the earthquake, Elio and I exchanged anxious e-mails, help-lessly fretting over Junior's safety from New York and California. And Elio had already started tapping contacts in Haiti to try to find Junior. So it was bittersweet this morning when, standing in the lobby of the Villa Creole, I managed to reach Elio and let him know that I had found Junior.

"You should hear him talk about his son," I said. "He is an amazing father. He's determined to make sure Christopher doesn't end up on the street." I had to stop and catch my breath on these last words, not wanting to cry in the hotel lobby. "That is so wonderful to hear," Elio replied. It was the first time I heard him relax since we had connected in Haiti. And once again Junior had given us occasion to laugh and marvel at his ingenuity. I told Elio how Junior had been making his living repairing cell phones. "You can bring him any phone from the U.S. and he can 'unblock' it to make it work in Haiti. Many people need a computer to do this. Junior does it without one. He taught himself."

"I should have brought my iPhone!" Elio remarked.

"He has worked on those," I said. "But he prefers Blackberries. They have GPS embedded in them, and most iPhones still don't." I said this last tidbit with a tone of mock knowledge. I am certainly unaware of the finer technical points of cell-phone capability. The fact that Junior is aware of this distinction at once makes us laugh and does not surprise us. This is one of the qualities we both love so much about Junior. "He is the same little ingenious boy as always," I said.

I stop to ask Elio and Heiner something that I have been trying to clarify since this morning. "Junior told me that before his son was born someone by the name of Javiel gave him US$200 to buy clothes and provisions for the baby. Could that be Javier Hernandez?" Heiner nods his head in agreement. "Yes, I believe that is correct," he says. I give him a quizzical look, asking him to help me understand the connection between Javier, the formal intellectual, and Junior, the streetwise cell-phone repairman. "Before Javier left Haiti he gave a very moving speech at his farewell dinner to a room full of UN colleagues. He spoke about Junior and described how after years of working to try to create a climate of respect for human rights in Haiti, he realized that Junior had absorbed the message best of all."

We are sitting poolside in an incongruous setting that could easily pass for one of the more affluent French Caribbean islands of Guadeloupe or Martinique. Fashionable Haitian couples and international staffers are sitting in groups and alone at tables. It's hard to believe there is a major humanitarian disaster right outside the restaurant gates. We are halfway through our dinner when a soft rain begins to fall and we must change tables and go inside.

Our conversation is both compressed and far-reaching. It feels like every word must count because we won't have all the time we need to catch up after so many years. I tell Elio and Heiner what I know about Marcelo's final days. How he died in 2008, less than two weeks after he had been diagnosed with a rare form of leukemia. By then he was remarried and the father of a one-year-old son. He had started a new life on the West Coast, working as the Air France station manager overseeing the airline's new Seattle base. I tell them how I reached out to his new wife and she shared with me that after his death she found out she was pregnant with his second child. Eight months later, she gave birth to a beautiful baby girl. In the photos I have seen since of his children posted on Facebook I have been amazed at how his son is an exact replica of Marcelo's baby pictures. I can see Marcelo's spirit reflected in the gaze of both his children's eyes.

After I speak, I listen intently to Elio and Heiner's every word of their final memories of Andrea. I ask if Andrea's home collapsed. It did not. What if she had made it home that day? I protest. Impossible, says Heiner. She rarely left the office before 8:00 p.m. To illustrate the point, Heiner says he and Andrea had been taking weekly salsa classes, and she often complained that the 6:30 p.m. start time was too early. Elio tells me that he and Andrea had gone to a restaurant not far from where we are sitting to watch election returns on the night Obama was elected president. The restaurant had large-screen televisions and Elio says the mood was joyous as Haitians and expats watched riveted as America elected its first black president.

I am grateful for these memories. As we say goodbye outside my hotel I find myself trying to express how transformative the years we spent together in Haiti were. There is no need to fill in the silence. Heiner and Elio nod. We agree that professionally and personally these were the most indelible years of our lives.

CHAPTER 15

Hotel Montana

Junior and I are walking up the hill leading to the Hotel Montana. I don't know what I am going to find, or if I will be able to see anything at all. I am nervous about coming face to face with the devastation that jolted me awake back in California, and yet I am also worried that I won't be allowed to see anything at all. That would be the worst predicament. To get this close and have to walk away would be like going to the funeral of a loved one and being asked to leave without paying last respects.

I've read press accounts that access to the hotel site is restricted by tight security. And as a stay-at-home mom, I don't have an active press credential. During all of my late night Internet searches, I never managed to actually see an image of the destruction. I still can't imagine how such a pillar of Haiti's development community, with so many of its citizen soldiers trapped inside Trojan Horse–style, could crumble, collapse, and pancake into an entirely different state of matter with such devastating speed and efficiency.

Our arrival at the base of the Montana hillside got off to a jarring start as the tap-tap bus in which Junior and I were traveling skidded on the road's pebbly surface to avoid a head-on collision with a dump truck. Traffic on both sides of the road was funneling into a single lane to accommodate heavy machinery being used to buffer the eroded hillside that had been denuded by the earthquake. Looking up, I saw the carcass of a home partially dangling over the ridge above us. Our tap-tap driver and the driver of the dump truck only bothered to stop at the last moment.

We start walking up the hill, first passing the private villas leading up to the hotel entrance. These homes always struck me as rarefied constructs of 1960s and '70s American modernist style, rather like idealized facades on Hollywood movie sets. I used to find myself wondering if anyone really lived there. They seemed like a kind of fantasyland. Now, the villas look like something out of a Greek tragedy. Junior and I stop to linger at one of the properties. The home's front portico and wrought-iron screen are still stylishly standing, while the actual home has crumpled and heaved upon itself. In the backyard, there is a green swing set that no longer has swings. A swimming pool is half empty with stagnant green water. An August 2004 issue of *Vanity Fair* lies on the ground, opened to the magazine's trademark "Proust Questionnaire" with former NPR host Bob Edwards juxtaposed with an ad featuring a negligee-clad Paris Hilton. The scene is eerily quiet and feels slightly decadent and vacuous. Looking at the ruins there are only questions. Were there children who played on this swing set? I'm still wondering if anyone actually lived here. It doesn't quite feel real.

We reach the entrance to the Montana. I brace myself for the possibility that we might have to turn right around and head back down the hill. A platoon of American soldiers is guarding the gated entrance. I introduce myself and explain that I have come as an American who used to live in Haiti. "I have so many memories from this hotel. This was our gathering place. I just want to pay my respects to all who lost their lives here," I say. An African-American army specialist in charge of the operation has been listening. He appears to have been moved by my simple plea. He looks me over carefully and Junior greets him with a friendly and respectful handshake. "I'm tired of turning away so many people," the soldier says unexpectedly. "And today is our last day here. A private security company will take over the post tomorrow." The soldier introduces himself as Tyler. He is both professional and clearly mindful of the sensitive nature of the site. Perhaps he too is seeking a way to pay his last respects. He agrees to lead Junior and me on a visit of the grounds, stopping first to outfit us with white hard hats. As we walk past the guard gate and up the hill to the former entrance I feel crushed by what I see. For two months I have tried to imagine this scene. A huge, neatly piled mountain of rubble now stands in place of the main building. All that is left standing is an imposing three-hundred-year-old mahogany tree that's older than the Republic of Haiti itself. It's a jarring composition, these two forces of nature standing side by side in uneasy harmony. Many of the hotel's adjoining buildings have been tossed helter-skelter on the hilltop in an Armageddon-like scene.

Standing amidst this scene of devastation, I linger in silence and think of those who drew their final breaths here. The destruction is so complete and yet I feel an unmistakable life force and energy surrounding me that is both powerful and positive. My thoughts are with those whose stories I have come to know from a unique community born on Facebook, the "Haiti Earthquake Hotel Montana" page, which now has more than 12,000 members.

In the first days after the earthquake, search teams posted updates on their rescue operations and families wrote messages to their missing loved ones. The site has grown into a healing space where relatives, friends, and colleagues share their memories, photos, and love for those who lost their life here, and whom I now regard as friends. I am thinking of Stephanie Crispinelli, Courtney Hayes, Britney Gengel, Christine Gianacaci, Patrick Hartwick, and Richard Bruno. The four American college students and two professors from Lynn University in Florida were participating in a course titled "Journey of Hope to Haiti," which had as its mission to feed the poor, aid the sick, and comfort the hurting via hands-on visits with orphans, handicapped children, adults, and the elderly. The course description included this promise: "Surrounded by the hungriest and poorest people in the world, you will experience kindness and beauty that will make you question everything you believe in and appreciate everything you take for granted." The experience made good on this promise. Just thirty minutes before the earthquake, Britney Gengel, a journalism student with a natural gift for storytelling and who had previously dreamed of being on television, texted her mom this message: "I want to move here and start an orphanage." She was days shy of her twentieth birthday.

I would have liked to have met the lost members of the Journey of Hope. The stories and descriptions I have read about each of them paint a picture of an engaged and committed group seeking meaningful connections. Stephanie Crispinelli, nineteen, collected sneakers and athletic equipment to send to boys living in a Jamaican orphanage after she played soccer with them in 2009 and saw how little they had. Courtney Hayes, twenty-three, was known for her empathy. A biology and pre-med major, she once wrote a note on an exam to her chemistry professor, thanking him for the test. Britney Gengel was a bright light who seemed to draw people in with her warmth and excitement for life. She loved Christmas, and her younger brother told one interviewer he still has a collection of loud Christmas pajamas that Britney convinced him to wear with her. Christine Gianacaci, twenty-two, raised nearly $3,000 on her own for a cancer charity event, and she was deeply moved by a trip to Jamaica the previous year. She dreamed of having her own radio show. Patrick Hartwick was Lynn University's dean of education. He saw his mission as helping each student discover their unique skills and talent. His vision, described by a colleague on the university website, completely resonates with me: "He believed in the power of education to eradicate ignorance and promote justice." Professor Hartwick had two children and his wife had previously passed away in 2008. He was fifty-three years old. Richard Bruno had worked as a U.S. Embassy doctor in Nigeria, Germany, South Africa, and Saudi Arabia. After serving twenty-one years in the foreign service, he began a new career as an assistant professor at Lynn University, working in the Institute for Achieving and Learning. Known as a consummate global citizen who was a passionate advocate for human dignity, social justice, and international cooperation, Dr. Bruno had participated in several Doctors Without Borders medical missions to Haiti. He was a proud father of three daughters who managed to impart a sense of "you can do it" to the students with whom he interacted. He was fifty-nine years old.

Standing here atop this devastated hillside, I think about how this space has become a true cathedral, a gathering spot and final resting place that continues to bring people together. I am thinking of Sandra Liliana Rivera Gonzalez, a Colombian airline employee who had moved to Haiti a few months before the earthquake to embark on a new career, helping to improve security at the Port-au-Prince airport. I am thinking of Diane Caves of the Center for Disease Control in Atlanta, who was on a three-week assignment to help implement an antiretroviral treatment program for AIDS victims in Haiti. I am thinking of Sylvie Leroux of Montreal, who has posted tender online messages of love and longing for her companion of twelve years, Roger Gosselin, a former professor working as a health and development consultant. On the eve of his trip to Haiti, Roger had enlisted Sylvie to join him on a quest for the perfect shoeshine brush for a Haitian shoeshiner he had met on a previous trip whose brush had only a few hairs left. The shoeshiner's warmth had touched Roger and he was determined to find him an ideal replacement. I am thinking of Chrystel Cancel of France, who was in the hotel lobby talking with her fiancée, Eric Nyman, on Skype, when the earthquake struck. Chrystel was one of the final guests to check into the Montana. She had just arrived from the couple's home in Panama, on an assignment with USAID to assess tourism development opportunities in Haiti. Eric had asked her to marry him three days earlier.

And my thoughts are with the Varese family of Uruguay and Guatemala: Marylinda and Fabiana. At the time of the earthquake, Daniel, thirty-one, was home with three-year-old Mateo in the family home at the Jerome apartments on the Hotel Montana complex. The Mexican rescue team known as "Los Topos," *the moles,* searched around the clock, mostly using just their bare hands, for fifteen days until they finally found father and son. Daniel was holding Mateo in his arms. Marylinda and daughter Fabiana returned home to Guatemala where Daniel and

Mateo were laid to rest in matching white caskets bedecked with bright flowers. Four blue and white balloons flew from Mateo's small casket, in commemoration of his fourth birthday, which occurred just days before his funeral.

I have not sent a message to any of the families, but I have mourned each of their loved ones and I have watched in awe as they have picked up and moved forward, committed to honoring their loved one's dreams, in some cases pledging to create new hope on the very soil that devoured their lost kin. As I look out over this field of destruction, which has been reshaped by the construction crews, I feel buckled by the mountain of collapsed concrete that so suddenly entrapped so many. I keep thinking, *there was no way out.*

I feel so connected to each and every one who lost their life here. This fortress on the hill brought together so many of us from around the world who were drawn to Haiti's unique blend of beauty and pain, eternal need and dignity. We would come here to regroup, draw strength, enjoy the spectacular view and the best rum sours in town—and then go out into the deep reality of Haiti to connect with our own humanity and hope that in some way our efforts made a difference. Standing here now, I want to tell those who spent their final moments here: You are part of a global chain. Your sacrifice mattered and it will be built upon.

Tyler motions that it is time for us to continue moving. He directs Junior and me over to the once glistening swimming pool, now filled with debris. Oddly, the roof of the restaurant where Junior and I last dined is still standing, although most of the building collapsed. It's a large oval orb hovering in the air. Tyler explains that rescuers have dubbed it the "Spaceship Enterprise," and no bodies have been recovered from this site. It is presumed that everyone in the open terrace restaurant managed to escape before its collapse.

As we prepare to leave, I recognize one of the owners of the hotel, Garthe Cardozo-Stefanson. The Montana began as Garthe's childhood home, before growing from a twelve-room hotel in 1946 into one of the finest hotels in the Caribbean. With her shock of gray hair and her sturdy construction-site boots, Garthe tells me it is easier to come to work each day than to stay home and reflect on her losses. She is grieving for the enormous loss of life at her hotel, including guests and longtime staff members who were like family. Most painful of all—she lost her seven-year-old grandson, Aile, whom she was raising as a son. The body of the front desk manager was found draped over the little boy, in a final effort to protect him. "He used to love to come here to play computer games in the office," she tells me. "What will you do next?" I ask Garthe. She tells me she hopes to rebuild. The road ahead is daunting. Simply clearing the rubble could take years and cost millions. And yet, at age seventy she will do what everyone in Haiti must now do: Begin again.

Chapter 16

Junior's Journey

Today Junior and I are searching for a home. We are looking for the place that came closest to being our shared haven—the house in the historic neighborhood of Pacot. I want to see if the house is still standing and if it resembles the memory in my mind's eye. Walking up the curving road leading into this historic district, I am surprised to see that most of the ginger-bread-style homes with wood latticework, shuttered doors, and spacious verandas withstood the earthquake. As we approach the yellow house behind the mango tree on Rue IV, I am thrilled to see it appears intact. But the home is vacant and shuttered—it feels empty.

A guard allows us to tour inside. The room I am most interested in seeing is the upstairs study, with the arched barn-style doors that opened to a balcony nestled among the mango tree's shady branches, my favorite aerie. It was here where I would often write in the afternoons, drinking coffee from a small metal pot, while Junior would draw at a small desk by my side. Those were some of my greatest moments of contentment and connection with Junior. Stepping inside, we find the room is dark and bare. We unlatch the wood doors and light fills the room. It is as I remember it. Junior and I stand still and for a moment we are transported. Before going downstairs, we pause at the veranda at the back of the house, which looks out to the sea in the distance. The view from here always seemed so timeless, like looking through a portal and capturing a glimpse of Port-au-Prince in 1910. As we walk downstairs, the guard points to deep cracks in the stairwell and I wonder if the home's foundation is still sound. The Haitian doctor and his wife who owned the home have both died, the guard tells us, and their children live abroad. I wonder what will become of this gracious retreat.

Junior and I continue on our way. Our next stop is the Hotel Oloffson, where we have lunch on the veranda. Here, Junior begins to tell me the story he could not articulate as a child: how he became homeless. I listen quietly as Junior relates his most painful memory. I learn that he was born in Camp Perrin, in southern Haiti, the illegitimate child of a young village woman and the local judge. When Junior was about four years old, his mother, Betty Louis, cheated her half-siblings out of an inheritance and ran off with a boyfriend, leaving Junior to be raised by the very relatives she had defrauded. One of Junior's aunts, Marise, was very bitter over the stolen money and would torture Junior as punishment, making him kneel on an old-fashioned salt grater for what felt to Junior like hours at a time—the sharp spikes burning salt into the cuts on his knees. One day, Marise was so angry over the stolen money that she began to whip Junior fiercely with an electrical coil. He still bears the scars on his right upper arm, shaped like a snake. Fearing that he would be killed, Junior fled the house without a single *sou*, or cent, for his journey. He was five years old. Junior raced to the marché, where he crawled on top of a bloated tap-tap bus. The bus traveled to the provincial capital of Les Cayes. It was in the market there that his Aunt Marie Louis—Betty's only full biological sister—went and found Junior and brought him to her home in Port-au-Prince. The market, with its warmth, energy, and abundance of fresh produce, was a central gathering spot in the region—and a natural magnet for a runaway boy.

I can tell that these are memories that Junior has kept buried very deeply. As he speaks, his eyes glisten with emotion and he casts his eyes far off in the distance, as if watching a reel with images of his young self in his mind. It seems like a good time to take a walk, get some air, and continue our talk in a contemplative setting. We head next to the remains of the National Palace, a site where even in its ruined state, people gather to reflect and stroll. Junior continues his account. Soon after arriving at his Aunt Marie Louis's home in Delmas, he realized he was not being treated the same as his two cousins, a boy and a girl. The cousins got to bathe each day and wear clean clothes. The cousins got to go to school. The cousins had toys to play with. Junior dreamed of going to school. And he dreamed of playing with their soccer ball. Instead, he had to stay home and mop the floors, do laundry, and go to market. When the family was out, the door was locked and he remained outside until whenever they returned. "They didn't beat me," Junior says. "I was just treated differently. I felt like a slave."

What Junior didn't realize as a child was that he had been made into one of Haiti's 250,000 indentured child servants, or *restaveks*. The term literally means "to stay with" in Creole—and the practice continues throughout Haiti to this day, ranging in execution from outright exploitation to a misguided form of foster care. Poor families will send a child to go work as a servant for a family, often relatives, in exchange for food and shelter. The UN considers the practice "a modern form of slavery" and child welfare advocates in the country—including former restaveks— are working to eradicate the tradition, but it remains legal.

One day, Junior grasped at some childhood freedom and fun. His aunt, her security guard husband, and his cousins had been out of the house all day. Junior found the soccer ball outside and went to play in a nearby field. Just as another player was setting up the ball for Junior to make a goal, he felt a strong whack across his back that knocked him over and left him winded. When he looked up he saw his aunt, Marie Louis. "Don't ever play with my children's toys again," she warned.

Junior was instantly reminded of a folk expression in Creole: "If you hit me with a broom we are no longer married." At that moment, he felt he had lost the little family he had.

As the sun begins to set over the collapsed palace, Junior has his arm loosely slung around a dusty-looking homeless boy who has gathered close as we have been talking. "We are no different, he and I," he tells me. "I am washed and have clean clothes. He does not. But we are the same." The boy with the powdery face breaks into a smile. The destroyed palace is such a shocking symbol. I keep coming back to it. No matter how long I stare, the revolutionary impact of it doesn't fade. It has a kind of power over me. I ask Junior what it means to him.

"There are some people who say that we needed to get rid of this for the country to advance," he says.

"What do you think?" I ask.

"I think we just needed to change the people inside. This was our national heritage," he says.

And then he touches on the central paradox of modern-day Haiti, which has officially been "free" since becoming the world's first independent black republic on January 1, 1804.

"We have our independence but we are still underdeveloped. It's like we are still slaves. It's like we have modernized slavery."

❍━❖━❍

Today, Junior and I are at the Plaza Hotel, the former Holiday Inn. This is where I worked when I reported for Reuters. The hotel has mushroomed in size in the days since it was my haunt—and the front entrance has been barricaded shut in response to repeated street protests and upheaval. All traffic is now routed through the back, giving the hotel a slightly fortress-like feel. There is a buzz and energy here that I haven't seen elsewhere in the capital. I feel as if we have stumbled on ground zero of the disaster response. Aid workers and television producers are racing around with a sense of urgency, while others sit languidly in planning sessions over drinks at the bar. Some are here on medical missions, as evidenced by their green scrubs. The CNN team is also housed here and we see some members of their team. Sprinkled throughout this eclectic crowd are a number of people milling about who look like they just flew in of their own accord on personal assignment as disaster tourists. Junior and I try to find a quiet table in the courtyard to continue our talk. We order fresh limeades that seem to get lost in the Beirut-meets-Brooklyn scene. Soon we notice that a cameraman has his lens fixed squarely on us as he squints behind the machine. Perhaps it's because we seem engrossed in a moving conversation. I glance at the cameraman, wondering if we are going to end up in his B-roll. He waves away

151

my concern and says he's not actually filming, which we don't believe. Junior and I continue talking, as the circus continues around us.

Even after the beating with the broomstick, Junior did not flee. He knew of nowhere else he could go. It was only after witnessing a shoot-out on the streets near his aunt's home, in a prelude to the coup that would oust Aristide, that Junior once again ran for his life. This time he ended up near the Paramount Theatre in downtown Port-au-Prince. A large flock of homeless children called this home. Junior felt as if he had entered an altered universe. Many of the kids spent their days getting high on glue. Junior was frightened. He jumped on a tap-tap bus and rode up the hill to Petionville, Port-au-Prince's most affluent suburb. Junior, now six, had been here before with his aunt, and it was a familiar place. Although Petionville was considered upscale, there were pockets of poverty throughout. Junior settled in at the marché, sleeping in empty tap-tap buses at night. He would soon meet another little homeless boy of about his age, his friend and companion, Fritznel Plaisimon. Fritznel would become Junior's entire family—both a brother and a best friend. The two boys were bonded by their status as *sans mamans,* motherless orphans. The stigma of being motherless is such in Haiti that the term *san mamans* is also used interchangeably to refer to ruthless killers and criminals. The weight of this social taboo is akin to not having a conscience or a soul. But Junior and Fritznel found a way to fly beyond the reach of the curse, making a pact not to follow the other boys in the streets. They would survive as lone wolves, being kind and friendly to everyone they met—but not getting too close. In the evenings, they retreated to their den in the empty belly of a parked tap-tap.

From the start, Junior found a lifeline in the kindness of strangers. "Tout mount te renmen. Tout moun te apresye m. Se Bondye." *Everyone loved me. Everyone appreciated me. It was Bondye.* "People used to always give me money. I hardly ever had to ask," he continues. The owner of the Public's supermarket, where I first met Junior, would pay a market vendor most days to prepare plates of warm food for the fraternity of young homeless boys who camped outside his store. And Junior and Fritznel formed alliances with restaurants that would give them a plate of cooked leftovers at the end of the night. Junior found nourishment for his mind with the help of UNICEF. The global organization arranged for him and his homeless brethren to attend a series of schools on Delmas and in downtown Port-au-Prince, paying for tuition and transporting the boys by bus. In this way, Junior was able to cobble together a sixth-grade education—but it wasn't much of an education. "We ate, we played, but they didn't teach us anything," he says of his primary school. "We were there, just happy little kids." His second school downtown showed greater promise, but militants had attacked a nearby orphanage run by Aristide, and Junior and his fellow classmates feared for their safety. "We thought we would be killed," he says. At a third school, located on the airport road, Junior says he learned rudimentary reading and writing, a skill he is still struggling to master. I ask him if there was anyone who made a difference in his education. "I can't remember anything about anyone who stood out," he says. The street would prove to be his greatest teacher. "There are many people who think that if you are raised on the street, you don't have a brain," he says. "Au contraire. You hear more things. You see everything."

Once I left Haiti to begin a new life in Florida, Junior returned to the apartments in Petionville where I was living when we first met. He found the building's guardian who remembered him fondly and allowed him to make his home in a small shed next to the rooftop pool for free—for two years. And then, when opportunity finally appeared in the form of the government-backed soccer league, Junior tapped the courage to return to the home of his Aunt Marie Louis on Delmas. He finally felt as if he were an equal. "I made peace with her but that does not mean I needed to be her friend," he tells me.

Junior's soccer team, "Sweet and Fresh," dominated the league and he experienced a small taste of stardom. After traveling with his teammates to Cuba, Puerto Rico, and the Dominican Republic, his shining moment came at the season finale on the Champs de Mars—the public plaza in downtown Port-au-Prince that is now a sweltering refugee camp. Junior tells me how he scored two of the team's winning goals against the rival team of homeless boys from the slum of Cite Soleil. President Rene Preval was in the stands and personally congratulated the team after the match. Junior had his photo taken with President Preval "even though he is no good," he says. Of Preval, he adds: "He does not have a concern for the country."

Junior's life was taking off and he was seeking new experiences. He met Fanfan and together they embarked on a new life, moving into the one-room home in Monoquil, where they lived together for a year. "We were like two children playing house," Junior says. The annual rent for their home was US$100. Junior was starting to earn a meager living by buying and selling used cell phones. The cell-phone dealers congregated in a familiar space: in front of the ice-cream shop at the base of my old apartment. Many of Junior's customers had returned from abroad and were selling their old cell phones and needed to program their newly upgraded models. Junior would guide the customers to small shops where clerks would consult a computer code to reprogram the devices. Junior earned a small commission for the referrals, and he soon began to observe closely how the conversion was done, eventually memorizing the codes. "Because it was a number, it was easy to remember," he says. Soon, he was no longer accompanying customers to the shops. He was programming the phones on his own. Whereas the shops charged an average of US$15 for the service, Junior's fee ranged from US$3 to $10.

An invisible hand aided Junior in his transition off of the street. Javier Hernandez, my former mission colleague who had once suggested I conduct an investigation into Junior's background, became one of Junior's most loyal patrons and mentors—Junior clearly having met his test of honesty and character. As Javier was preparing to leave Haiti for a new posting with the United Nations in Colombia, he found a friend, also named Javier, from Spain, and deputized him to check in on Junior and to help him in case Junior was ever in hardship. When Javier #2 was preparing to leave Haiti, he tasked another colleague, named Carol, with the role. It was Carol who delivered Junior's first laptop, an Acer Pentium 3. The device elevated Junior's perspective and capabilities, introducing him to the Internet and allowing him to tap cell-phone codes for Motorola, Samsung, and Nokia, which a friend loaded onto his computer. When I ask Junior if the codes are copyright protected he suggests the intellectual capital is part of the public domain, much like library books. "They are codes for everyone," he says. "They are from programs." After the earthquake, a shaken Carol came looking for Junior. "She was so happy to see me," Junior recalls. "She said she would let Monsieur Javiel know that I was alive."

When Fanfan became pregnant, Junior felt he had the chance to start the family of which he had always dreamed. He promised Fanfan he would find a stable job with a fixed income to support their new family. The job he found was as an assistant at a brothel. His job was to act as a guide and to accompany the Dominican girls on their daily outings to the supermarket and to the beauty salon. Junior already had a facility for language, speaking a bit of both Spanish and English, and he was able to communicate with his charges. He was paid US$20 per day—a good salary given that Haiti's annual per capita income is $1,200.

The job led to the unraveling of his relationship with Fanfan, who was advancing in her pregnancy and still living in Junior's home. Junior had fallen in love with one of the Dominican prostitutes, a sweet "girl next door" type named Patricia. "Everything she had she shared with me," Junior recalls. For a while, Patricia wanted to continue working as a prostitute, to be the primary breadwinner for Junior and herself. But eventually she quit and Junior was fired from his job for a kind of embezzlement.

Junior did his best to balance his ever complex personal life, staying in touch with Fanfan after she moved back into her family home and remaining committed to the ideal of being a loving and involved father. With this in mind, he set out to his birthplace of Camp Perrin on a special quest. As a street child, he had no papers and he wanted to give his son a family name. He needed to find an official record of his birth—or to at least find someone who would claim him as his or her own. Arriving in the fertile countryside, he learned that many of his mother's half siblings had immigrated to Canada. Only a few relatives remained behind. Feeling further abandoned and alone, he erupted into a fit of rage—never had he felt so much anger released from his body. With his fists pounding the rich soil of his birth, Junior demanded to know what had happened to his mother. Two of Junior's male relatives tried to comfort him, telling him his mother had most likely not died. They believed she had left Haiti, but they never heard from her again. The emptiness in Junior's heart was not erased, but the moment was a catharsis and he found a measure of peace. Junior's relatives put Junior in touch by phone with an uncle in Canada who agreed to sponsor Junior with his paperwork and to give his nephew a new identity. And that is how Junior Louis was reborn as Junior Davilma.

Christopher Junior Davilma was born at a Doctors Without Borders clinic in Port-au-Prince, with Junior at his side. Both mother and father agreed on the name, but it was Junior who proposed the name for his firstborn. He chose Christopher for its roots in divinity. "I know it is a sacred name that is protected by *Bondye,* because I know that *Bondye* is also called Christ. That is why I chose it. Christopher is the son of *Bondye.*"

After the birth, Junior did his best to try to be a doting and loving father—although he felt guilty about not being able to provide for his son financially. Patricia also adored Christopher as her own son. They shared parenting responsibilities with Fanfan, who quietly harbored her jealousy of Junior's new girlfriend. One day, Fanfan showed up at Patricia's tiny apartment, on the pretext of needing money to buy milk for Christopher. Fanfan handed Patricia the baby, immediately triggering a powerful reaction. Patricia's arms broke out in a bright red rash and her arms felt as if they were on fire. Fanfan had attempted to perform a vodou curse on Patricia. The spell sent Patricia rushing to the hospital— and she fled to the Dominican Republic by bus the very next day. It was only after she crossed the border back to her home that

Junior learned that Patricia was pregnant. They have since lost touch. But Junior still thinks about the child he hasn't met—and he silently hopes he has a daughter.

Junior's greatest heartache was yet to come. His best friend, his brother, Fritznel did not survive the earthquake. He was living in a small cinder-block home with his aunt and cousin—within sight of Junior's own small home—and was watching television at the time of the tremblor. "He loved soccer," Junior explains. What torments Junior is that Fritznel's body has not been recovered. There were no rescue operations in his neighborhood, except for what the residents themselves were able to accomplish. He fears that Fritznel's spirit will be trapped if his body is not found and buried. And his face burns with anger and shame at the thought that no one else seems to miss him. Fritznel's aunt and cousin don't seem to be mourning him. It's as if Fritznel's life didn't count. Junior decides he will have his own ceremony to honor Fritznel. He will do this on the remains of his own home because he cannot reach the site where Fritznel is buried; there is too much debris stacked on top. Fritznel loved fruit—mandarins, banana, and pineapple. Junior will gather fruit and perhaps some of his own clothes and present this as an offering to his brother. He will pray to *Bondye*. "I will ask *Bondye* to protect him on his journey. And I will tell Fritznel that I will never forget him."

CHAPTER 17

Nature and Art

I am on a quest today to find traces of pastoral Haiti—bright sugarcane fields, neatly tended rows of crops, children attending village schoolhouses, women riding horseback to market, people living simply off the land, just as they did hundreds of years ago. My trip to Haiti would not be complete without a visit to the countryside. I need to return to Leogane and Petit Goave. This is a meditative journey. I am hoping to restore my vision of Haiti and to catch a glimpse of the future that is embedded in the past.

This morning I called Junior several times to coordinate a meeting place so I could pick him up and take him with me on my outing. But his phone was not charged and he did not answer. Reluctantly I went on my own with Pierre. In some ways, I think this was for the best. I will be doing some time traveling today and it will be good to sit quietly with my thoughts.

Arriving in Leogane, I see deep, curving gashes carved into the road. A sign promising the opening of a new international university stands beside three large, buckled slabs of stacked concrete. The three-story building now sits just a few feet off the ground. Further ahead, a convoy of green World War II–style military jeeps is driving over a bridge. The road is sending some powerful clues. We are driving through the epicenter of the Enriquillo fault line. Just six miles below the surface here is where the earth's trembling began, triggering the 7.0 earthquake.

Arriving in town, one house after another has collapsed. I see a series of A-frame cardboard homes that have been erected on the dusty streets. It appears residents have moved into temporary shelters just in front of their former homes. From a distance, the town has managed to retain its picture-book charm, but most of the buildings are destroyed—collapsed but still standing. The energy and activity of once-thriving shopkeepers and artisans has been replaced with emptiness in the streets. The "Lovers' Barbershop" is one of the casualties. But the town's old-fashioned dry cleaner's—which I had always found intriguing that a small provincial town had such a thriving and established dry clothes press—has survived.

I want to go first to the St. Rose de Lima Catholic Church. In Haiti's rural towns, the church still operates much as it did in medieval Europe. It's where people often turn to first when they need help. When I was monitoring the human rights situation in Leogane, I used to stop at the historic church, originally built in 1510, and call on the priest, Pere Fritz Savageur, to glean his insights and see if he was aware of any cases of persecution. As sources went, he was always very cautious and mild mannered, but I continued to call on him during my weekly visits because I knew the significant role the church played in the fabric of daily life. Approaching the site of the church, I do a double take. It has vanished, completely removed from the landscape. All that remains are the altar and the tile floor. I had no idea this living piece of history had collapsed—and I can't believe how speedily it has been swept up and carted away.

I meet the new priest, Pere Marat Guerand, sitting on some recovered pews. He is a thoughtful man, and more fiery than his predecessor. It's evident he is getting increasingly frustrated by the inertia surrounding him. Leogane has lost more than 3,000 residents and 80 percent of its infrastructure, he tells me, and the town is filled with aid workers snapping pictures on digital cameras as they drive around in air-conditioned SUVs. A man of faith, he is mindful of the divine presence in his midst. On the day of the earthquake, Pere Guerand was in the church courtyard, overseeing food distribution to four hundred children. He heard a loud crashing noise. The jolting vibration that followed sent him and the children bouncing "up and down, like balls." Not one life was lost when the church and rectory both collapsed into rubble and ash. Pere Savageur also survived the quake, he tells me. And yet, sitting next to the few recovered church artifacts—some ballpoint pens and two large brass church bells—his loss is palpable. St. Rose de Lima would have celebrated its 500th anniversary on Aug. 23, 2010. And now, Pere Guerand finds himself in the humiliating position of having to beg for handouts for himself and his parishioners. Apart from a one-week supply of food, he has yet to receive any help. He still does not even have a tent to sleep in. During our talk, he repeatedly tries to call a certain "John Brown" on his cell phone, whom he believes is a Canadian peacekeeper. He's been told this is the person who can provide him with plastic sheeting to shade the 1,900 worshippers who attend his Sunday mass under the blazing sun. The secretary keeps putting him on hold—and the calls keeping getting cut off. "Il me roule," he says angrily in French. "*They are playing me.*

This is not serious. I ask myself why all of these people have come to the country." I take notes during my talk, which I later e-mail in the form of a report to Elio. I am no longer reporting for a United Nations mission, but I see it as my duty to help the town of Leogane regain its dignity.

On the road to Petit Goave, the dried-out husks of sugarcane fields give way to greener groves of banana trees and palms. But the path of destruction continues. We drive past a collapsed vodou *peristyle* temple. Further up the road, a Presbyterian church has equally succumbed to the pressure. The deep gashes in the road continue to mark our trail. Turning a corner, we see an improvised village of nomadic tent homes made of palm fronds, sticks, and plastic sheeting tucked behind green foliage. The dazzling Caribbean Sea shimmers in the distance. As we enter the city limits of Petit Goave, Pierre skillfully drives around a series of large boulders, triggered by a landslide after the earthquake, that are blocking the road. An old peasant is hobbling by on the side of the road, carrying a large straw bag on his back and carrying a walking stick and a shovel. He wears long brown shorts and a straw hat—and no shirt. His name is Jean Rene and he was born in 1920. He is now ninety years old. The earthquake confounded him. He had never experienced one in his lifetime, but it did not fundamentally change his life. He lost no relatives or close friends—and he is still hungry, struggling to make an existence off the land.

In town, the brightly colored pastel buildings are crooked and tottering—and there are many of the now familiar voids. The once notorious Relais de l'Empereur hotel has been wiped out, the site completely cleared. It is an empty white space. Across the street, Spanish United Nations peacekeepers driving a forklift are busy clearing another now-vanished relic.

As I want to make sure to get back to Port-au-Prince before nightfall, I don't have time to try to find former contacts and allies. And Petit Goave still doesn't feel like a safe enough place to come into town and start asking for people by name. Locating my former sources would need to be done more discreetly and quietly. Before heading back, we pull over to the side of the road to buy some of the town's trademark delicacy, *Douce Macoss,* a fresh caramel paste sold in slivers of wax paper. I can use the sugar pick-me-up right now. As I sit back and finally feel a cool breeze on my face, I think of all the times I made this drive before. It's not that I want to go back in time, not really. And yet, there are aspects of my life from my time in Haiti that I wish I could carry into my life now. The friendships. The shared sense of purpose. Working in an international environment. And living in a country of tradition and ritual, where life is connected to the land and nature. I came hoping to experience this communion with nature once again—and yet I have mostly seen a path of physical destruction that I fear could threaten Haiti's frayed cultural and social fabric.

Back in Port-au-Prince that night, I go to dinner alone. I consider myself an optimist and a dreamer. But I am not feeling very hopeful right now. My talk with Pere Guerand in Leogane is weighing on me. He's right, I think. He is being played. I am writing in my journal and having a dinner of chicken, rice, and fried bananas with a rum punch that is too sweet. The restaurant is empty when I arrive but soon fills up. A Haitian American from Miami takes a table across from mine and we soon start talking. His name is Jean St.-Lot Gervais and he is the son of a former Haitian diplomat. Our conversation naturally shifts to the current situation and I confide how I am feeling. He offers some insights that are strangely prescient. "We all think we can come down here and change or fix it," he says. "And yet it changes us! We keep coming back because we can't figure it out." His pep talk comes with an admonition: "We all have a light inside of us. We must use it. Don't lose hope. I don't want to step in the shit or to let the shit hit me, either. There are a lot of forces within and without Haiti who don't want to see it succeed. Yet, many of us see the potential and we must help Haiti reach the ideal of her beautiful beginning."

⚬━┿━⚬

I'm meeting Dr. Percque for breakfast this morning. I waited several days after the quake—until he changed his Facebook profile picture to the image of a Haitian flag—to contact him via the online network. I was too afraid he might have lost another loved one, or that he himself might have been harmed in the earthquake.

Once in Haiti, I had dropped by during his early-morning office hours to greet him, and we made plans to meet the next day over breakfast. His marriage has not survived Haiti's heartbreak and his wife, son, and now ten-year-old daughter are living across the border in the Dominican Republic. (The move was initially prompted by telephoned kidnapping threats during Haiti's spate of high-profile kidnappings a few years ago.)

On the afternoon of the quake, Dr. Percque was preparing to fly to the Dominican Republic the next day to celebrate his daughter's tenth birthday. He was standing in his driveway when the earth began to shake. That night he went to his Petionville clinic before rushing to the embassy to perform triage surgery on the scores of walking wounded who arrived during the night.

At daybreak, he returned to his clinic to recover two badly injured State Department Foreign Service officers pulled from the Montana, who had been hand-carried on makeshift stretchers composed of a wooden door and a ladder. In the days ahead he perfomed combat medicine to save the lives of earthquake victims. Luckily, he was one of the few doctors in Haiti to have access to pain medication for his patients. The wounded were a blurred sea of humanity. Percque can recall virtually no faces of the victims he tended. He stares blankly at the survivors who have come back to thank him. He doesn't remember ever seeing them before. Over breakfast, he relates a feeling that I hear echoed by expats during my visit to Haiti. Despite all the civil unrest and political violence they have endured, Haiti has never felt so unstable and unsafe as it does now.

Dr. Percque, has long resisted leaving his birthplace. I ask him about this. "It's a curse," he tells me. "It's like the James Michener novel *Caribbean* set largely in Haiti. The French slave masters used the decapitated heads of Haitians to play soccer—and the Haitians later did the same with their French masters. This country is soaked in blood. And once you fall under its spell, it's in your blood." Plus, Dr. Percque knows that time is precious. Certainly the quake has imparted this lesson to all. But Percque has another visual reminder. He has been diagnosed with a rare disease. "I don't know how much time I have," he tells me at breakfast. I look at him in protest, not wanting to believe his words. And then he gently takes my hand in his and I see that his fingers are bloated and bulging like a giant's. The veins look as if they might burst, as if that Haitian blood is looking for an escape.

After breakfast with Dr. Percque, I drop in on American art gallery owner, Toni Monnin. Toni arrived in Port-au-Prince by way of Paris, where she was studying and teaching English, in 1976. Fate in the form of an earthquake brought her to Haiti. She and a group of girlfriends were planning to travel to Guatemala when a 7.5 magnitude earthquake struck, killing 23,000 people. Travel plans were scrapped and Port-au-Prince was chosen in place of Guatemala City. During the trip, Toni met and fell in love with another transplanted expat, Swiss-born art dealer Michel Monnin. The couple has been together thirty-four years, making Haiti their permanent home, and they have two ethereal and accomplished daughters, Gaelle and Pascale. When I note the irony that it was an earthquake that originally brought Toni, who was born and bred in Dallas, to Haiti, she exclaims: "That's Haiti!" It's a refrain she repeats several times during our chat and I find myself adopting it as my mantra during my stay.

Toni is close friends with Hotel Montana owner Garthe Cardozo-Stefanson and she becomes emotional when the conversation turns to her friend and the loss of her grandson. "Garthe considered him her own son. They were incredibly close," she tells me. Toni had gone to the Montana to have lunch with Garthe just a few days before the quake. She feels an overwhelming sadness for her friend, even though she survived. I tell her I understand the feeling. I felt the same way about a former colleague, who was at the UN compound when the quake struck. I was so worried that something might have happened to her. But even after I knew she was alive I still felt so sad for her. I stumble on some unexpected emotion as I try to describe this. "That's Haiti!" chimes Toni. She is sweet and offers to refill my water bottle. "My friend has made her life here. She's not ever going back," I explain.

"Neither am I," says Toni. We both wonder aloud if we will ever see Haiti rebuilt in our lifetimes.

And because Toni knows that you can't survive for long in Haiti without a highly developed sense of humor, she decides to tell me a funny story. It takes place at the Montana, during the hotel's golden days. "I saw Brad Pitt's underpants," she says with a twinkle in her eye. "I couldn't help it!" It was 2006, and Brad and Angelina flew in for an overnight visit from the Dominican Republic to support Wyclef Jean's charity. The power couple was staying in the Montana's presidential suite and Garthe asked Toni if she would stage a private gallery exhibit for them. Toni worked painstakingly to put together a world-class offering—and then Brad and Angelina were a no-show because they ended up staying out late at a vodou ceremony. All was not lost. The next morning, they toured the exhibit and Toni had a private audience with the couple. "Angelina was very reserved. She didn't say a lot," recalls Toni. "Can you imagine, constantly being picked apart? She wore very little make-up and a simple black tank. She was stunning. It was the time of 'the bump.' You could just barely see it. Everyone was wondering if she was pregnant." Of Brad she says: "He's just very natural. He got excited by some art and called out, 'Hey Angie, look at this!'" And that's when she saw it. Brad Pitt crouched down to look at a painting and Toni saw the drawers of one of the world's most desired men. She was in the right place at the right time. That's Haiti!

⚓

My trip to Haiti is nearly complete and I still have a very important mission to accomplish. I need to visit the Hotel Christopher to say goodbye to Andrea. I smile as I think of how Andrea would have enjoyed Toni Monnin's story of Brad Pitt—and I wonder if she might have had a similar story of her own. As one of the most seasoned members of the UN mission in Haiti, she had brushes with many high-profile visitors and celebrities on fact-finding and goodwill missions. As I approach the former UN compound—which consisted of the five-story hotel and a collection of separate office buildings and villas—I feel as if I am entering an altered universe. Junior is by my side and together we survey telephone poles twisted every which way and buildings smashed and strewn at unnatural angles. When I reach the actual hotel site, I am startled to see a lone office with a burgundy chair behind a desk exposed from the rubble, as if still officially open for business. I wonder who sat there. So many people took their final breaths here. One hundred and one lives lost.

My thoughts are with Andrea. At the time of her death, I had not been in touch with her for some time. She was one of the few mission members who did not reach out directly to me after Marcelo's death. I understood that completely. It was in many ways an awkward situation. I was no longer Marcelo's bride. Andrea was herself a child of divorce, and I sensed a certain pragmatism in her silence. I had only been on Facebook for about a month at the time of the earthquake in Haiti—and for days before the tremblor struck, I had been seeing her photo pop up on my profile page, with the online social media site exhorting me to "friend" her, sensing our shared network through its complex matrix system. I was slowly branching out, usually crafting a personal note to friends scattered near and far. I lamented that I did not get the chance to write that note to Andrea.

I am seeing her now in my mind's eye. She is smiling and surrounded by bright light. In her final photos posted on her Facebook, which was open book accessible to all, she looked so radiant. I sensed she was in the prime of her life. Here she was riding with Matt Damon in the back of a relief vehicle, guiding him on an aid mission. Here she was smiling broadly with singer Wyclef Jean as he took a swig of coffee from a white cup. Here she was with Chilean President Michele Bachelet during a visit to Haiti, looking like best friends. And here she was teaching a course on the proper use of force to a group of Haitian police officers. I remember what Junior wished for his friend, Fritznel, and I too ask *Bondye,* God, to protect Andrea on her journey. I am comforted by the thought that she is no longer here. She is free now—back home with her family and loved ones in Chile. I pull out the white candle that I have been carrying in my purse all week. When I instinctively grabbed it from my pantry before leaving for the airport in California, I did not stop to think that lighting a candle in a debris field might actually be dangerous. Instead of lighting the candle, I slip it into the crevice of a lone cinder block, a fallen piece of UN headquarters, which cradles the candle as if in an embrace.

○—━—○

When I sit down to have my last talk with Junior on the eve of my departure, he astonishes me with his wisdom and insights. Spoken as a true Haitian survivor, he riffs on the importance of sadness to achieve true balance in life. "Even if you are sad, you must make your life. You must go on," Junior says. "If you don't have sadness, life will not have true balance. There is a time for sadness, a time for happiness. Life will never finish. Each time a person dies, there must be a person to replace them. People die. The world does not."

I ask him how he learned all this, being raised without parents. Junior tells me that his survival instinct was never to follow "what the others did" in the street. And he tells me that our meeting made a pivotal difference in his life. "It's because you always recognized me," Junior says. "You didn't know who I was and I didn't know who you were, either. You trusted me without even knowing me. You let me into your home. We went and ate ice cream together. You let me come in and sit down. You introduced me to everyone, and I will never forget that."

During this meeting, as a torrential rain falls, Junior tells me of his dreams for his son and for Haiti. Christopher is his "whole heart" and everything he does now is for him. He will do everything possible to make sure his son does not live a life on the street. Junior knows I always loved his drawings, and for this goodbye he has brought me one of his latest. It's a drawing of myself and Elio. Looking closely at the drawing, I see that Junior's son, Christopher, is in the middle between towering Elio and tiny me. Junior is in a small, hovering oval on the left side of the picture. His hand is holding up his chin. He is reflective, wondering, and concerned for Haiti's future and that of his child. As for his homeland, Junior notes that Haiti is now worse off than it ever was before. If Haiti does not improve now it never ever will. "The earthquake has given us some hope that change is coming, but the earthquake also crushed our hopes," he says. "If this had to happen, everybody hopes something more beautiful, *pi bel*, will emerge."

A week after I leave Haiti, as I am preparing to fly back to California from Florida, I receive an e-mail from Elio telling me that Junior was run over by a truck on Sunday morning as he went to buy milk for his son. Junior survived the quake, but is now crippled. He will need operations and will not be able to walk for at least three months. After days of calling, I finally manage to reach Junior on his cell phone. "San," as he calls me, "You have to help me get out of here."

CHAPTER 18
Return II

Reading the State Department Travel Warning to Haiti is a sober-ing exercise certain to cast doubt—like buckets of cold water—on even the most fervent traveler's plans. I read the warning dated December 9, 2010, in the run-up to Christmas as I begin plan-ning my trip for next month's commemoration of the one-year anniversary of the earthquake. The consular briefing sums up with bureaucratic precision what I have read anecdotally in news reports: A number of Americans have been robbed and attacked as they left the airport. Two Americans were shot and killed in such incidents this year. Kidnappings as a means of extortion are also on the rise. In some cases, the victims have been raped, physically assaulted, and killed. One line from the warning keeps standing out. *No one is immune from kidnapping, regardless of one's occupation, nationality, race, gender, or age.* I know some people read these government-issued warnings and think they are com-plete exaggerations. My read is slightly different. I believe these things are unlikely to happen as long as one exercises good judg-ment and caution. But I don't kid myself. The risk of "wrong place, wrong time," which can strike anywhere in the world, is especially heightened in Haiti. I know you can do everything right—be aware, vigilant, culturally sensitive, and well-intentioned—and still end up in the Haitian mush pot.

Still, it's hard to take these warnings at full face value. At the very least, they have taken on a kind of muted, surreal quality. I haven't been able to reach Junior for three weeks, placing the prospect of my trip in the air. The last time I spoke to him was the night of Haiti's doomed presidential election. By then it was becoming increasingly obvious that the race would be determined by a street battle. Madame Mirlande Manigat, a Sorbonne-educated professor and former first lady favored by the Haitian establishment, would politely be invited to advance to the second round. But the title of second place would need to be slugged out, gladiator style, between the competing city-states of Ruling Party vs. Dispossessed Masses. Whichever side could amass more followers in the streets and create a greater state of generalized chaos would be determined the winner. Representing the ruling party is the public works official, Jude Celestin, whose fleet of dump trucks and tractors oversaw the crude disposal of dead bodies and rubble following the quake. Representing the legions of displaced tent dwellers is Michel Martelly, a pop singer known by his stage name of "Sweet Mickey," who promises to invoke his same brash stage persona, and his penchant for dropping his pants during performances, to take on the status quo. I managed to reach Junior by phone in his tent in the Place Boyer on election night. He sounded both giddy and braced for backlash. It was a marked contrast from my previous calls with him in the weeks before, when he had vowed to refrain from the political process. "Let me tell you something," he had said then. "Anyone who is in politics in Haiti becomes part of a mafia . . . I am not going to vote to make somebody rich." But in our last call, he had sounded notably energized, even as he predicted the vote would be stolen. A nationally televised political debate, in which Martelly had challenged his establishment opponents to declare what they had done for Haiti in the past twenty years, had been a game-changer, Junior said. "We had no choice but to vote for Martelly," Junior said of his vote, and that of his brethren. He sounded almost apologetic for voting for a political novice. "We voted for change. We don't know if it will lead to anything better."

As predicted, Martelly was excluded from the run-off following days of hushed ballot tabulating, with official results placing him safely out of power's reach, in third place. Weeks of violent street protests followed, paralyzing the capital and shutting down the airport for days. At least three deaths have been reported in the clashes. Throughout this ordeal, I have been calling Junior's two cell-phone numbers. One is dead. One sometimes rings and goes to voice mail. I imagine his phones falling from his pockets as he runs for cover from the spray of tear gas and gunfire. But I secretly worry that Junior may have been swept up in a raid and is languishing in a jail cell. I fear for his safety and wonder if I will have to start searching for him all over again. Also gnawing at me is the combination of guilt and fear that as the mother of a three-year-old child I am assuming an unreasonable risk to return to Haiti. It sounds silly, but I pay careful attention to see if some warning sign manifests telling me I should not return. When none comes, I tell myself that I will find safe passage amidst the hundreds of journalists, aid officials, and private citizens coming to pay their respects to Haiti's vanished quake victims. I am committed to helping Junior and his son get their lives on track. I know that my friendship with Junior has deepened my understanding of humanity and made me a better person. I want to do the same for him.

I celebrate a quiet Christmas with my husband and son at our new home in Scottsdale, Arizona, where Tom has been transferred as part of a restructuring at the Associated Press. On Christmas Eve, we eat tamales and have a glass of Italian prosecco before visiting two homes transformed into winter wonderlands of icicle lights, Victorian window displays, choo-choo trains, reindeer, elves, and imaginary snow in the Southwest. A magical atmosphere is palpable. Alexander, clad in his flannel pajamas, approaches Santa Claus with wonder in his eyes and thinks long and hard before settling on his wish. "An orange light saber," he announces finally.

Five days later, my friend Elio sends me a New Year's message via Facebook. Junior has managed to reach him at his UN office. He is broke and lost his phones. Junior asked Elio to please let me know that he is safe. I feel like this is the sign I have been waiting for.

I'm still pretty sleepy when my morning flight touches down in Miami but I notice people intently scrolling on their smartphones and I overhear someone say there has been a shooting in Arizona. It's not until I step off the plane and see the television screens that I realize CNN is reporting that a congresswoman has been killed. The name Gabrielle Giffords does not immediately resonate. Since moving to Arizona three months ago, I profess to having a bit of an ostrich-in-the-sand mentality to the state's politics. I find much of the official rhetoric, particularly in regards to immigration, to be so distasteful and polarizing that I haven't spent much time learning all of the local players. Instead, I have focused my energy and attention on the unexpected beauty of our new surroundings. On our first day in our new home, our neighbors across the street, a Czech-born doctor and his wife and two children, came to our door with homemade cards and a casserole to welcome us to the neighborhood. Alexander and I soon found a playful refuge in the rich array of children's programs at the Scottsdale public library system. Tom initiated our quest to explore new farmers' markets and local foodie culture. And our greatest sense of community has come from my son's international school, which offers bilingual education in Spanish and French, and acts as a magnet for a dynamic collection of cultures from around the world.

Even as I stare at the screens, I do not grasp the gravity of the situation. The possibility that Giffords may have been targeted for her politics seems unfathomable. In my travels and work as a journalist I have come to truly understand that it is the core building blocks of democracy—the rights to free speech, free assembly, and the peaceful transition of power—so embedded in our political DNA, that truly define us as a nation and make the American body politic a beacon of hope to so many around the world. And yet I also know that until the passage of the Voting Rights Act of 1965, those core values and protections did not extend to all. The lynching of African-American men from magnolia trees and the imposition of Jim Crow laws of the South, relegating blacks to separate rail cars, supermarket checkout lanes, telephone booths, schools and libraries—officially sealing their status as second class citizens—is a reminder that ours is still a young democracy.

I know polarizing rhetoric can have deadly consequences. But right now my instinct is to ascribe other, more banal, motives for the Tucson shooting. Perhaps the congresswoman got caught in the crossfire of rival drug traffickers on a Saturday morning outing to the supermarket? Or maybe she was the victim of a deadly love triangle—or was targeted by a stalker. It's not until I'm scanning the luggage carousel for my faded olive green suitcase that a fellow female passenger from Tucson tells me Giffords was likely targeted for her politics. At that moment I feel the full sting of shock and indignation. "Are you kidding me?" I say. "Yes, and as Democrats go, she is actually pretty conservative," the woman tells me.

I'm suddenly feeling afraid for Alexander and I'm again questioning our move to Arizona. Before moving to the state, I had braced myself for the vitriol and was relieved to arrive and find many like-minded, kindred spirits. But now, the memory that floats to the forefront of my awareness is of a man I saw at my local supermarket shopping center over the Christmas holidays who was walking proudly on the sidewalk with his wife, a gun strapped prominently into a suspender-like contraption on his midriff. I was tempted at the time to roll down my car window and make a comment along the lines of, "Is that really necessary?" but I exercised restraint because Alexander was strapped into his car seat in my backseat, and it's generally not a wise idea to taunt someone with a loaded gun.

I immediately call home, knowing Tom will be working full throttle on this major national news story. He tells me he has been mobilizing photographers to cover this quickly breaking story. Alexander has inevitably overheard snippets of his phone conversations. Without fully understanding the situation, Alexander has offered to "get the bad guys" with his light saber.

By the next morning, when I board my connecting flight to Port-au-Prince, I know that Giffords is clinging to life and at least seventeen others have been shot. Six people have been killed, including a nine-year-old girl. The tragedy in Arizona does not make me feel any "safer" about going to Haiti but it does make me realize risk is more widespread and embedded into daily life than we are willing, or able, to acknowledge. I scan the departure gate and notice a number of news photographers queuing up to board the flight. Once on the plane, I see the flight crew scrambling to find spots to accommodate the trove of television cameras. I am seated in an alcove of the plane that has just two passenger seats, and which brushes up against the crews' jump seats during take-off and landing. There is a feeling of openness and curiosity on these flights, which beckons the question: Why are you going down there? The three flight attendants, two male and one female, seated next to me at take-off open up and share that the Haiti flights are their preferred assignment. Passengers on these flights are so filled with optimism as they prepare to embark on some of their most meaningful life work, they tell me. It's a stark contrast to the grumpy passengers irritated about cramped seats and heightened security checks on most other flights. To illustrate the point, they relate an anecdote about a medical emergency on the previous day's flight. When the pilot made the announcement asking if there was a doctor on board, more than twenty hands shot up in the air. As I prepare to disembark, the female flight attendant hands me a large plastic bag brimming with crackers, roasted nuts, and hummus. These weren't the snacks I was served on the flight. She has given me the food from the first class cabin. "Anything that doesn't get eaten needs to be thrown away," she says ruefully. "It seems like such a waste, especially when there are people who need so much right now." I have told her and her colleagues about Junior and his son. "Please give these to your friend, or anyone in the camps who might be hungry," she tells me.

Walking through the old terminal, the deep gashes from the day of the earthquake remain etched in the glass doors. The Compa band retains its place, performing on cue for the newest flock of visitors. Their expressions seem less dour than from my previous visit, yet their eyes remain ever watchful on the tip jar. Once inside the hangar functioning as the arrivals terminal, I check to see if Gattine, the soft-spoken airport official I met ten months ago, is at her post. Her moving story of digging her son out of the rubble in the darkness after the earthquake has lingered in my heart. To my surprise, she is there, seated behind a desk, her hair tucked in a neat bun. She stares at me quizzically for a moment when I greet her—and then her face breaks into a warm smile. It is a complete coincidence that I have stumbled on her today, she tells me. She has been out of work for more than two months due to a back injury, which she attributes to the earthquake. As she accompanies me in line to passport control, she offers a quick update on her life. She is no longer living with her extended family in a courtyard under a plastic tarp. Together with her husband and son, she now calls an apartment home. The pieces of her life are slowly reassembling themselves into a new mosaic, and yet as I embrace her and prepare to step out into the hot, gusty air outside, I sense a certain melancholy in her.

Once outside, I quickly spot Alek, a thirty-something Bulgarian hostel manager who will be my host on this trip. I've never met Alek, but I recognize him from photos posted on the hostel's Facebook page. He is standing with a Haitian colleague holding up a wooden sign that reads: "Art Hostel." During my last trip, when I visited with American art gallery owner Toni

Monnin, she had told me she was converting part of the property into a hostel that would be run by a pair of young Balkan expats. This information had proved to be a vital tidbit when I scrambled to book hotel reservations, as I deliberated my trip during Junior's brief disappearance, only to find that the few functioning hotels were already filled to capacity for the earthquake anniversary.

Our trio makes its way to Alek's white jeep in the parking lot. We've just started rolling after a push-start when Alek's cell phone buzzes. It's his housemate, a Brazilian working for the UN mission. Is there any way Alek can swing by the airport and pick him up? He's just arrived back from his Christmas holiday in Rio. The Brazilian housemate has no idea Alek is right outside the terminal, about to embark in his Chitty Chitty Bang Bang mobile back to Petionville. He emerges from the terminal wearing a small straw hat, the kind that has recently become a fashion statement from the beaches of Ipanema to the dance halls of Brooklyn and the streets of Port-au-Prince. We squeeze in together and settle in for our drive up toward the hills. Cigarettes are lit and stories are exchanged. I have the impression I have just stepped into an indie film. The film would be about a Bulgarian and Brazilian room-mate living in an unnamed post-war landscape together negotiating access to water supply trucks and the underground party scene, while otherwise remaining unscathed and unfazed by the shrapnel ricocheting around them. I'm grateful to take cover in their orbit. I suddenly can't remember why I was so worried about my drive from the airport into the city. It's a Sunday afternoon and the streets are fairly empty of people. As we weave our way up the Delmas thoroughfare I am surprised to see that there has been a cursory attempt to remove some of the rubble from this main artery. In its stead are heaping piles of trash, a monument to the presidential stalemate paralyzing the country right now. The sky has grown overcast and the sight of all of the trash weighs on me. I'm not sure if it's just a matter of my eye needing to adjust to Haiti, or if the country has slipped even deeper into the muck. I'm afraid it's the latter. A farewell message from my colleague Leigh in New York, a fellow editor with the custom publishing company where I have started working in Arizona, comes to mind. "Please give my love and devotion to that indestructible little country," she wrote.

We arrive at the arched wooden door of the Gallerie Monnin and proceed to the courtyard, which formerly housed the Café des Artistes restaurant. This was one of the trademark stops on the Petionville restaurant circuit in the 1990s, with its inviting outdoor seating area and French brasserie fare. It's also where I used to take aerobics classes in the afternoons, when the security situation permitted. The four rooms overlooking the courtyard have been reinvented into the Art Hostel. I know from studying the hostel's Facebook page that this seemingly sleepy courtyard is the site of some lively concerts and shows that look as electric as a Portland rave scene. I have joked with Tom that I will be staying at a nightclub. But Alek tells me there are no concerts scheduled for the rest of the month, although he may have a few friends over later in the week to keep things from getting too quiet.

I drop my bags off in my room and Alek negotiates for me to pay the cook $40 so she can slip outside and procure me a brand new cell phone with a prepaid calling card. I'm excited to be "connected" on this trip. Once that transaction has been settled, Alek next calls a trusted moto-cab driver who promptly pulls up outside the gallery's massive door, which is like an ancient wooden portal connecting the haven of the gallery space to the hub of cars and street life outside.

After all the weeks of wondering and worrying, I am finally on my way. I hop on the motorcycle and head with the driver to the tent camp at the Place Boyer in search of Junior. I'm suddenly feeling a bit nervous. Was it perhaps naïve of me to think I could just waltz right into a refugee camp and find Junior simply by asking for him by name? Pulling up to the camp, I take a close look around. It looks much like it did last March, except people appear more haggard. Two women sitting on a cement mooring that once bordered the open public plaza, and which now signals one of the main entrances to the tent camp, listen carefully to my introduction. They have never heard of Junior but they are sympathetic to my quest and offer to sit with me while I wait in hopes that Junior might pass by and see me here. The women's gentle presence is welcoming and I am eager to hear their stories. The reports of rapes in the camps are becoming increasingly alarming and I am concerned this horror may have reached the Place Boyer, which at first glance appears to be one of the more livable camps. I'm seated with three generations—Guerline, a mother in her thirties, and Milta, a grandmother cradling her infant granddaughter in her arms. Guerline begins her first-person testimony. As she speaks, the elder Milta nods her head gently to signal her understanding and support.

Guerline lost her husband and her home in the earthquake. Her husband, Fritz Augustin, a security guard, was on the job at a "gwo bilding," a *big building,* that collapsed. "Everyone inside died," she tells me. She was in her home in a hillside shanty in the Canape Vert neighborhood of the capital. It, too, collapsed, but she was able to escape without serious injury. Now she lives together with her four daughters, ages four to thirteen, in a tent. Her oldest daughter, Carly, used to have "little problems," she tells me. She suffered from headaches and was sometimes challenged at school. But since the earthquake, she tells me, Carly has descended into a vegetative state. She no longer talks and spends most of her time alone in the family tent. "She is traumatized," Guerline explains. I ask about security conditions in the camp. Have there been cases of *kadejak,* or rapes, I ask? Her response is chilling for its raw vulnerability. "At night, you sometimes hear the cries of people when intruders slice open their tents with machetes to steal from them or rape them," Guerline replies. I ask her if she can imagine a new life outside of this camp. "It's only *Bondye,* God, who can help us because here we don't have a government," she replies. Sometimes she returns to the memory of what life was like before this. "Before the quake, I lived better. I was able to eat. I was in peace," she says. "Life here is really difficult. People don't have any resources. They don't have water or food. They don't have anyone to talk to or to give them advice."

Still, I can't help but wonder. *How* does she survive? *How* does she provide for four children? Guerline, whose hair is neatly swept up in rows of curlers, tells me she is a hairstylist. She is able to eke out a small sum of *gourdes* each week by styling the hair of fellow survivors caught in the same tumultuous cascade as herself. She also has a frayed support network to draw upon. As one of seven children born to a mason father and homemaker mother, she has one brother and a sister who have managed to avoid the fate of camp life. Her sister, a market vendor who lives in a "popular," working-class neighborhood of Petionville, watches Guerline's children for her on Sundays. Despite the chasm threatening to engulf her, Guerline's spirit shines bright. Today she is manning the soft drink stand of a friend, to make a little extra pocket change. The mere act of putting her hair in rollers represents a gesture of self-preservation and hope for the future.

Milta, a former secretary and mother of six grown children, cradles her sleeping granddaughter Stephanlie in her arms. The child was born just three months before the earthquake and Milta seems to be physically shielding her from the dust and desperation swirling around her small frame. The matriarch sits quietly and patiently on the cement ledge, as if biding a punishment. But it's clear she is a wide-eyed observer of everything that goes on around her and she offers an unvarnished account of camp life. "Nobody comes to see us. When people say they are going to help us it is a lie," she says plainly. "During the *fêtes,* the Christmas holidays, not a single person came here to help us. We don't see a possibility to get out of here." As I listen to her words, I realize life in this temporary, permanent shelter is perpetuating the trauma of quake survivors. It's like they are still trying to escape from the wreckage. Milta puts it this way: "It makes us remember things that made our hearts cry a lot. We lost a lot of family, friends, and many homes were destroyed."

Guerline offers to show me her tent. She takes me by the hand and leads me into the labyrinth-like maze of white and blue plastic bubbles filling every pocket of open space. When we arrive at her shelter, I realize it is not even a tent. It is a large piece of plastic tarp suspended over four wooden poles. Inside there are some dirty blankets and a few crusty pots on a loose dirt floor. It looks like someone dumped a bag of cement on the ground. Guerline proudly holds up a piece of corrugated tin and tells me this is her "baryè," her *gate.* This is her security system against roving thieves and rapists. I'm speechless. I've been in a lot of shanties and slums in Haiti, but these are the most rudimentary living conditions I have ever seen. I am trying to imagine how four children can live in this squalor. It might seem odd, but my thoughts drift to my dog Humphrey, who lived with me here in Haiti, in the house on the Rue Chavannes, literally around the corner from where I now stand. Humphrey, my gentle, sensitive, and ice-cream-loving golden retriever, passed away this summer, months shy of his fourteenth birthday. He did not spend even one day of his life in such miserable conditions. One word comes to mind and I cannot push it away. INHUMANE. No human being—no child—should ever live like this.

I know poverty is not unique to Haiti. I know there is terrible, crushing poverty in parts of India and Africa, where people must sometimes supplement their diets by eating locusts and termites. But that doesn't make this acceptable. Haiti is just five hundred miles from the United States. And from where I have been sitting, talking with Guerline and Milta, I have been looking directly at the Haitian headquarters of the American Red Cross. Their office literally looks down on the Place Boyer. Americans donated a staggering $1.4 billion to assist survivors of the Haiti earthquake. Of those private donations, $479 million, the largest single amount, was given to the American Red Cross. I know they have their fancy balance sheets and reports. Officially, they have dispersed more than half of those funds. I hope the millions that remain to be spent can make a meaningful and lasting difference for the now estimated 1.4 million people waiting patiently in their tents, who have been told the world has shown unprecedented generosity on their behalf. I don't mean to imply that there are easy fixes. Figuring out how to best help Haiti, and the Haitian people, is a quagmire I first stepped into eighteen years ago. I know this is really, really hard. Haiti has a complex social reality and poverty was already endemic before the quake. But what I believe in my heart is that this situation is immoral. I believe the international community can do better than this.

Guerline turns her attention to my quest. She wants to help me find Junior. She again takes my hand and I follow her bright halo of curlers to another tent. This one is not a home. It functions as a cell-phone store. Two young men and a woman are seated behind a desk, with brand new cell phones, chargers, and phone covers neatly stacked around them. They listen intently to my description and then shake their heads. They have never heard of Junior. A gentle spinning sensation spills over me. I am being tumbled in an ocean wave. There must be at least three thousand people living in this camp. Junior is here somewhere. How am I going to find him?

As we exit the tent, Guerline begins asking each person we encounter on the narrow footpath between the haphazardly pitched tents if they know Junior. After just a few tries, a man lights up. He thinks he knows whom we are talking about. The man leads us a short distance down some steps and around a corner to where an old woman is scrubbing her granddaughter's soapy face over a bassinet in a makeshift courtyard between a cluster of tents. "*Wi,*" Junior is her neighbor, the old woman says, barely looking up from her task. The woman tells us she often makes tea for Junior in the mornings. "He lives there," she says, pointing to an orange tent right next to where we are standing. "He's not here right now. He has gone to see *petit li,* his child. Come back this afternoon, after 5:00 p.m." she advises.

I feel as if I am flying. I can't believe I have pinpointed Junior's tent like this. When I arrive back at the Place Boyer, pulling up to the plaza at 5:00 p.m. on my moto-cab, Junior is standing there with Guerline and Milta. He has been waiting for me. We embrace and walk together to his tent. As we approach, I am surprised to realize Junior does not live alone. A young woman wearing a coral-colored halter top and jean shorts, her braided hair pulled back into a ponytail, emerges from the side of the tent. With her caramel-colored skin, lithe and rounded figure, and her long legs, she looks like a model from a painting by Haitian artist Fritzner Alphonse. "San, this is Samantha," Junior introduces me. They naturally gravitate toward each other and I can see there is genuine tenderness between them. Standing arm in arm, they are a handsome couple and they radiate vitality. If I lived in a tent, without running water or electricity, I would look like an absolute mess. After talking together for a few moments, I can tell that Samantha is educated and she did not grow up in a shanty. I wonder about the circumstances that have led her to this camp without relatives. Junior opens the front flap of his tent and shows me their invented home. It's a stark contrast to the tent I visited earlier today. Junior has a queen-sized air mattress, with neatly tended blankets and pillows. A colorful, woven scarf is folded in the shape of a triangle and hung artfully over the bed like a headboard. At the top of the tent, a thin cord is strung around the perimeter, functioning as an ingenious closet system. I can see pieces of Junior's hip wardrobe wallpapering the tent walls. As tents go, this one looks comfortable and homey. It occurs to me that the violent poverty of Guerline's tarp home might in itself be a form of self-protection. By so clearly stripping her home of anything of value, Guerline may be warding off the evil eye of potential thieves and attackers. If my theory is correct, it would be the first time I have witnessed Poverty as Magic Sword. It makes me think of how vulnerable women are in these camps and of the sacrifices they make for their children.

Junior and I go to sit and talk over dinner, and I give him pocket money for his and Samantha's immediate needs. Back at the Art Hostel, more than half of my suitcase is filled with basic necessities for him and Christopher, including shoes, pajamas, clothing, coloring books, toothbrushes, trail mix, art supplies, and fixings for a birthday party for Christopher, who turns three this week. I remember Junior telling me that Christopher's birthday had occurred just days before the earthquake. It seems especially important to celebrate life this week. In the days ahead, we will embark on the search for a new beginning for Junior. Our master plan, which we had begun discussing by phone before our communication was disrupted, includes safe housing, education, and most elusive of all, employment.

As we sit down to a dinner of grilled chicken, *diri ak pwa,* or rice and beans, and fried plantain, I tell Junior how worried I had been about his safety and how strange it seems now to be sitting with him. And I again marvel at his uncanny ability to speak in poetry. "Destiny has a beautiful secret behind it that neither you nor I know," he tells me.

CHAPTER 19

Zwazo

When Junior was eight years old, and used to sleep in the gallery of the yellow gingerbread home I shared with Marcelo in Pacot, it often startled me to see him sleeping in his troubled state—as if his body was somehow poised and ready for conflict. As an adult, there are moments when I see flickers of him retreating to that numb place. He has told me that he still sleeps in the same rigid fight or flight pose. "It's not good. I should let my blood circulate better," he told me recently. Sometimes when I first see him in the morning, he will be in that distant world, as if still emerging from the threat that deep sleep can pose to someone living on the street and fighting for their survival. This is the case today. It isn't warm, optimistic, and aware Junior who arrives at the Art Hostel to embark on the quest for his new life. Instead, he is distant, cold, and curt. His deep brown eyes, which often seem to look right into my soul, are like mirrors or glass marbles, reflecting a void.

I sense numb Junior is feeling resentful of me. I feel it instinctively. But I don't know why. We sit sharing a cup of coffee in the courtyard of the Gallerie Monnin complex. I decide to broach the matter directly. "Is everything okay? I feel like something is bothering you," I query, speaking directly into the glassy marbles. "I didn't sleep well last night," he says, both diplomatically and tersely. And that's when it hits me. The rain! How rude of me! As soon as I first talked to him by phone this morning and the moment he first walked through the gallery's massive wooden door, I should have asked him how he and Samantha fared during last night's sudden and cataclysmic torrential downpour. Junior was my first thought as soon as I awoke in the middle of the night to the sound of gushing water. I immediately pictured him on his air mattress, and I fretted over the thought of Junior and Samantha becoming totally engulfed in a puddle of mud. The rain was so thunderous, it taunted anyone to try to fall back asleep. I sat up in bed, my mind whirring, cocooned in a feeling of anxiety and powerlessness. My thoughts flowed next to Guerline, Milta, and all the other earthquake survivors clinging to flimsy plastic shelters. By now, the threat of rain might actually be commonplace to tent dwellers, and I tried to imagine the ingenious strategies that mothers have most certainly concocted to keep their children from becoming totally drenched. The only redeeming thought was that at least the force of nature would hose rapists and thieves back into their dens.

Earlier in the night, it had taken me a long time to fall asleep, as I had been forced to listen to a macabre concerto of feral cats howling below my window. Their haunting, guttural cries, contorted in a fury of anguish and longing, had seeped into my consciousness and prevented me from being lulled into a gentle sleep. Now the pounding rain was mocking me, reminding me of my status as a Have in a land of Have Nots. I had my own bed in my own private room and I could derive little comfort from that.

I tossed and turned for the rest of the night until the first light of day appeared as a welcome reprieve from a futile and exhausting exercise. By the time I finally spoke to Junior by phone and he appeared through the wooden portal, it seemed like an eternity had passed since the howling tempest of the night before.

The truth is, I didn't get a good night's sleep either, and that is why my awareness is jarred and temporarily delayed as we sit down to coffee. But I can't really say that. It wouldn't make any sense. Instead, I do my best to convey that I have been genuinely concerned about him and Samantha and that I only slept a few hours last night. He seems to appreciate my gesture and, together with the prescriptive power of the aromatic Haitian coffee, he re-emerges from his numb state. We are ready to start our day.

Our plan to find a new beginning for Junior has several planks. Finding secure housing and a job will be the most challenging, as both are virtually nonexistent. Junior has a lead on a house that is within walking distance from the Place Boyer, which we will visit later this week. Today we will focus our efforts on education. Given that Junior has, at best, a formal sixth-grade education, we are trying to find the best way to empower him with the knowledge that will be his true freedom. Our plan is to enroll him in a school where he can get the equivalent of a high school education, in addition to enrolling him in private English and art classes. In my mind, I have dubbed today's outing our "Ivy League" tour, as we will be visiting one of Haiti's most elite secondary schools and I'm hopeful for the possibility of advancement and social integration it could provide. It's a lot to take on, but we have decided to adopt the approach of the popular Haitian adage, "Piti piti, zwazo fé nich li." *Little by little, the bird makes its nest.* Junior the *zwazo* is about to take flight.

Our first stop will be the Union School. This is where many of the country's mulatto elite send their children to school. Originally founded in 1919 as the Colony School, the school's founding mission was to educate the children of U.S. Marines during the ill-fated American occupation. The campus did not even admit Haitian students until 1943, when the school was renamed the Union School. These days, the school boasts as many as seventeen different nationalities in kindergarten through high school. And the curriculum could satisfy two of our goals, as the primary instruction is in English. Junior and I had planned to hop on a tap-tap bus heading down Canape Vert, one of the two main arteries connecting Petionville to downtown, but every bus we see is so full that we end up embarking on an hour-long trek by foot to the school's campus in the Juvenat neighborhood, a once-upscale quarter that is now mostly elegant in name.

The walk is an interesting jumble of contrasts. We are keeping a brisk pace and talking as we go, maintaining a watchful eye on the road to dodge the mixture of rubble leavened with the heaps of trash strewn in our path. I am curious to know more about Samantha. I sense she is a survivor and, like Junior, she seems to have retained an open spirit. I wonder if she is someone with whom he can finally forge a sense of family. This walk, as we leap-frog over obstacles in our path, seems like a good time to broach the subject. I'm surprised by the detachment of his response.

"Samantha, she is nice. She is cool. I like that. But I don't really know her," Junior tells me. They have been living together for a few months. She is from the town of Croix-des-Bouquets, on the northeast outskirts of the capital. Only about a ten-mile drive from the airport, Croix-des-Bouquets has managed to retain the charm of the Haitian countryside. The town is best known for its fantastical metal sculptures made from recycled oil drums. Both of Samantha's parents have died and she has a surviving sister who lives in downtown Port-au-Prince, with whom she is not in touch. Junior does not know the details of her losses. "With girls, there are a certain number of questions that you don't need to ask because it upsets them," he explains. "And you know, there are some things girls won't tell you. You just have to accept them." But does he feel there is the possibility to grow closer in the future, I ask?

Here, the specter of education, housing, and employment, all the things I wish for Junior, cast their shadow over his dreams and ambitions. Until he can get a steady footing on the shifting ground below his feet, Junior cannot imagine making a life, of laying roots, with someone. He pauses, as if to search for the words, and says, "I would like the force to create personal activities." Once he has a safe physical exterior, he will finally be able to cultivate his rich, inner life.

As we continue on our path, we notice a group of bystanders staring over an abyss. We approach to take in the view. An upside-down tap-tap bus lies below us in a debris field. The crowd murmurs about how the driver came too fast down the road a couple of days ago and belly-flopped into the bed of cleared rubble. It's unclear if there were any passengers onboard. The sight of the crumpled wreckage makes me grateful to be walking.

Throughout our walk, Junior has been doing his now familiar politician routine. He stops to shake hands, rap knuckles, and flash peace signs with male acquaintances as he goes. Once the peers are out of earshot, he reiterates one of the core components of his street survival strategy. "San, I am friends with everyone, but I do not get too close. I do not follow what the others do. It is too dangerous. That is why I prefer friendships with women." He says this last sentence without any trace of irony or bravado. I know he is serious. This is how Junior has managed to avoid the deadly trifecta of drugs, guns, and prison.

One male friend who pulls up on his motorcycle appears to be an exception. I can tell that Junior has a genuine affection for him. He is a baby-faced man in his thirties. "This is Lucky," Junior says proudly. I recognize the name right away. So this is the friend who rescued Junior after he was run over by the truck. In the days after the accident, it was Lucky who drove Junior to the internationally staffed hospital in the countryside and stayed by his side, helping him advocate against an amputation and making sure he had something to eat each day. Lucky tells us about his new job, working as a chef at one of the fanciest area hotels located above Petionville. His name matches his sunny disposition. Once Lucky drives away, Junior tells me: "You know, Lucky used to live in the United States, in Chicago. But he had to come back. His family is still there." I understand what Junior is telling me. Lucky is a criminal deportee. The news is unexpected. I try to line this information up with the image of the person I just met. Lucky hardly seems like a criminal. What was his offense, I ask? Junior shrugs. "I have never asked him. Sometimes people just make mistakes," he replies. As is so often the case in Haiti, things are the exact opposite of what they seem, a reminder of the duality and complexity of life. It turns out one of the very few people Junior feels he can trust is a criminal deportee.

We arrive at the fortified entrance to the Union School. A quick flash of my U.S. passport gets us past the guard gate without any questions or calls to the front desk. The manicured grounds resemble an American high school campus and I can tell that

Junior is excited by the possibility of studying here. As we walk past the main quad, a slogan painted in block letters announces, "We're Building Character," and I learn that the campus is the home of the Panthers.

We make our way to the secretary's desk and I can see the disdain etched on her face as I describe our quest. She is looking at Junior as if he is a piece of trash dragged in from the street outside. I think of the irony of how upper-class Haitians want their children educated in some of the best universities abroad and are counting on enlightened principles for their children to be accepted as equals and not subjected to racism. And yet, those same principals don't seem to apply in Haiti, the world's first independent black republic, founded by freed slaves. I also take a moment to reflect and try to see the situation from other vantage points. In the eyes of many, including Haiti's land-owning class and some foreigners, Junior may appear at first glance to be a street tough or a member of a criminal gang. That impression stems in part from his rap-influenced fashion style and swagger, but it is rooted in something much deeper and more universal. Although Junior lives in a "black country," he too is subject to the burden of black men everywhere, who must learn to absorb the cold stares of those unable or unwilling to acknowledge their humanity. I think of the slim gold volume of W.E.B. Du Bois's timeless text, *The Souls of Black Folk,* which is sitting on my bookshelf at home. Du Bois first published this masterpiece of American literature in 1903, and although he was writing about the dehumanizing treatment of black Americans, his writing is transcendent and relates to this current moment. One of the underlined passages in my copy reads: "It's a peculiar sensation, this double-consciousness, this sense of always looking at one's self through the eyes of others, of measuring one's soul by the tape of a world that looks on in amused contempt and pity." As the secretary sizes up Junior with her imaginary tape measure, she may have genuine reason to fear Junior's presence, given Haiti's fragile state of political unrest mixed with post-apocalyptic natural disaster. As the official gatekeeper, it is her job to look out for the safety of her students. And yet, unless Haiti's elite institutions open their doors to the tent dwellers in their midst, the country will remain unsafe for everyone.

Perhaps this exercise has been moot. We learn that the Union School has no continuing education program and Junior is too old to enroll in the high school. I later learn from the school's website that they have an open admission policy "without regard to nationality, race, creed, or religion" and admission to the school requires other hurdles, such as report cards for two previous years and a letter of recommendation from a member of the board of trustees, or a member of the Union School community.

As we prepare to walk away, I see a flyer for evening English classes and I inquire if this might be a possibility for Junior. The secretary can think of no reason to disqualify him. She reluctantly directs us to another office across the hallway. We get the needed information and deliberate. A part of me is all for breaking down barriers. Junior clearly wants into this world and is undeterred by the secretary. "I could meet a lot of important people here," he tells me. I know that is true. But there are some drawbacks, as well. For starters, the class meets only once a week and the courses are held in the evenings. Junior and I both question how much English he will learn with such an infrequent class schedule. And we worry that the school's distance from the Place Boyer could put him on the road after dark and potentially place him in harm's way if the current political impasse is not resolved soon. I don't mention it, but I also worry that throwing Junior into this milieu so early into his transformation could be damaging. Studying in an environment where one is unwelcome or made to feel like an outsider could make learning all the more difficult and be unhealthy to his self-esteem. We have another English-language school to check out this afternoon. We agree to keep an open mind.

As we are trudging up the hill back toward Petionville, Junior glances at the lunchtime traffic and says we might be able to squeeze in a quick visit with Christopher before Fanfan's relatives pick him up from preschool. This is a surprise and a treat. We hadn't talked about visiting with Christopher today and I had no idea the school was right on our path. From the outside, it appears to be a child-friendly place with a large courtyard. The school is named after an imaginary boy and girl playmate and it has a charming logo that looks as if it came from the pages of a children's book. Parents, some dressed in office attire, are starting to line up to pick up their children. When the gate opens, I can see children dressed in royal blue shirts and navy blue shorts skipping in the courtyard. Junior checks his wallet and tells me he did not bring the school-issued ID needed to get Christopher out of school. He's not sure who from Fanfan's family will be here. It could be Fanfan, or her cousins. This news injects a bit of anxiety into the situation. I am keen to meet her, but she is not expecting to see Junior and me here, and I don't want any drama or a situation that might frighten Christopher.

Moments later, the cousins arrive. They are two young men of about twenty years old, both friendly and low key. They greet Junior warmly. We sit and wait with the other parents. One by one, children start to emerge from the green metal gate. I'm looking around, watching the entire scene unfold around me, when I suddenly notice Junior is seated next to me with a sweet little boy. This must be a friend of Christopher's, I think. Junior doesn't say anything but he gives me a funny little smile. Is this Christopher? I ask, perplexed. He smiles and nods. I'm confused. Christopher had dreadlocks. This little boy has a shorn head and a prominent scar on his forehead. The cousins are holding the school release card, which has Christopher's photo on it. Junior hands it to me so I can see it, but it only further confuses the picture. The first name listed on the card reads "Jeffetey" and the last name is one that I have never heard of. I'm utterly perplexed. Is this child Christopher, or is Junior simply winding me up for fun? The little boy is tucked happily into Junior's arm eating some biscuits. I give Junior a quizzical look as if to say, "What is going on?" Inside, an avalanche of doubt is starting to set in. I find myself wondering if anything Junior has shared with me is true, or simply an extension of a highly evolved imagination, perhaps the product of the trauma of life as a street child.

"Is this your child?" I ask him. "*Wi,* San. I can explain," he says. Then he looks at the little boy and says, "Ki jan ou rele?" *What's your name?* The boy smiles nervously, not understanding what is really being asked. He doesn't reply. Instead, Junior answers for him. "Yes, this is Chris." Next he addresses the cousins. "Is this Chris—or is this Jeffetey?" Like the boy, the cousins sense the question is best left unanswered. I can see that Junior is getting frustrated now. The contradictions of his life are colliding. "Look, this is something his mom has done to try to get back at me," Junior explains, annoyed at having to explain this indignity and perhaps sensing that his trust is being questioned. "When

Christopher was born, I gave him his name and we agreed on it. But when his mom enrolled him in school, she gave him a different name. I have asked her to correct this with the school administration, but she won't do it," Junior says. "What name appears on the birth certificate?" I ask Junior, still not convinced. He tells me Christopher Junior Davilma is the name that should appear on the record, but Fanfan is the one who recorded the birth and he has never seen the document. The birth certificate has been in the possession of Fanfan's sister and Junior has been asking to see it for some time. "They won't give it to me," he says.

As confounding as this tale sounds, I'm willing to believe it. Christopher is playing with some of his classmates on the steps where we have been sitting, giving us a chance to talk. I want to express my concern about the situation, without meddling or putting further pressure on Junior. "Perhaps you should speak to the school about this," I suggest gently. "I think it could be quite confusing to a child to have two different identities." I look over to where Christopher has been playing. He wears a Disney *Cars* backpack and carries a Pokemon lunchbox. I marvel at the power of Hollywood blockbuster franchising. These are the exact same cartoon archetypes to which Alexander would respond. How I wish Christopher and Alexander could meet as children.

Even more troubling than the identity crisis is the scar visible on Christopher's forehead. I would have remembered seeing this last time. It looks like an inch long gash, possibly from a piece of glass or a razor. "Junior, what about the mark on his forehead?" I ask. "That's from *envie*," he says nonchalantly. I am again confused. "You know, when a woman is pregnant, and she wants to eat something but she can't find it. She scratches her belly and it makes a mark on the child," Junior says, as if this cause of birthmarks is common knowledge. I raise an eyebrow and Junior sighs. He tells me perhaps the mark on Christopher's forehead is new. He fesses up that he has some concerns about Christopher's safety. He tells me that neighbors have told him they have seen Christopher out as late as midnight playing by himself on the steep steps leading up to Fanfan's family home in the favela and he once tumbled down the maze of steps. I shudder at this news, and the account that follows.

Earlier this year, Junior continues, Christopher was left all alone in the family cave when a fire broke out. He survived by crouching in a corner. "If you ask him, 'Chris, kote ou te kache?', *where did you hide?*, he will take you by the hand and show you," Junior says. "I don't want to have any conflict with Fanfan. It's not good for Christopher. That is the main reason I want to have my own home. These people are negligent. It's frustrating," he says. He tells me that after the two incidents, Christopher has primarily been living with his aunt, Fanfan's older sister, where he has better supervision. But he says Christopher doesn't like to be left all alone in the aunt's care and he worries that she, too, may be mistreating him. This is the first time I have heard of these concerns and I am very worried. Junior adds that Fanfan's family often does not consult him on decision-making. They recently cut off all his dreadlocks and asked him what he thought afterward. "Why are you asking me now?" was all he could muster. "It's because I don't have family that they know they can get away with this." Junior's account makes me reflect about how in Haiti, one is not accountable to the state. One is accountable to family and community. And then it hits me: Christopher is his only real close blood relative in Haiti. Junior is doing his best to find his way and lead Christopher. He can't do it alone.

Junior holds Christopher, placing his hands on the boy's bare forehead. He tells him that he will visit him tomorrow and to be strong. They say goodbye by rapping knuckles. Junior and I head to lunch around the corner at Marie Beliard, my favorite bakery in Petionville. We have hot-pressed sandwiches and cappuccinos, and I hope that the warmth of this environment can bolster Junior's spirit after what he has just shared with me. I love how this café melds both the Haitian and French traditions. The beautiful cakes and confections it produces for baptisms, weddings, and birthdays are created with the artistry and importance due life's meaningful milestone moments. And being a bakery, it has a broad reach, preparing daily bread, baguettes, croissants, and *pain raisin,* for a broad swath of society. It's a wonderful place to recharge and people-watch. This is one of Haiti's unifying places.

Our last stop of the day is the English language school next to the police station in Petionville. The feeling here is very different from the Union School. There is an old-fashioned language lab where students wear large sets of equally old-fashioned earphones and listen to cassette tapes to practice vocabulary and sample dialogues. There are a lot of students and there is no sense of snobbery. It actually feels very democratic. Classes take place five days a week and students must spend time in the language lab practicing their lessons. This school exudes a palpable feeling of social mobility. From where we stand in the hallway, we can overhear one of the afternoon classes engaging in a group exercise. *Is that your sister? Are you a lawyer? Are YOU a lawyer? Yes, I'm a lawyer.* The class is wrapping up and the teacher steps out of the classroom. "Hi, I'm Carl," he introduces himself. He speaks perfectly clipped English and I like the way he addresses Junior, treating him like an intelligent and capable partner. Carl does a quick evaluation and gets a sense of Junior's ability. Together they craft a plan. Carl will start Junior in the beginning class and will tailor the assignments to his ability. Junior's first day of classes will be on January 13, the day after the earthquake anniversary. As we leave, Junior is already thinking about what he will wear to his first day of school. He has a white shirt that he somehow wants to get ironed. "You must dress up for your first day of school," he tells me.

CHAPTER 20

Anniversary

The sound of singing stirs me from a light sleep. The words are not distinct but the chorus drifting in from outside my window is ethereal and soothing and as soon as I open my eyes I realize that "the day" has come. I could not be here in the days after the earth shook, when thousands lay buried in a suspended state between life and death and every moment mattered. And that's why it became so important to me to be here on this day. Being here in person is my own way of standing with Haiti, of quietly expressing that every life lost mattered.

I quickly shower and am dressed and ready to go when Junior arrives at the hostel's arched wooden doors. There is no time for us to sit and drink a cup of coffee. We are heading to the Eglise St. Pierre here in Petionville, a beautiful, yellow church that seems like it would fit in perfectly in a small New England town. It has always been one of my favorite Port-au-Prince landmarks. There is something about the way the light dapples its amber walls in the sunlight that signals it as a healing place. That its historic stone walls are still standing is a source of comfort, a testament to the strength of enduring places. On the day that Junior and I sat and celebrated his survival over a bowl of *soupe giromon,* pumpkin soup, he revealed that this was the space to which he had returned over the years when he wanted to have a closer communication with *Bondye.* Now we are walking briskly uphill in order to be there in time for 8:00 a.m. Mass. When I step on the street I expect to see a procession but there is none. I cannot identify the source of the mellifluous singing, which has continued as a constant soothing infusion for over an hour now. Junior points to a crushed hull of a building across the street. "That is a church," he tells me. "They are singing inside." As is so often the case in Haiti, things are not as they appear on the surface. Throughout this day, I will repeatedly hear singing in the distance and not be able to pinpoint the source.

We approach the Eglise St. Pierre, walking past the flower stall where I had spontaneously selected a bright bouquet for Junior as I prepared to reunite with him in March. Today, there are memorial funeral wreaths at the ready. Pastel-colored ribbons cascade down the sides of the floral spirals with the message "Hommage aux victims du 12 Janvier 2010" written in gold glitter. The time on my cell phone reads 8:03 a.m. Already there is an overflow crowd gathered on the steps of the church. I can see that most people are dressed in white. Music from the service is being piped into the courtyard. The mood is calm and reflective. This is one of those rare instances when all sectors of Haitian society have come together. I see entire upper-class families standing on the stone floor next to women and children from the camps. A man on crutches holds his straw hat in his hands. Everyone is respectful and introspective. I sense in the crowd a feeling of relief to have a place to gather and express what doesn't have a name. *Goudou Goudou* is the word that has emerged in Creole for the day the earth trembled, the word literally echoing the sound of the rumbling mountains, trees, and soil. We lack a similar animist word for this moment of loss, sadness, and reflection on the chasm that swallowed an ocean of lives. Together we are standing here seeing the past and the future, collectively etching a line to infinity in our minds' eyes.

Junior and I are standing side by side in the courtyard. I have a printout of three photos in my purse that I have been waiting to give him. My friend and former colleague Paige Jennings, an American from Kentucky who went on to work as the lead Haiti researcher at Amnesty International in London after leaving our human rights mission, dug deep into a trunk of photos tucked in a hallway at her home in Ireland one night as her three children slept in order to find these. Just as I had been tasked in the early days of our human rights operation to reach out to journalists and monitor conditions for press freedom, Paige's portfolio was child welfare. She always had a special awareness and sensitivity to the plight of Haiti's street children. It was a bond we shared that went unspoken until she reached out to me via Facebook after learning that I had found Junior. Paige had watched out for many of Petionville's street children, offering them guidance, support, and a loving presence. Junior was certain she would remember his friend and brother Fritznel, who died in the earthquake and whose name had rung familiar to me, but whom I could not recall by face.

Paige wrote to me that Fritznel had gone by the name of Michael as a child, a nickname she believed he had adopted in reverence to singer Michael Jackson. She recalled how even as a child, Junior would act as the wise elder, constantly correcting his best friend. "His *real* name is Fritznel. Call him Fritznel,"

Junior would implore, to which Michael would respond: "Call me Michael." Paige noted, "I got the feeling that he did it gently to wind up Junior, who was otherwise clearly the leader!" And she shared with me the heartbreaking memory of her last meeting with "Michael" during a return trip to Haiti, when he was navigating one of life's most difficult transitions, from boy to man, on his own. "Michael had become a teenager and he told me, with real sadness and a bit of bewilderment, that people on the street were starting to be afraid of him, to see him as a threat as he wasn't little and cute anymore," she wrote. "It was so gut-wrenching, to see this kid that no one had ever lifted a finger for, actually feeling hurt that people had that misperception. It was like, what was he supposed to do, once he'd lost the vulnerability that had been his one 'asset' with passersby? Live up to their expectations, and mug them?! He wasn't a kid to do that kind of thing, and it upset him that they would make that assumption."

But Michael's identity was again thrown into question during a subsequent phone call when Paige reached out to Junior to offer her condolences over his death. In a very patchy connection, Junior appeared to suggest that Michael had died before the earthquake. Or at the very least, he seemed uncomfortable talking about it. I've been carrying the three photos that Paige's husband scanned at his architecture office, the first of Junior at around age nine, the second of Fritznel/Michael at about the same age, and the third of another boy who lived on the street and was their friend. I've so far resisted giving them to Junior on this trip, as I've worried these photos could send him into a place of pain or numbness. The principle of *gusimbura* seems to apply here. Author Tracy Kidder writes about this Burundian social custom in his book, *Strength in What Remains,* about the extraordinary journey of genocide survivor Deogratias. It is the act of reminding some-one of something traumatic and it is a social taboo to be avoided in a country of endemic poverty and political violence. And yet I remember how vividly Junior grieved that no one seemed to care or take notice of his dear friend and brother's death. I know he has no trace left to remember him by. This seems like a safe place to unearth this memory. "I have something for you," I tell Junior, handing him the folded piece of paper from my purse. His initial response catches me off guard. He unfolds the paper and stares at the photos and then breaks into a deep, hearty laugh. "Fritznel, Mike," he exclaims, pointing at the center photo. It's as if the immediate association was a flashback to his childhood, briefly short-circuiting the memory of death. After a moment he grows quiet, reflective. "This will help me talk to him," Junior says, before folding the paper and placing it in his back pocket.

From our spot in the courtyard I see some open spots in the pews. I'm eager to enter the church, to feel the embrace of this healing space. Spiritual hymns are playing while congregants take communion. The morning light is being filtered and reflected by the church's amber walls to create a golden haze. It's perhaps an irony that I rarely attend Mass in the United States, and yet I seek out historic churches in my travels for the sacred spaces and refuge they provide from modern life, a place to hear the quiet thoughts inside us and connect with those who came before us. In truth, I have doctrinal differences with the Catholic Church, which I believe render it exclusionary and out of step with the world we live in today. And regardless of any personal schism, I know I am just much more comfortable with a spirituality that is not prescribed by a rigid code or defined by a single name. But here in Haiti, and elsewhere in Latin America, I take comfort in how Catholic tradition and ritual provide a framework for transitions, hardship, and loss in daily life. It's quite possibly in my blood.

On a trip to Colombia in 2005, I visited the Marquez family crypt at the main cemetery in my parents' hometown of Medellin. I was surprised to see small buttercup flowers reverentially placed around the entire doorframe of the crypt. It was All Saints Day, and although people had placed flowers at many of the crypts and tombstones in the cemetery, this seemed different. My uncle Tomás and Aunt Alicia, who were accompanying me, were equally intrigued. Just as we were wondering aloud a custodian came by and answered our question. "Someone special is buried here. People routinely come here to place flowers in her honor." We all knew whom he was talking about. It was my paternal great-grandmother, Maria Jesus Bravo Echeverri, who was renowned for her expansive, cerulean blue eyes and was affectionately known as Mama Jesusita. She was a deeply religious woman who was believed to have prophetic visions and was known for her lifelong commitment to the poor. When she died, humble people in the neighborhood came and asked to have a small piece of the blanket that comforted her during death, to seek her protection and vision. According to family lore, there was even a local effort to have her canonized as a saint. When we returned to the apartment of my Aunt Inés and Aunt Clara that evening, two of my very sage aunts whom I consider keepers of the family history, they nodded knowingly. They were well aware of the tradition of strangers placing offerings at the family crypt.

Now here in the Eglise St. Pierre, I look around at all of the faces surrounding me. I see people from all walks of life. Sprinkled throughout the crowd are women dressed head to toe in white. Some are spiritual leaders, known as *mambos*, or vodou priestesses. But regardless of people's external appearance, there are many assembled here for whom their reverence of vodou deities, or *lwa*, is seamlessly intertwined with their belief in Catholic saints. Take for example the spirit *Aza Athiassou*, who is said to live in darkness at the bottom of the ocean. He incites followers to prayer, meditation, and concentration and he has been described as "the supreme woman." He is also a "Master Thief" who steals from thieves to give to others. His Catholic correspondent is the Holy Spirit. Another oft-cited presence in Haitian life is *Erzulie Freda*. She is a fickle lover who appreciates offerings of rice pudding, is fastidious about cleanliness, and demands that her suitors be impeccably dressed. Erzulie ensures the fertility of the fields and she is said to be in love with her stepson. Her Catholic correspondents are Our Lady of Mercy and Our Lady of Charity. Far less charitable is *Ogoun Shango*, a cruel hermaphrodite who dresses in blue pants and a braided red jacket. Because the stars on his epaulets are blinding, it's necessary to look him right in the eye. Shango favors distilled sugarcane "fire" water, a whiskey-like substance known as *clairin*. And he is a fine dancer and cigar smoker who revels in cruelty but who also resolves the hardships of his devotees. His Catholic correspondent is Saint Michael the Archangel. These three examples are drawn from the book *A Practical Directory of the Loa of Haitian Vodou* by Mercedes Foucard Guignard, an ethnologist, anthropologist, researcher, storyteller, and playwright who goes by the nickname Deita. In her introduction to the book, Deita explains her motivation for writing a directory to Haiti's vodou spirits, citing as inspiration *Papa Simbi*, a gracious deity who is the essence of the waters, and who counsels against giving false information to the "non-initiate or the uneducated." Her white pages–like directory to Haiti's spirit world, along with the writings of sociologist Laennec Hurbon, one of Haiti's most noted intellectuals and cultural interpreters, resonates with my experience of Haiti. I've come to realize that whether one practices Catholicism, Taoism, or vodou in Haiti is of no real relevance. What matters is that this is the belief system rooted into the collective imagination. These are the symbols and the markers, which give shape, depth, and meaning to daily experience. Vodou is the mythology of Haiti and more than anything it provides a fundamental grid to source the duality of life here.

My attention shifts now to the priest who is addressing the congregation. He is speaking in a very gentle, calming voice, and I find him perfectly suited to be today's messenger. I am being lulled by his sonorous tone when I am suddenly jolted awake. For the past year, words have failed to stand up to the violent collusion of poverty fused with nature, which conspired in such a devastating loss of humanity. The toll: 230,000 lives snatched in thirty-five seconds. And now, in this moment, the priest has found a way to distill meaning from this senseless tragedy. He has handed each of us a gift to take out into the world. "Respect l'amour. L'amour triomphe." *Respect love. Love triumphs.*

Junior and I sit for a moment in silence, taking it all in. As we are preparing to leave I see a familiar figure. It's Carole Devillers, the French photographer and longtime Haiti resident who was my colleague and Holiday Inn officemate when I reported for Reuters in Haiti. Carole now lives in Florida and today we will be reunited as a team. I have commissioned her to make a portrait of Junior at his tent home in La Place Boyer. Like a portrait artist, I want Carole to record Junior one year after the tragedy and render his spirit and his milieu in this tent encampment, before this moment in time fades away. I'm hoping her portrait will give me a deeper look, a new perspective, to add to my understanding of Junior's complexity. Our meeting place was to have been the front steps of the church, but we have run into each other right at the center of the nave as Junior and I form part of a human chain slowly exiting the church. We embrace in a strong hug. It's wonderful to see Carole again after fifteen years. She looks just as I remember her. She wears her long dark hair piled in an elegant and efficient bun and wears her signature bandana around her forehead. Her celestial blue eyes retain their softness and sense of wonder. Carole knows and loves Haiti so deeply. I love seeing this mythical landscape through her eyes.

Junior, Carole, and I walk on foot to the camp. A man and a woman standing on a wood-frame stage are leading a crowd of mostly women in prayer and song at the perimeter of the plaza. The spiritual hymns are meditative and reflective and yet two little boys in the crowd cannot repress their exuberance and joy for life. The boys arch and twist their bodies in a happy jig, spreading their bliss to all around them.

We enter the maze of tents dotting the plaza. After walking down a narrow cement path framed by hanging clotheslines, we turn a corner and arrive at Junior's place. It's perhaps not surprising that Junior's tent stands out from the crowd. Most of the tents are standard issue white or blue. Junior's is a vibrant orange, like something you might actually pack to go on vacation, and looks slightly more secure. There is a small padlock, similar to a luggage lock, securing the zipper handles that provide entry through the tent's front flap. But the tent was not a handout. In trademark Junior fashion, he bought his from a street vendor, being judicious in his choice. I don't think Junior chose to buy this as an extravagance. It just so happened that by the time Junior found himself needing a tent, the major aid groups were no longer giving them away. I believe he financed the purchase by tapping into the US$350 in seed money my friend Elio gave him to start a cell-phone business after he was run over by the truck. I haven't pressed Junior on it because I know it's a point of contention between the two of them. Several months after Elio returned to New York, Junior phoned him at his United Nations office to report he was broke and needed help. "What happened to the money I gave you?" Elio asked, no doubt exasperated. "Why didn't you use it to start a business?" Junior said he had used the money to pay for Christopher's preschool. Elio and I both sensed there was more to the story. Although I understood Elio's frustration, I also understood that $350 in seed money was not enough for Junior to rebuild his life *and* start a new venture. The accident, which left Junior dependent on crutches for three months, made it impractical for Junior to continue staying with his friends, the young middle class couple, in the hills. And much like the fifty-pound bags of rice and industrial-sized containers of cooking oil stamped USAID that often end up for sale at roadside market stalls, the remaining inventory of tents donated by good Samaritans around the world were simply absorbed into Haiti's thriving black market. Junior bought his deluxe model for just under US$40.

Once we arrive at the tent, I stand back to allow Carole and Junior to enter into a comfortable rapport. It doesn't take long to realize that Junior is making peace symbols and otherwise posing from his reclined position on the air mattress inside his tent. Carole and I notice that when I talk to Junior he seems to become more natural, and so we agree that I should engage him in conversation. The presence of two foreign women with camera equipment soon attracts a small crowd, and I notice a subtle shift in Junior as he snaps tersely at passersby to keep away. This is not the gentle Junior I know who routinely addresses strangers with a warm greeting of *sè'm* and *frè'm*, my sister and brother. My own small talk with Junior may even be contributing to this change. In recent days I have noticed Junior's abiding sense of fashion and how carefully he eyes clothing from the roadside *pepe* vendors. "If someone doesn't dress well in Haiti, it's because they don't want to," Junior had remarked. "You can find anything from the *pepe* vendors. Kenneth Cole. Gianni Versace. It's all there." It got me wondering who his favorite style icons are. How had he ever acquired this rarefied taste? Now, I have him listing off the names of his favorite Haitian rappers, whom I have never heard of, and some of whom live in Miami. This conversation only seems to be heightening Junior's swagger, despite his assurances that his icons all have "pawol pozitif," or *positive lyrics*. I feel as if I detect a transformation in Junior. He is acting like a celebrity refugee, a shift no doubt triggered by the photo shoot and his awareness that his life is somehow on the cusp of change. Despite the growing pains, Carole manages to capture a range of Junior's depth of expression. At first, Junior appears somber, reflective of the anniversary. In one image, he casually brandishes an aluminum baseball bat. It seems menacing at first, until Junior explains this is his security system. "San, I don't believe in having guns," he assures me. And then we stumble on something that makes us laugh. Junior's face lights up, revealing all of his beauty, hope, and vision.

Next we visit the children at the camp school. It's a one-room schoolhouse in a blue UNICEF tent pockmarked with holes to provide ventilation. Junior has cited this school as an example of the lack of international aid in the camps. Not even here, he has told me, are they providing a hot meal for the children. I am intrigued to learn who is operating the school, and I am secretly hopeful that we will learn about a little-known service being provided to children. Certainly, the international community cannot ignore the plight of the children in the camps. We arrive just as a crowd of about seventy children is assembling. A masterful teacher, dressed in white linen pants and a white T-shirt, in honor of the anniversary, is leading the children through a lively, healing, and cathartic exercise to understand the meaning of the day and to help them release their pain. "Last January 12, a lot of people cried," he begins. "But this January 12, I want you to give me a little smile." He puts his finger over his lips and raises his eyebrows up and down in a mime-like manner. Giggles reverberate from the crowd. "Now, on January 12, a lot of people left," he continues. "We will never forget them. We *cannot* forget them. There were a lot of *ti-moun* [children] who cried. There were a lot of *gran-moun* [adults] who cried," he says, before drawing close to the assembled circle. "Now children, let me tell you something. Yes, we cried. But that was in the past! I am not crying anymore. It's true that my little friend went away. It's true that my *maman* went away. It's true my *papi* went away. My brother went away. Nonetheless, I am still alive, okay?" The teacher begins jiggling his body in a jitterbug fashion. "Children, touch your body," he instructs, as he shimmies, wiggles, and twists as if he has ants in his pants. The children erupt in laughter and play. "Okay," he pronounces. "If you are here, it means you are still alive!" Next, he invites a little boy of about nine years old to stand up and sing a song. The boy's a cappella rendition washes over the mass of huddled children like a healing rain. "Y'ale. Yo pap retourné. Yo kité. Tout moun ap plenyé. . . . N'ap kenbe fèm. Nou pral wè demen." The sweetness of the boy's voice masks the bitter message. These are hardly the words of a children's song. This new generation has just been inducted into the rites of the Haitian survival anthem. *They went away. They won't return. They left. Everyone complains. . . . We'll stand firm. We'll see them tomorrow.*

Junior has been alternating between admiration for the teacher and petulance. During the exercise, he actually scolded some of the children for spilling beyond the rope barrier of the classroom and onto the dirt footpath. I'm not entirely sure what is festering inside Junior today. Although it saddens me, his mood does not break the spell of the magic I have just witnessed. As I have watched the teacher's interaction with the children, I have felt reassured that UNICEF has tapped one of the very best trainers I have ever seen in action. I approach him after the exercise to congratulate him and learn more about his work. I am startled when he tells me that the school is his own grassroots operation. He started an organization to aid disadvantaged children two years before the earthquake. Now, with a roving staff of seven and threadbare financial support from the Haitian government, he runs schools at seven different camps in the capital. His organization does not even have a website. Confused, I point to the UNICEF tent and ask about his affiliation with the global children's organization. The teacher, Clarens Alexandre, is diplomatic in his response. UNICEF provided the tent, plastic floor mats, and some soccer balls for the school. When they have foreign dignitaries visiting, UNICEF officials often come by to showcase the work he is doing. "We would like to do more with them," Clarens tells me.

As we are speaking I am feeling a mix of intuition and inspiration swirling inside me. For months, I've been brainstorming to try to connect Junior with an international organization that could mentor and train him to work with Haiti's displaced children. And now, here is this wonderful schoolhouse operating literally in Junior's backyard—with virtually no international support. UNICEF essentially provided the "branding." What I've been observing and feeling these past few days in Haiti is now gelling. The "old model" of international organizations coming into Haiti and setting their own priorities for projects, the model that brought me to Haiti, has for the most part not worked. The groups pay their top salaries to their experts. Haitian capacity is not developed. And yet, here is Clarens and his team finding solutions on their own with utmost professionalism and sensitivity. Here they are, nurturing the minds and spirits of these beautiful, displaced children.

I have just one question. "Why do you do this?" I ask Clarens. He quietly tells me the story of his son, who was born with a muscular disorder and has never been able to skip and play. "Every time I see a child I imagine it is my own because I have only one and he cannot walk," he tells me. The weight of his words crushes me. It's impossible to express everything I am feeling in this moment. For more than two years I have railed against the limits of modern medicine, longing so deeply to have another child, a dream thwarted by my husband's unsuccessful vasectomy reversal and the cost and emotional toll of fertility treatments. I understand the instinct to see a child and imagine it as my own. Standing here with Clarens, I know I have found a very special mentor for Junior.

Our next stop of the day is the home of Junior's "sister-in-law," Nahomie. This is Fanfan's older sister and currently Christopher's primary caregiver. Junior and I want to make sure we have some time with Christopher on this anniversary, but because Junior's relationship with Fanfan's family is strained, our visit has not been coordinated and there is no guarantee that Christopher will be there when we drop by. I have a vague memory of Nahomie from my visit last March. I remember her as a friendly presence enveloping the darkness in the family cave located high in the shantytown of Stenyo Vincent, named after a former Haitian president who staunchly opposed the American intervention of Haiti. Junior tells me that Nahomie has moved, together with her husband and young daughter, to a new place not far from the main family abode.

When we arrive I do a double take. Nahomie's home lies directly between the stunning mansions hugging the hillside and the shantytown. The geographic location and infrastructure of her home places her on the tiny sliver of the social grid occupied by Haiti's middle class. Stepping through the door, I instantly recognize the classic trappings of a bourgeois Haitian home: There is the slightly stiff and uncomfortable sofa with two matching upholstered chairs and a coffee table. And perhaps even more important, the signature wooden stand in the corner, housing blue and white ceramic figurines dancing cotillion-style atop crocheted runners, as if in the court of Marie Antoinette. (I have never seen these figurines for sale in Haiti's outdoor market stalls, and yet they are standard issue in proper homes. Perched alongside vases of plastic flowers, these Limoges porcelain knock-offs are markings of culture and sophistication and they telegraph the lingering hold of the French colonial era.) I see that Nahomie's home has added a modern twist to the classic middle class Haitian home. Apparently, there is a new marking of social mobility and worldliness: A portrait of President Obama watches benevolently over the room. The word "Leadership" is etched in bold letters under his visage. Obama's presence is especially notable given the country's current political morass over the contested presidential election results. In the days ahead, Jean-Claude Duvalier, aka "Baby Doc," will return to Haiti after nearly twenty-five years of exile in France, meekly seeking to commemorate the earthquake anniversary with the dispossessed millions among whose ranks his family dynasty tortured and embezzled at whim. And former President Aristide will write a public letter from his exile in South Africa, alerting the world of his intention to do the same.

We step outside and the pleasant balcony with sweeping views of the capital and the port below surprises me. We learn that Fanfan came by this morning to take Christopher to church. It's unclear when she is expected back. I get a closer look at Nahomie now. She is heavyset woman, not yet thirty, with a beautiful face and a sturdy body offset by gentle curves. Her demeanor is purposeful, hardworking, and amiable. She has bleached the floors on the patio outside and has just finished washing a bassinet full of clothes, while her three-year-old daughter plays at her side. Beads of sweat pool at her bosom. As she pauses from her work to speak with us, a kindly woman steps out from the kitchen to announce that the afternoon *repa,* or meal, is now ready. A hearty smell of a rich stew and vegetables wafts out of the kitchen. Again I find myself doing a double take. Nahomie is able to afford domestic help and yet here she is doing rigorous physical labor. I ask her if she will be going to church or otherwise participating in anniversary events today. "Oh, no. I have too much work to do," she tells me. She is clearly the diligent and industrious foil to her party-girl sister, Fanfan. I am intrigued. Nothing I am seeing is consistent with the image Junior led me to expect of a potentially negligent and abusive caregiver. Again I am confronted by the brainteaser that is Haiti. Reality is a constant puzzle, existing on multiple layers, and Haiti challenges you to decipher it.

I sit down with Nahomie at a wrought iron table on the balcony to engage her in a hushed conversation, discreetly out of earshot from Junior. I am determined to square this circle and gulf the divide between perception and reality. I learn that Nahomie's husband is a lawyer. She herself completed high school and she, too, dreams of becoming a lawyer. It's a goal she hopes to realize by emigrating to Canada with her husband and daughter within a few years. Nahomie also briefs me on the family history. Her parents, her deceased father and surviving mother, were both cooks and her mother continues to work at a downtown restaurant. The family settled in the hillside favela of Stenyo Vincent in 1978. Together with her husband and daughter, Nahomie temporarily moved back into the dank family home for a few months following the earthquake. She feared her downtown home, although not destroyed, was structurally unstable. She felt safer in Stenyo and she remained there until this comfortable apartment home became available.

Nahomie also unwittingly offers some inconsistencies to Junior's accounts of reality: Christopher's birthday is in July, not January. She knows this without consulting the Blackberry she fingers idly in her hand. In fact, Christopher was born on July 18, 2006—exactly two weeks and a day after her own daughter was born, and the children have been raised as siblings, she tells me. Next, I gingerly raise the issue of the jagged line on Christopher's forehead, bracing to hear a heart-wrenching account of how the sweet-natured toddler went tumbling down the favela stairs on a starry dark night when nobody was looking after him. Here, however, Nahomie corroborates Junior's account. "That's *envie*," desire, she explains sweetly. My expression is less incredulous this time. "How exactly does that work?" I ask, nonchalantly. "If a woman is pregnant and she craves something, but cannot find it, sometimes she scratches her belly and that leaves a trace," she tells me. Of course. I am at least heartened that Junior and his sister-in-law are sticking to the same story.

Next I move on to the topic of the two names, but already I have lost some of the fire in my belly to insist that both sides of the family call the child by a single name. Who am I to think that I will be able to single-handedly reverse Haitian cultural practices? This question causes Nahomie to shift briefly in her chair and here I am treated to her innate lawyering skills. Yes, Christopher has two names, she acknowledges head on. His mother named him Jeffetey and his father named him Christopher. Pausing for a moment, as if to reassure me, she adds: "But we call him both names." This is the Haitian custom, she adds. She herself has two names. Her given name is Nahomie and her family also calls her "Caloune." I'm not entirely convinced. I suspect she is doing her best to equate the universal penchant for nicknames with an all-out power struggle between Junior and the boy's mother. I am curious to see what the boy's birth certificate states, which Junior tells me is in Nahomie/Caloune's possession. But I stop short of insisting on seeing it. At this moment, I have decided that building rapport with Christopher's primary caregiver is more important. I press my case gently. "I think it would be in the boy's best interest if everyone called him by the same name," I say, looking her in the eye. She nods and I know she understands my point. I have one more question. I ask her to tell me about the time fire broke out in the family home and Christopher survived by holing himself up in a corner. Here, Nahomie simply shakes her head, claiming ignorance. It's impossible to know if she is simply deflecting my question, or if I am asking her about something of which she has no knowledge.

My exchange with Nahomie has made me realize that there are some aspects of Christopher's welfare that will take me longer to decipher, and there are some things I may never know. And yet, I am satisfied that I have been talking with a sage, thoughtful, and reasonable caregiver for Christopher. I trust my gut instincts. I like Nahomie. And yet—I also know that a relative caring for a niece or nephew in Haiti can result in socially sanctioned disparity. Junior himself stayed with an aunt who made him into a domestic servant when he should have been attending kindergarten. I do not dismiss Junior's concerns about his son's living arrangement and well-being. But our visit has convinced me that Nahomie's home is a far better alternative for Christopher than living in Junior's tent or Fanfan's cave. This is the best situation for the short term, until I can help get Junior into a stable home. But even then, Junior won't be able to do it on his own. He will need to rely on his son's extended family for help with child care.

Junior has been sitting in the living room, with Obama watching over him, stewing quietly. I am pretty certain he feels betrayed by my having this conversation, but I am hopeful I might be able to help him bridge the divide between him and Fanfan's family. I make a point of thanking Nahomie for all she has done to care for Christopher and we make plans to return the following day to see him.

Junior and I emerge into the searing afternoon light, walking briskly and silently down the winding steps that connect

Stenyo Vincent to Jalousie, a neighboring shanty that gleaned its name from its lofty location, looking down on its affluent cousin, Petionville. The mounting tension snaps on a sparsely populated street corner. "She has one face with you and another with me!" Junior declares angrily of his sister-in-law. I've never seen Junior so agitated. I feel as if I am having an argument with my teenage son. I try to make him understand what I know he does not want to hear. Be grateful that someone educated and stable is caring for your son, even if it is not the ideal situation, I plead. You need to try to have a better relationship with Fanfan's family, for Christopher's sake.

I get the impression I have ignited the kindle to Junior's burning frustration. "You know the problem! They never loved me!" he erupts. We stand staring at each other as if seeing each other for the first time. Ah-ha. Now I understand. The true wound has just been uncovered. Junior's feeling of invisibility and rejection by his former girlfriend's family—and on a deeper level by society at large—is festering, exposed, and burning. I can see now that the swagger and high fashion are all part of a carefully constructed self-esteem campaign, for which I admire him tremendously. By tearing open this wound, I have revealed the vulnerability and pain that Junior bears as a scar from his years living on the street as a *Sans Maman,* a Without Mother.

They never loved me. Those words trigger so much in me. Growing up, how often had I felt that dull pang that I wasn't getting the love I needed? Later, in marriage, I remember the feeling of invisibility and solitude when Marcelo's family would brush past me during their joyous reunions at Ezeiza Airport in Buenos Aires or during their interminable and slightly tribal gatherings spent huddled in a circle, passing a gourd with *yerba mate* tea and telling stories, at the family home in Argentina's agricultural heartland of Neuquen. I had married Marcelo's mother's professed favorite son. How could she spare the energy to build a deep bond with me when she was gasping for air each time she saw her son? And Marcelo, equally guilt-ridden at making his life on a distant point of the hemisphere from his family, struggled to negotiate the divide between his parents and me. It wasn't until after his death, after sending cards, letters, and photographs expressing my grief to Marcelo's parents at his Washington state home, that I finally connected with my former in-laws by phone. At the start of our phone conversation, Marcelo's mom told me she had just applied dye to her hair. During the course of a three-hour conversation with Ibel and Jorge on alternate receivers, we cried, laughed, and exchanged memories. "Sandra, we need you to know that we loved you," they said, each completing the other's sentence. At the end of the call, Ibel, a retired school principal who for years annually marshaled her admiring pensioner colleagues on all-inclusive trips to such distant points as the Nile in Egypt and elephant riding in Thailand, laughed, "My hair is going to be purple after this call."

There is so much I want to tell Junior at this moment, and yet I also know that there are certain life lessons you have to learn for yourself. I do my best to encapsulate what I am feeling. "This is the way it is everywhere in the world. It's just like that. Most people don't think their husband's or wife's family cares about them. And you may not know about it until it is too late."

Even as he loses his temper, I feel empathy for Junior. He has never had family to tell him hard truths. It's 2:00 p.m. I've had nothing but a bottle of water today and I am feeling weak. I imagine Junior has not eaten either. We are around the corner from one of the few businesses open today, a "fast-food" Haitian eatery specializing in Creole cooking. I know a plate of warm food and some rest will help restore a sense of balance. As we are ordering our meal, he snaps once again, this time barking at the clerk behind the counter to add some *accra*, or fritters made from fried malanga root mixed with black-eyed peas, to his plate. My patience is wearing thin. "That is not how we talk to people," I scold Junior, in the same tone I might use with Alexander, a toddler just learning to negotiate social situations. His eyes bulge with indignation. "You've got problems!" he blares in English. I sigh and shake my head sadly. I know what he is trying to say. I have been known to be hypersensitive to tone of voice. He's not the first to tell me of this "problem." But I know I am not imagining this. The young woman behind the counter has rolled her eyes and looked at me as if to say, "What's with him?" We sit down together in the outdoor courtyard and cool down, eating lunch in silence. I'm feeling sad. This is not how I expected this day to go. And yet I don't fight it. I know it's impossible to steer events in Haiti. This is just the way it is. And, yet, on some level I know it is good for us to be experiencing these growing pains. Successfully negotiating a conflict is an important point of growth for any relationship.

We stop briefly at the hostel before catching a tap-tap bus downtown. We need to push past this stress and tension and focus on the significance at hand. Our first stop will be the former United Nations headquarters, the crumbled remains of the Hotel Christopher. The bus drops us off at the bottom of Canape Vert, a somewhat verdant and residential thoroughfare connecting Petionville with downtown. We have to walk a winding, sinewy trail of destruction through the neighborhood of Bourdon to reach the Christopher. The path of devastation is dramatic. The private neighborhoods have not seen bulldozers on the same scale as the main streets. I feel like I am walking on the razor edge of a fault line. This is one of the capital's hard hit quarters of destruction. During the span of just one year, some of the debris is already starting to take on a look of a prehistoric ruin with verdant growth reclaiming the rubble and cascading its tendrils around it.

We stop briefly at a construction site just steps from the gate to the gaping hole and pile of debris that is now the Christopher. There are several rows of what appear to be classrooms. Crews are hard at work on this national day of mourning to complete final touches. Junior and I stop to briefly talk with the head engineer. He tells us this is a college-level academy to train future diplomats. His construction is considered anti-seismic. It is designed to withstand the shock of a future earthquake. No cement has been used in the construction. I take this as a sign of a new flower growing from the ground.

Since we are relying on public transport, it hasn't been practical to walk around all day with a large bouquet of flowers or a ceremonial wreath. And from my last visit here, I found comfort in the thought that Andrea is no longer here. She is in Chile now. On her soil, with her family and friends. I caught a glimpse on Facebook recently of a gathering of her family and loved ones coming together to celebrate her at an outdoor barbecue. It looked warm, casual, and lovely, and it made me happy to see that.

Maybe it's because of the tension today with Junior—or the fact that overall there are so few tangible signs of progress, considering all the suffering happening in the camps—but my spirit feels deflated. Perhaps that's why I haven't shown up today with a clearly articulated thought, or "message" for Andrea and the others who perished here. I wish I could somehow have some solitude to capture it. It bothers me a bit but I try to simply stay in the moment. I stand here and stare at the remains of the site. The shell of a building still standing, like a silhouette rising from the hotel remains, bears a certain resemblance to the Acropolis in Greece. I soon find myself staring off into infinity. I hear the familiar echo of song rising from the hillside down below. It's comforting. The natural thought that develops is that I try to imagine what those final moments were like for Andrea and her colleagues in this building.

That's where I am when I suddenly notice the sky has grown just a shade darker. I instinctively pull out my cell phone. The time is 4:55 p.m. That's it. The anniversary occurred two minutes ago, without my even noticing. Junior and I had expected to be in front of the palace gates at this time. Instead we are here. I was standing with Andrea, who had stood by me and helped me escape from harm's way on that dark night many years ago.

As I have been standing here quietly, Junior has been excitedly gathering pieces of rubble all around me. I can see he is searching for pieces with innate artistic form. He has befriended the Indian UN peacekeepers on duty and asks them for permission to remove these physical traces. They shrug and indicate a universal sentiment: "Be my guest." I worry for a moment that perhaps the significance of this afternoon is being lost on Junior. As always, he seems to have an innate ability to read my mind. "San, you see this piece," he says, showing me a large, brick-like shape, the largest of his collection. "I will make this for Andrea's family." He points to the speckled lime surface, showing me his vision. "Hotel. Andrea. Flower. Sad," he says, pointing to the piece of rubble like a canvas.

We head next to the palace. Our journey here to the Hotel Christopher site has united us again and I can tell there are no hard feelings on either side. We both seem implicitly to understand how hard it is to survive in Haiti and there is no need to discuss at this moment the growth we experienced this afternoon. We walk to the main road, Avenue John Brown, named in honor of the American abolitionist who was hung for treason by the state of Virginia in 1859 after organizing a slave revolt at Harper's Ferry, a precursor to the American Civil War. The street is eerily quiet. There is not one car in sight. A lone motorcycle rider coming down the hill agrees to deposit us near the former palace. As we zigzag through the empty streets, the wind blowing through my hair, I catch sight of ripe breadfruit bursting like fertile nests hanging from a tree. They appear as if torn from a still life by Colombian painter Fernando Botero, a corpulent symbol of abundance and possibility. On the Champs de Mars public plaza by the palace gates, tent cities exist alongside an enormous Haitian flag and parked bulldozers. I spot a man in his seventies walking by with a pink T-shirt that reads: "Keep laughing. This is your girlfriend's shirt." His expression is somber, as if unintentionally dead-panning. This is Haiti reminding me to laugh. She is tipping the other side of her mask of tragedy.

Junior and I stroll. There has been no formal event or commemoration here at 4:53 p.m. Instead, a steady stream of people has been strolling through to bear witness in their own personal way. The mood is one of anticipation, expectation of an imminent transformation, and of marking history with your own eyes. I remember walking down the Champs Elysee in Paris on

December 31, 1999, my four-year wedding anniversary with Marcelo, with the same expectation that the world was about to undergo some intangible transformation. Instead, we had a meal with friends of friends in an apartment near the Eiffel tower and walked with throngs of revelers into the early morning light.

Certainly, this Belle Epoque relic, Haiti's *Palais Nacional,* designed in 1912 by noted Haitian architect Georges Baussan, who trained in Paris, has all the grandeur of a European palace, even in this state of shambled vulnerability. At this moment I make a little prayer to the mischievous Marassa Twins to invoke their spirit powers to preserve this living piece of history exactly as it is: a living relic powerfully connecting Haiti to its past and present, honoring all those who died. This lovely beauty, her face cracked, her spine crushed. She can no longer stand. And yet, she is regal, dignified, and grand. Her scars perfectly mirror the pain and struggle of her noble people.

Nightfall descends quickly. The sky is shrouded. Together with the strolling crowds, Junior and I are reading the large panels depicting architectural renditions and planning announcements that have been erected on the palace grounds, acting as a screen to reframe the crowd's vision. The sight of the crushed palace is now filtered through dreamscapes of what Port-au-Prince's future could look like. They might as well put up images of the Champs Elysee in Paris. For now, these renditions are utterly disconnected from the grim reality of Haiti's capital.

We linger, standing at the final screen. "That, Junior, is exactly what Miami looks like," I say. It's a drawing that could be Lincoln Road, the Miami Beach pedestrian mall, with its vibrant cafes, bookstore, shops, and street life.

As I say this, a young Haitian who is standing there with his arm casually looped around his girlfriend says irresistibly, "It's nice there, isn't it?" I pause, wondering how best to offset the expectation that I have just unwittingly created. "Yes, it's nice," I say. "But like everywhere in the world, they have problems, too." The four of us form a little pocket of understanding. And then Junior and I hail a moto-cab and ride back up the hill to Petionville and into the ocean of night.

Chapter 21

The English Teacher

I know now that Christopher's birthday is not until July, but that is of little relevance. We will continue with our plan to have a birthday party for him today. I think of how occasionally Alexander and I have had "pretend" birthday parties for him, making a carrot cake and putting some of his miniature Disney characters on top and then pretending to call his friends from preschool to invite them over to come celebrate with us. Why not have a birthday party in January for Christopher? What matters most is to celebrate his life and to make him feel loved.

Junior and I go to the Marie Beliard bakery, where we have been having lunch most days. We've spent plenty of time staring at the bakery case, studying the cakes and delicate pastries. Junior has already identified his favorite. It's a two-layer yellow cake with a cream filling, topped with fresh fruit: peaches, grapes, and cherries. We order the cake and pick out an orange candle shaped in the number three. I have the rest of the fixings that we need for the party back at the Art Hostel. I've packed a Thomas the Tank Engine plastic tablecloth and plates, some sparkly blow-out party favors, stickers, and toy cars.

After our visit with Nahomie yesterday, we have been granted an audience with Christopher for today. The plan is to drop off the party fixings at Nahomie's and then walk the short distance to the family cave to pick up Christopher and bring him back for the party. Fanfan is also in on the plan. She is watching Christopher this morning and she will hand him over to us. I am excited and a bit nervous to finally meet her. I'm still not quite sure what to expect.

Junior and I are climbing the favela steps to the shanty when he suddenly stops and begins to laugh. We are just outside the entrance to Fanfan's family home and he is listening in on a high-pitched tirade echoing from inside the home. I hear the voice of an older woman yelling. I can make out something about "a *petite putte* sleeping in my bed." Junior shakes his head. Fanfan was out all night and must have come back early this morning with one of her friends and crashed out on the large mattress at the back of the cave, Junior tells me. The voice is droning on in a long monologue. We step into the home and the voice stops. It has been Fanfan's mother railing on and putting her foot down.

We walk in and say hello. The mother nods her head and retreats into the shadows. We make our way to the back of the cave. Fanfan is there with Christopher. What a contrast. It's Madonna and Child—as in Madonna Ciccone and child. Fanfan's head is framed in a perfect cascade of dark curls, as if she just left the beauty parlor. She wears a pair of tight jeans that impeccably frame her heart-shaped body matched with a form-fitting V-neck T-shirt. She comes across as a highly sexualized figure engaged in one of the most maternal acts. She has just taken Chris out of a basin of water and is wrapping him up with a soft bath towel. After carefully drying him off, she reaches for a bottle of Johnson

& Johnson's lotion, which she rubs over his body, and then she dusts him off with baby powder. Chris is like any other happy child. After his bath and powdering, he stands up on the large mattress and begins bouncing up and down, bounding back and forth between his mother and father like a happy sprite. Following his bath, Fanfan dresses Christopher in an outfit composed of some of the clothes I have brought him, starting with a pair of superhero underwear, a pajama shirt, because Chris likes the alligators, and a new pair of pants and shoes. I hang out with her as she gets Christopher dressed for his birthday party. I am eager to win her trust as I want to get to know her better and learn more about her. The moment presents itself and it seems that she too is hoping for the chance to reveal herself, to tell her side of the story. Junior seems to expect this and doesn't seem bothered that I am sitting and talking quietly with Fanfan in the back room. We sit on the bed into which the *petite putte* had crawled this morning and talk.

Even now that I am in her presence, I am nervous to talk with Fanfan. I worry that she does not know me, that she will not understand my relationship with Junior, and she won't feel comfortable speaking honestly. As a form of icebreaker, I ask her to tell me about her first impression of meeting Junior. "When I first met him I thought he was a *massissi*," she tells me, giggling. I ask her to repeat the word, wanting to make sure I understand what she has said. "Do you know what that means?" she asks me. Yes, I say, confused. We are talking in hushed voices. I remember that *massissi* means "gay." Part of the reason that I don't immediately recall the word is that it seems out of context. It's not making sense. For a moment I think that perhaps she has said this as a way to "get back" at Junior, to question his sexuality, literally behind his back. Perhaps it will give her some pleasure to see me write this taboo word down in my green notebook. I look at her closely to see if she is saying this in jest. "Why did you think that?" I ask her. "Because he was always with the *blancs*," she tells me. I am again startled by this response. I don't understand how Junior's hanging with the foreigners could signal him as being gay, how that would have any bearing on his sexual preference, one way or the other. I reflect on this for a moment and realize that this association has marked Junior as part of the "other" in his social circle. And I take it a step further, thinking about how Junior's artful and exuberant fashion sense could also make him stand out as an individual and mark him as different. I come to realize that *massissi* in this context is synonymous with *other*. Part of Junior's survival strategy has been to have a very strong sense of self. To run counter to the crowd. To not follow what the others do. Like a gay man, he has had to chart an often lonely, brave, and authentic self-revealing course. Yes, he is *massissi*, I think. He is part of this tribe.

Fanfan is continuing now. She is in a comfort zone. Keen to share her knowledge and confide. She was with Junior for two years, she tells me. She learned he was not gay. I ask her if she is certain that Junior is her son's father. She does not hesitate. "Wi. M' te remen," she says simply. *Yes. I loved him.* Then she again giggles like a schoolgirl. "He left me when I was pregnant. He left me for a Dominican with long hair." I realize she is telling me about Patricia. I didn't know if she would want to talk with me about the vodou spell she tried to cast on Patricia, to confide in me in this way. But she is talking freely, as if she has been waiting to get this off her chest for some time. "He had the police arrest me because I fought with him. I wanted to get him back." I want to press her on this, to see how close her account compares to Junior's. "You mean, with *bagay mistik,* a mystical act?" I ask. "It was not me. It was my friends who wanted Junior to take care of his son," she continues. "They did something to make her go away. They are the ones who made the powder. They put it on the front door to make the girl go away and never come back. They put it in a tiny *bidon,* a vial. She stepped on it and she started shaking all over. They took her to the hospital. She could no longer stay in Haiti. She went back to her country." Fanfan's narrative has the dramatic tension of a classic fairytale or an opera. She has been telling this story with a certain element of pride, as if she is finally getting the chance to right a wrong. I hear no tinge of remorse or shame in her account. I ask her if she regrets what happened to Patricia. If she thinks it was wrong to harm her in this way. "I don't regret it because that girl didn't have the right to see my child," she says.

We continue the conversation. I am curious to know how her relationship with Junior is now. When Junior talks about it, he is so detached and disinterested it is hard to detect if there is any hostility between them. I am looking for some assurance that they are both looking out for Christopher's best interest. She says she is fine with Junior but her main concern is that he never gives her money. She adds to her grievance list that Junior doesn't ever bring anything for Christopher. She tells me she has an American friend who helps her pay for Christopher's school and he gives her money. Christopher's school is pricey, at nearly $900 a year. I remember that Junior told me he didn't have his school-issued identification card the day we dropped by to visit with Christopher and I now sense that was a face-saving explanation. In the months after the earthquake and following his accident, Junior simply did not have the means to pay for this kind of private school education. What money he did have he needed to spend toward his survival. I ask her if this American is her boyfriend, her *ménage*. No, she tells me demurely. He already has a girlfriend. "I am his friend."

As we talk she is putting on long, dangly chandelier earrings. Seeing her like that makes me wonder what she dreams of. "If I had money I would like to go to school and have my own beauty studio," she tells me. "And if I was still with Junior I would have another baby. It is not something I would do on my own." I wonder if she still longs for Junior, if she harbors a secret wish for them one day to get back together and become a family. She answers the question without my having to ask. "I don't love him as a *ménage*, but I love him as a friend," she says. Her dreams have moved beyond Junior. "I dream of Christopher going to school and being able to live *a l'aise*, freely, and for me to be able to offer him all that he wants because it is in my hands that he lives." Her words make me think of how the dreams of mothers are so universal and cut across the jagged peaks of geography, class, and culture.

With Christopher freshly bathed and dressed we head down the steep steps and walk the rutted dirt path back to Nahomie's house. Christopher rides on Junior's back, piggy-back style, and the bond between father and son is so apparent, so pure. They move together, swaying their bodies in a single motion. Arriving at Nahomie's, we place the tablecloth on the balcony table, overlooking the sweeping views of the capital. We bring out the cake with the orange-colored candle and we sing "Happy Birthday," a hybrid rendition in French, Creole, and English. Christopher is beaming, basking in the love around him. After he blows out the candle, we share a piece of cake and then he has fun blowing the noisemakers.

I am flying back to Arizona tomorrow and Junior and I still have so much we want to do. We sit and chat for a while, playing with Christopher and enjoying the moment. After a while, it is time to go. Junior has had his first English class today and I want to go and meet with his instructor, Carl, to see about arranging private tutoring on the side. Maybe this would be the best way to help Junior fill in the gaps of his education. As we are pressed for time, we arrange to leave Christopher at home with Nahomie. Her young daughter, Christopher's cousin, will be home from school soon and he will have a playmate. We say our goodbyes and as Junior reaches down to kiss Christopher on the forehead the little boy freezes and pleads with his daddy not to leave him there alone. It's a moment of pure expression. Of course, this could be nothing more than separation anxiety. But I sense fear from the boy. Junior and I look at each other, silently registering what we have just seen. We agree to walk Christopher back to the family cave where he will be under the watch of his grandmother. As we trek back, Junior says: "You see what I mean? He doesn't want to be left alone with his aunt." It is impossible to ignore the instincts of a child. We will make sure that Christopher feels safe and is comfortable before working through our to-do list of the day. And at the same time, Christopher's response gives greater urgency to our tasks. His anguished look is a reminder that Junior needs to be fully empowered to best protect and provide for his son. Back at the cave, Junior again kisses Christopher and says goodbye. This time, the little boy immediately becomes immersed in a pile of laundry, which he substitutes for a toy, and seems not to notice when we leave.

We arrive at the school and find Carl in one of the empty class-rooms. I'm eager to have a chat with him, to learn more about him, and confirm if he will be the right fit to be one of Junior's mentors. Junior already has homework from his first day of classes and he heads over to the language lab to don the big floppy headphones and listen to a dialogue in English. Carl and I head outside and sit on the steps to have a chat. I recap how I first came to Haiti and how I came to know Junior. I tell him I am committed to helping Junior start a new life and how I feel an enduring wonder about Haiti. "It's the best school ever," Carl says. "You want to know about life, about others, also, the people that you live with. Haiti is the best place to teach you." I'm still so intrigued and want to understand how it is that he speaks such clearly enunciated English.

Carl begins his story. He was born Carl Handel LaRoche. His father worked as a "fixer" and assistant to a French journalist. In 1996, when Carl was nineteen, his father found a scholarship for him to study in the United States. He moved to New Jersey and became a student at Atlantic City Community College. The experiment ended in 2001 when Carl returned to Haiti. Life in the United States had become too alienating. "I don't really like life in the United States. Life there is so crazy." Although I can understand and relate to what he is saying on an intellectual level, I have yet to encounter a Haitian of modest means who returns to Haiti willingly from the United States for quality of life reasons. I ask him to elaborate. What was it exactly about American life that he had found to be challenging? "Taxes," he replies, cryptically. "First of all, everything is about taxes. You go to the store and each thing you buy you have to pay taxes. I'm not used to that." His response is unexpected. "Was there anything else?" I ask. "Or did you return to Haiti to avoid paying sales taxes?" "Well, also the law," he continues. Each new layer is more curious than the last. With this new response a little yellow flag is flashing in my mind. And yet, the fact that he has casually volunteered this information, self-reporting that what he most disliked about life in the United States was paying taxes and the rule of law, I wonder if perhaps he is some kind of contrarian who simply couldn't adapt to a society so much more structured and regulated than his own. "What was it about the law?" I ask, trying to sound casual. "I had a girlfriend," he begins. "She told the police I hit her, and that is just not true. She was supposed to be the mother of my child and unfortunately we lost a child together. She fell down the stairs and said that I pushed her. That's not true. I wasn't even there. She was trying to get me arrested. I didn't get arrested, though. Thank God. God was there. God was my witness. The police officers that came to take the report realized she was lying. She couldn't prove anything."

Carl says this incident was the catalyst that got him thinking about packing up and returning home to Haiti. "I told myself, if she could do that to me, I couldn't trust anyone in the States." And then his mom called him and reminded him that he already had a child. "You have a son in Haiti and he doesn't even know you," she said. The boy was nine years old. Carl decided it was time to come home. The boy's name, Carl Hendy, is a variation of his own, prompting Carl to reflect on the musical origin of his middle name. "Yeah, 'Hallelujah,' by Handel, right?"

Hearing him describe his pregnant girlfriend falling down a flight of stairs gave me the chills. Instinctively, I think he did push her. Perhaps it was the way he said, "She couldn't prove anything." And yet, it's possible the investigation was inconclusive and he decided to return to Haiti so as not to risk getting framed for that—or a future accusation. Reality can be so multi-layered and unknowable in Haiti. I keep an open mind and also make a mental note to keep my eyes wide open.

Carl tells me that when he returned to Haiti he started teaching French, math, and physical education at the New American School, a high school that followed a U.S.-style curriculum, in the downtown neighborhood of Turgeau. He worked there for three years. He left that job to work as a translator for the United Nations. "It paid really good, but I didn't like it. I felt too stupid. Everywhere I went, I was just repeating what other people said." He has again intrigued me. I've never met a Haitian who voluntarily left the United States before "making it" and who then came back to Haiti and quit a relatively high-paying job out of principle. I think about how the personnel records of local hires most likely vanished in the collapsed rubble of UN headquarters and I find myself wondering if he really worked as a translator and if he really left on principled grounds. Carl tells me he now lives with his mother in the working-class suburb of Marianni, on the outskirts of the capital. It's got to be at least an hour commute on tap-tap buses to Petionville where he now teaches, and he starts each day bright and early. I find Carl to be an enigmatic and fascinating character. I don't necessarily believe anything he has told me. I would definitely classify him as an unreliable narrator. Still, I have one more question. I am curious to know what his relationship is like with his son, who he tells me is now sixteen. "Not too good, not too bad," he says. "He loves his mother more than me."

Despite my doubts, there is something about Carl's contradictions that seems to inform his teaching style in a way that I admire. He is part of this downtrodden class and yet he is educated. When he speaks to Junior he addresses him with a kind of dignity. Not in a feigned way. But simply accepting him as someone capable of learning, as someone who has a contribution to make. Carl agrees to my offer to tutor Junior on the side, in addition to being his English teacher at the language institute. Carl will compose a general education curriculum, focusing on the subjects of English, French, and math, with an emphasis on helping Junior learn to read and write. Our conversation flows next to the texts that Junior will need. He writes them down carefully in my notebook, with the estimated cost in dollars for some of the texts from the leading book distributor in town.

Oxford Picture Dictionary—$40

An English grammar book—$30

An American English expressions book—$30

A French grammar book

A French reading book

A math book

His love of books and his thoughtful disposition as a teacher have outweighed my concerns about his dislike of taxes and law and order. I know I should probably exercise greater caution, but the fact is I am leaving tomorrow and I am determined to find teachers and mentors for Junior. I take his employment at the language institute as a form of reference. I offer to pay Carl $200 to cover both the cost of the texts and his tutoring fee for two months. It seems like a modest amount, given the cost of the books alone will probably total about $100. The one caveat is that I have to pay Carl with a check drawn from my American checking account. I brought enough cash to cover expenses on this trip and to give Junior some financial assistance. But I've been surprised by the extent to which Haiti is increasingly becoming an all-cash economy. Even the Art Hostel doesn't accept credit cards. Money evaporates quickly in Haiti and because of the travel warning and the risks associated with the airport road, I didn't feel safe being flush with a lot of extra cash. I remember from when I lived in Haiti that most of the major banks offer savings accounts in U.S. dollars. I ask Carl if he has such an account. He does not. "Why don't you go to one of the banks now and see if you can open an account with my check, while I am still here," I advise. "In case I need to go and sign anything or show some identification."

Carl dashes off and Junior and I continue moving through our to-do list. We go to a nearby bookstore where I am perusing titles, on the lookout for texts on Haitian history, culture, and current events that are virtually unavailable in the United States, when my phone rings. It's Carl. He sounds different. He's talking fast. He couldn't cash the check. I assume he's worried that I will leave Haiti without paying him. Junior and I agree to meet him at the language institute. When I see him, I notice his demeanor has changed completely. He looks desperate, as if his life depends on this sum of money. For someone who presumably walked away from a high-paying translator job and who doesn't really care about money, this doesn't add up. I ask him to give me the check and he hands it to me like it is a worthless piece of paper. I tell him I will try to cash it myself, but in truth I have already decided against this arrangement. The desperation I see in his eyes has heightened my perspective.

Later that afternoon, I return to the Art Hostel. Dr. Percque will be coming by the hotel to see me. It's strange to be seeing him on the eve of my departure. This has been a short trip and he and I have been in touch by Facebook and e-mail throughout, trying to coordinate schedules. But I know that there is a deeper reason why we have not yet seen each other. This has been a tough, emotional time. Not only is it the one-year anniversary of the earthquake, this week is also the anniversary of Marco's own personal apocalypse. January 10 was the twelve-year anniversary of his eldest son Jean Marc's death and the accident that forever disfigured his life. Earlier this month, on January 3, Jean Marc would have turned twenty-one years old. In a reflection of the constant yin and yang that is life, Marco has chosen to meet me on a happier day. Today is his daughter's eleventh birthday. She is the light that emerged from the tragedy. As we sit together over a cup of coffee, he pauses to take two of her calls. She is calling from the Dominican Republic, where she continues to live with her mother. Marco tells me he and his daughter have had an easy day-long conversation. In fact, this is how they communicate on most days. The love is so apparent in his voice. His face is illuminated as he talks to her, asking about her day, describing where he is and alternating effortlessly with her in their personal code of English and French. She is at a birthday party with her girlfriends and she is making sure that her papa is there with her.

Seeing Dr. Percque always evokes so much emotion. He has such a warm, passionate, and incisive presence. At age fifty-one, after more than two decades of service to the U.S. Embassy in Haiti, he is preparing to retire. His future is uncertain. And although it's not obvious by looking at him—he still has a commanding presence with his tall frame, thick brown hair spiked with peppery highlights, and his piercing blue eyes—his health remains fragile. He is battling three conditions that are snarling his body in spasms of pain and require periodic chemotherapy treatments. And there are concerns that the calcium deposits that have formed like lumps on his back, arms, and hands could reach his eyes and brain. His plan is to move to Montreal in the coming months, where he will be reunited with his mother and son, who has embarked on a promising future as an electrical engineer at a top university. It is his dream to have his daughter there with him, too. Marco will have greater treatment options in Canada, but the road ahead is uncertain. He knows he must make the most of this time.

While it would be facile to try to portray Marco as a kind of hero, Haiti has taught me to embrace the layers of nuance and contradiction inherent in every human being. I prefer to celebrate Marco as a survivor who was nearly crushed by his life experience and yet who has remained whole and full of desire for life. As we have sat talking today, we have again revisited the events on the day of the earthquake. He paused as he reflected on how he stayed at home until almost 11:00 p.m. on that fateful night before going to his clinic to tend to survivors. He lingered on that moment, glancing at me slightly in a way that signaled to me that he wanted me to understand the implication of that detail. I did and I didn't see the need to dwell on it. Perhaps I could have pressed harder. But I believe in unspoken conversation in certain instances. Here's how I understood his pause: Could he have left his home sooner to help save lives more quickly? Probably. But Haiti had already robbed him of everything that mattered. It shattered his family life and his health. He had no more to give. To some, he could perhaps be seen as emblematic of the jaded foreigner. Except he is not. He is not a foreigner. He was born in Haiti. And he is still so very much alive and rooted in this complex reality. Marco does have Haiti coursing through his veins. Like many Haitians and longtime expats, I sense he has a deep love-hate relationship with the country. It has ruined his life and yet, I sense that even he is reluctant to leave. It is his home.

I'm sitting in the courtyard after my visit with Dr. Percque, taking it all in. It feels like a flood has just swept through and I'm sitting silently in its aftermath. I'm wondering if I will ever see him again, and I am sending up beads of light and love for my dear friend.

Junior returns from going to check in on Samantha. I have my laptop with me and I begin showing him many of the pictures on my computer. I show him photos of our last days enjoying the beach in San Clemente before moving to Arizona. I show him photos of my visits to Disneyland with Alexander. He lights up when he sees Alexander wearing different hats in his photos. He gets a sense for Alexander's personality from the photos and I can see that he feels a genuine connection to him. "He has style," he tells me, approvingly. I remember that I have all the photos from my last visit to Haiti on my computer and he hasn't seen those, either, except for looking at the back of my camera screen when I took many of the pictures.

We are flickering through the collection when I happen on a picture of Jenny, the little girl with whom I fell in love when she took me by the hand in the hardened refugee camp that I visited last March. "That's Jenny!" Junior says immediately. I look at him surprised. I was never sure if he realized what an imprint this little girl made on my heart. "How do you remember her name?" I ask Junior, perplexed. He seems almost offended by the question. "San, her camp is not far from mine. I visit them whenever I go by to see how they are doing. They remember you." I am astonished and touched by this news. And yet, it makes perfect sense. Of course Junior would check back on this community. It is in his nature as a caring person and it is also part of the code of Haitian survival. People watch out for one another and help each other out. It is the only way they get by in the absence of a credible and functioning government or economy.

"How is Jenny?" I ask Junior, eager for any news on her fate. He tells me that they are fine. They are getting by. Jenny has a new *mere adoptif.* For a moment my heart jumps. Someone has adopted her! Junior elaborates. One of her aunts has moved to the camp, together with Jenny and her grandmother. I am relieved. That is as it should be. For months I have worried in the back of my mind about how she has managed to survive the rainy season and cholera epidemic in such dire conditions. I have wanted to visit Jenny this week but I've been held back by an inner conflict that might seem strange or nonsensical to others. If her grandmother had placed this little girl in my arms and said, "Take her with you," I would have adopted her in an instant. Knowing that, I've struggled with the thought that perhaps my intention to visit Jenny was not "pure." Perhaps a visit would be a veiled attempt on my part to explore that possibility further. I've been reluctant to drop back in on Jenny and her grandmother. I don't want to interfere in their lives. My relationship with Junior is the result of years of layered connections. With this little girl, it was a single episodic moment that burst my heart. And the truth is I know I cannot "save" her. Here I am trying to help Junior build a new life and that is a complex and still incomplete process. After days of deliberating, I had decided these concerns were silly. What mattered is that I care about this little girl and her family. I had made my mind up that I would try to go see her today but I simply ran out of time. So it seems rather prophetic that Junior and I have just stumbled on her photo and he is telling me this now. I look up and see that the sky is filling up with tiny dots of dark matter. Dusk is settling in. It's too late to go out and find her now. I feel like the curtain has just been drawn shut on my last night. "Junior, let's go see Jenny tomorrow morning before going to the airport," I say. There will not be a lot of time. Junior nods his head. He understands.

As we are having this conversation and continuing to look at photos, I hear a voice approach me from behind. "There you are," the voice says, tinged with a high-pitched note of satisfaction. It's Carl. He is joined by one of his colleagues from the language institute, a heavyset young man with a British accent who earlier offered a long, winding story of how he learned to speak English from a missionary. Carl wants to know if I have managed to cash the check. I tell him I am still working on it. I had accidently slipped earlier in the day and mentioned that I was going to see if the Art Hostel might cash it. "In case I am not able to cash the check we will simply continue with the plan that you will be Junior's teacher at the English Institute. I think we might hold off on private lessons for now," I say. Carl appears not to hear me. "Are you staying here?" he asks, closely surveying the surroundings. "Oh, no," I say brightly. "I'm staying with friends. I'm just here to have a drink." Carl looks right at me. "Well, have a very good night," he says, before glancing up at the row of guestrooms overlooking the courtyard.

Carl's visit has elevated my concerns about him into the red zone. The hostel's two other guests have just checked out today and I can't fathom the idea of staying here by myself tonight with a lone security guard pacing the courtyard at night. I instinctively go online and find the number for the Kinam Hotel, which is just up the street. It's the site where Junior and I met after my search for him last March. I dial the Kinam's number on my cell phone and I am amazed when a front desk receptionist answers. The country's ailing infrastructure occasionally surprises and comes through. As I suspected, many of the earthquake anniversary visitors have already checked out. Yes, they have availability for tonight, the voice on my phone says. I book a room.

I go tell Alek that I will be checking out tonight. I'll still pay for this night at the hostel and I would still love for him to drive me to the airport tomorrow. I tell him I've had an intimidating encounter with someone and I don't feel safe being the hostel's lone guest tonight. As I say this, I have a brief flash to the memory of being trapped in the barren guesthouse in Mirebalais. I will not do anything to risk ending up in that hell again. Alek looks sympathetic. He tells me there will be many people at the hostel tonight, including a French friend of his who works for the Red Cross. He is having many people over tonight. People will be here all night. I hesitate. The only way I will stay is if Junior agrees to stay at the hostel. Alek says he can sleep with pillows and blankets on one of the couches downstairs. I have carefully budgeted my remaining cash—as the hostel doesn't accept credit cards—and I don't have enough to pay for an extra room.

I share my fears with Junior. I tell him I now believe Carl is a criminal deportee from the United States, and I fear I may have exposed us both to possible harm by trying to contract him as a tutor. I tell him that I feel so foolish. How I am angry at myself. Carl spelled it all out for me to see. And I ignored the signs because I was so focused and intent on wanting to get him a teacher. Junior imparts two pieces of wisdom. "San, I know that you were afraid to come to Haiti, and still, you came anyway. That tells me so much." As for Carl, he says: "Li ka yon DP, et li ka yon bon moun, tou." *He may be a criminal deportee and a good person, too.* "Remember Lucky," he adds, reminding me of the friend who rescued him after his accident. Junior agrees to stay at the Art Hostel without hesitation, adding that it would be wasteful to pay for an extra room given that we will be up late talking and the club-like atmosphere will go on until at least 3:00 a.m. First, though, he needs to buy some food from a street vendor for Samantha and make sure she is safely secured in their tent for the night.

When Junior returns I have one last gift that I have been waiting to give him. It is a laptop computer. Apart from his home, his laptop computer was the most valuable possession he lost in the earthquake. I can see how excited he is by this and I find it rather touching that he didn't expect this at all. Once we start up the portable computer, I notice an interesting contrast. Junior is quite comfortable with the device, and yet at times he seems very hesitant on the keyboard. I set him up with a Gmail e-mail account. As we do that, I realize how many of the standard account security questions are not applicable to his life experience. The modern-day oracle is asking for the name of his first teacher and first boss. The questions seem superfluous to his life.

And then I introduce him to the marvels of Google Translate, which now includes Haitian Creole. I tell him how all one has to do is type a word and watch how it instantly translates it into other languages. I do a sample try. I write the Creole greeting, "Ki jan ou ye?" and accidently translate it into Vietnamese. Junior is delighted. Now it is his turn. I encourage him to try. He hesitates for a long time, staring at the keyboard. I realize he is unsure, shy, and embarrassed about his limited ability to write. After a long pause he tentatively types the word, *viv,* or live. Giving Junior the computer leads to an unexpected revelation. After his test drive of Google Translate, he confides: "Even a simple questionnaire with three lines, I can't do it sometimes. It's simple. But it's hard. It makes me feel like a burden on society."

It's my last night and Junior knows that I am going to want to stay up late talking. I also need to pack. The Art Hostel's cook, Jacqui, a talented and hardworking creative spirit who is also a dancer, a beadwork artist, and a landowner, will be making us dinner, but I don't see any activity in the kitchen and I suspect it will be some time before we sit down to eat. The courtyard is starting to fill with a very hip crowd that would fit in perfectly across the Atlantic in Miami. Junior and I go to my room upstairs, leaving the door open to keep an eye on the scene below. Junior is sitting at the table working on the computer, Googling random rap stars and soccer players. I am packing my suitcase. By the time I am done, the courtyard and balcony are overflowing with people and rock music is pounding. It's a pure rave scene. I step out for a moment and walk into a miasmic cloud of smoke. The smell is pungent. I see now what Alek meant about my not being the only person here tonight. I think for a moment that if Carl wanted to try to harm me, this dazed and hallucinogenic crowd might provide him the perfect cover.

Standing there on the balcony, I stop and ponder how I have learned things both about Junior and myself on this trip. I've seen a new vulnerability in Junior. I always recognized his confident side, but this time I also noticed how skillfully he masks his uncertainty in certain social settings, sometimes talking very quickly to fill a void, and how he learns to adapt by carefully studying the behavior of people he deems trustworthy, like when we would have lunch at Marie Beliard and he would deliberately mirror my actions. I also came to realize fully that Christopher is his only close blood relative in Haiti. I now comprehend how truly alone he is and how he is doing his best to find his way and lead his son to a better life. Reflecting on my journey, I think about how this experience has reminded me of how even in my twenties, I used to sometimes get tired and spacey when I was immersed in too much pollution, misery, and chaos. That is still true today and I know how important it is that I not push too hard or move too fast in this sensory-rich environment and risk missing important signposts and signals. And I realize how my search for Junior is connected to my search to expand and complete my family.

Morning comes and I quickly shower and dress. Junior, the security guard, and the cook have all slept on different couches downstairs. When Alek arrives in the Chitty Chitty Bang Bang mobile, I tell him that we will be making an unscheduled stop at one of the camps before going to the airport. He looks at me rather incredulously. It's about 8:00 a.m. when Junior and I jump out of the jeep and run to the camp entrance and right to Jenny's family tent. I feel like my spaceship just landed from another planet. Jenny's grandmother looks up and immediately acknowledges my presence. It has been ten months, but she seems to recognize me right away. "Where have you been? You never came back," she exclaims. "I don't live here," I offer gently. "I have returned for just a few days." Then the situation becomes apparent. Little Jenny is lying on a mattress that has been ingeniously propped up on a platform of wooden planks to avoid getting soaked and muddy in the rain. She is listless, feverish, and numb. She is being tended to by two younger women who have the grandmother's same expressive eyes. There can be no doubt that these are Jenny's two aunts. The little girl must look up into their faces and feel as if she is seeing the image of her mother in double vision. This is the *mere adoptif*, Junior introduces me. I am speechless. Jenny has three fairy godmothers watching over her. She has her country and culture. But maybe that wasn't enough. I feel as if Death is hovering here in the tent with us. I fear that I am seeing the ravages of cholera firsthand. I reach for the last of my cash in my purse and hand $40 to the grandmother. It is terribly inadequate. Please take her to the doctor this morning, I urge.

As we approach the airport, my cell phone rings. It's sycophantic Carl. He has learned that the Citibank by the airport can cash my check. "I have to go, Carl," I say, before turning off the phone. I say goodbye to Junior. I'm glad we stayed up late talking because it's hard to really know what to say right now. We hug and agree to keep moving forward with the plans for his housing, education, and art. I take my place in the check-in line that snakes outside the terminal under the piercing sun. I feel like an exhausted ultra-marathoner who just finished a hundred-mile race through the desert. I am filled with emotion and I can't shake the image of Jenny lying expressionless in her bed. My thoughts turn, too, to Dr. Percque, who is back at work today at his office just down the street from here in what is now the fortified bunker that is the American Embassy. I pray to Haiti to loosen her grip on them.

I feel as if I am standing in line amidst a group of foreigners waiting to return home from Disasterland. There is a certain absurdity to the situation that grates me. People are juggling their souvenirs and the overall feeling is one of euphoria mixed with a tinge of bravado. "There was a shooting at a roadblock in Martissant this morning," I overhear someone say. "I read about it on Twitter and I had my driver go around it." I'm in no mood for the small talk. Still, the woman in front of me seems not to notice. She chatters away. Tells me she is from Oakland. She travels to Haiti every few weeks with an organization she has started to teach Haitians about recycling. "I had a lot of high-level meetings this week," she tells me in a self-congratulatory tone. I find myself wondering how big her carbon footprint is. And I think of the little boy who approached me this week, offering to sell me a beautiful, bright, and intricately woven handbag made entirely from chewing gum wrappers. "Haitians are already very good at recycling," I say. She doesn't notice my dry tone.

I don't mean to be the grumpy traveler. All I really want is a quiet moment to take it all in. I know that all of us in this line are part of the same human chain that is grappling with the challenge of how best to help Haiti and the Haitian people.

And yet, I can't help but think that amidst all of the vital work being done by some of the major aid groups, there are also a lot of people who are undertaking their own personal pet projects without stopping to consult Haitians on what they most need. I think of the earnest aid worker I met at the Art Hostel who told me that he was in Haiti to organize online conversations between "people who live in slums and people who don't." Where are there no slums? I asked. "Places like Portland and Seattle, where I live," he said. Great, I thought. Forced pen-pal conversations. Did Haitians ask for any of this, I wonder?

The paradox of post-quake Haiti is that the country's needs are so overwhelming and the central government is so weak and nonexistent that Haiti is at serious risk of becoming an NGO nation, a multinational nation state run by foreign workers who decide the country's agenda from their air-conditioned offices, with little coordination among key players. Of course there is a lot of vital good that is being done. Groups like Doctors Without Borders and Partners in Health are floating the nation's shattered healthcare system. And I know that Haiti brings out the best in so many people. I think of the families who lost loved ones at the Hotel Montana. Many of them have invested in Haiti's future to pursue the dreams of their lost daughters, sons, wives, husbands, grandchildren, sisters, brothers, and friends. There is no obvious, single way to help. I will later stumble on a Tweet by Jonathan Katz, the Associated Press correspondent in Haiti, posted on the one-year anniversary of the earthquake. "Haiti will go on. It is going on. But survival is a gift. As long as some must fight for it, no one can take it for granted." His words perfectly describe my experience on the ground.

I think of how Carole has found a way to make a difference in Haiti while leaving behind a small footprint and a big impact. In 1984, she founded PATCH, Photography in Aid To Children in Haiti. She had been in Haiti for just one year and knew she needed to find a way to make a difference. Her idea was simple:

She would make greeting cards from her photographs and use the proceeds to fund small projects and help "patch" things up as she went. With just a few thousand dollars a year, she knew she could make a meaningful contribution. As she describes on her website, "This country had taken me by the hand, shown me its courageous and resilient people and its wonderful rural hospitality—it had stolen my heart. How could I not do something to help in return?"

Her simple idea led to the formation of a school in the rural central Haitian town of Haut Saut d'Eau. The Center for Hope, as it came to be known, opened its doors in 1989. The four-room schoolhouse was built with an incredible display of sweat equity. Children and their parents carried rocks from local fields on their heads and on horseback to the site where the school was to be built. The motivation was great as the town had no school. When it opened, the school provided education, uniforms, shoes, and hot lunches to one hundred students ranging in age from four to fifteen. But the dream appeared to be short-lived. After just two years, the school was shuttered due to political violence. Carole continued supporting other initiatives and she was soon swept up in covering the tumultuous political upheavals of the 1990s. She left Haiti in 2000 after Western news interest in Haiti plummeted and she could no longer make a living by selling her photos. But Haiti never let go of her heart. On a return trip, she again traveled through the remote town of Haut Saut d'Eau and was startled to hear people calling her name on the dusty road into town. It had been fifteen years since the school closed and yet, it turned out the seed she had planted had given new fruit. The Center for Hope had moved to a new location under the direction of the original head teacher, Placide Jean-Sommener. Placide had continued Carole's efforts and was providing an education to 150 students with a staff of five teachers. Needless to say, PATCH has resumed its patronage of the school, fundraising to help fulfill the school's annual $10,000 budget. The cost of annual tuition for one child is $3.75, as Carole notes, "the cost of a Starbucks beverage," and yet most of the local families can't afford it.

What I most admire about Carole's approach is that she hasn't lost her sense of wonder. And she seeks to help Haiti on Haiti's terms. She has made repeat trips to the country since the earthquake, launching a micro lending program to women in the camps. She gives an initial loan of $80 to $100, as she doesn't believe in giving handouts. She doesn't think handouts are good for self-esteem and she also believes they won't help people emerge from poverty. I admire her tenacity. I admit, I can't bring myself to ask people who have lost everything to sign a slip of paper telling me they will pay me back. I tend to give out cash as I go, which won't have the same measurable long-term effects as what Carole is accomplishing with her careful planning. To the women who are able to pay her back in six months, she issues a new loan. Already she has empowered several women, now on their third loans, who are supporting their families.

On the day of the earthquake anniversary, when she photographed Junior, Carole's backpack was filled with nail polish and other beauty supplies for a mother of two who had started a beauty salon in a tent camp located just across the street from the crumbled National Palace. The mother and her children hold a special place in Carole's heart. The oldest child, eight-year-old Rodeson, ran back into the family home immediately after the earthquake to rescue his younger sister, Anne. Both children survived, but little Rodeson's right foot was badly injured in the rescue operation and was amputated. A photograph of Rodeson and Anne from Carole's collection of PATCH cards tells their story. They radiate a pure joy in each other's presence. Little Rodeson's crutches are in the picture, but they are off to the side of his body, like wings.

If that is not enough, Carole is part of a unique effort to discover and preserve Haiti's caves, unique natural underworlds that retain traces of the island's pre-Columbian Taino culture, in hopes of renewing tourism to Haiti in a way that is both good for the economy and the environment. The Caves of Haiti project, of which she is a co-founder, has garnered support from UNESCO.

Before leaving Haiti, Carole and I met for a second time, when she photographed Junior one afternoon working on his art alongside fellow street artists. It was only then, as I watched Junior coloring in one of the sketch pads that I had brought for him from home, that I noticed how his drawings remain virtually unchanged from the childlike drawings he made for me as a young boy, and which I still cherish. Walking together afterwards, our conversation drifted to the topic of how best to help those we love in Haiti. Carole's eyes grew bright as she asked me, "Do you know the starfish story?"

"A little boy was walking on the beach, which was covered with starfish," she began. "He started picking them up, one by one, and tossed them back into the sea. An old man came by and sternly told the little boy to stop what he was doing. 'You can't throw them back into the sea. There are too many,' he said angrily. 'Yes,' said the little boy. 'But I can pick them up one at a time.'"

After returning home to Arizona, I contact the Atlantic City Police Department to find out if they have any record of a Carl Handel LaRoche. I learn that Carl was twice arrested for marijuana possession between April 1999 and September 2000. During that time frame, he was also held in contempt of court and violated the terms of New Jersey's Intensive Supervision Program, an alternative incarceration program to ease prison overcrowding. The department did not find a report of a pregnant girlfriend being pushed down a flight of stairs.

And I call Junior to find out if Jenny has survived. She is fine, Junior tells me. Jenny's family took her to a health clinic the same day I saw her. She was put on medication. She does not have cholera. Already, she is feeling better. Survival is a gift.

CHAPTER 22

New Beginning

July 2011

I smell the scent of roasting plantain as we are driving through the countryside on the way to Junior's hometown of Camp Perrin in Southern Haiti. We anticipate it will be a five-hour drive from the capital, and we've gotten an early start in hopes of averting the worst of rush-hour congestion that snarls all life into a mushroom cloud of pollution, dust, and grime on the outer ring of Port-au-Prince by 7:00 a.m. I am excited for this homecoming. Finally, I will get a chance to see the house where Junior was born and see with my own eyes the conditions that launched him on his flight as a child. Junior has told me that he has never stopped searching for his mother, praying to *Bondye* each time he finds himself at church to tell him what happened to her. I'm hoping our journey will reveal some new insight or glimmer of truth that can offer him healing.

Outside my window, thick groves of banana trees fill the landscape. This is exactly what I have been longing to see once again. The lush, emerald green fields and flashes of the sparkling

Caribbean Sea reveal themselves like a translucent watercolor painting, each color subtly blurring into the next. I see a group of children sitting in a circle under a shady mapou tree. A woman bathes in a nearby river. And rows of hand-woven straw hats neatly arranged alongside mounds of fresh mangoes line the roadside, beckoning travelers with the promise of nourishment and protection from the blistering sun. Tent camps also dot this landscape, together with traditional wooden A-frame village houses and cement structures that somehow withstood the force of nature during the earthquake. But there is a purity to life here missing from the alchemy of urban grit and abject poverty that tints most existence in the capital. Life seems simpler here. Rooted in tradition and living close to the land, Haitians seem closer to the ideal of their hard-won freedom. Junior leans forward from the backseat and signals the driver. "Something is burning. I think it's the engine." I look up and notice a plume of smoke coming from the front of the car. I am pulled from my reverie. Ahh. That was the scent I mistook for smoked banana. The visual color field had informed my senses.

A young man riding along the side of the road on a bicycle stops and together he, the driver, and Junior begin tinkering with the engine. An engine belt has burnt, which in turn has damaged the car battery. Junior soon delivers the dreaded assessment: We won't be able to make it to Camp Perrin. I am crushed, but I can see that Junior is accepting of the situation. In part, it's because he knows better than to force outcomes in Haiti, but I sense there is more to it than that. It's possible this return trip has more significance for me than for him. He has spoken reverentially of the beauty of his birthplace and he would have been a conscientious guide and host. But on a deeper level, I realize now that Junior already experienced his cathartic release when he traveled home to obtain his identity in preparation for Christopher's birth. In three trips back to Haiti since the earthquake, Junior has never expressed an agenda for our time together. He's open to what each day presents. I decide to follow his example. Standing under the shade of a banana tree, I stop to reflect on the situation. We are right at the entrance to the town of Grand Goave—midway between Leogane and Petit Goave. I think of how expectation and reality so often clash in Haiti and I can hear Toni Monnin repeating her wise mantra: That's Haiti!

I know the family of Britney Gengel, one of the American college students who died at the Hotel Montana, is starting an orphanage here in Grand Goave. Britney was the one who texted her parents thirty minutes before the earthquake to say she had just discovered her life's calling: to open an orphanage in Haiti. I've been inspired by her family's act of love. It would be completely understandable if they never wanted to set foot in Haiti again after their unbearable loss. And yet, they have committed to fulfilling her dream and are creating positive change in Haiti. The name they have chosen for the orphanage, "Be Like Brit," hints at their daughter's playful and can-do spirit. In the back of my mind, I've even wondered if Junior might somehow become involved with this orphanage, connecting him to his dream of helping homeless boys.

I have wanted to reach out to the Gengel family. I have felt a silent connection to Britney since I first learned of her story. She was studying journalism and was close to my age when I first arrived in Haiti. On her quest to make a difference here, she had stayed at the Montana, and she felt a deep connection to Haiti's children. Perhaps it was Britney reaching out to Junior and me today, inviting us to come by and have a little visit. I realize this is what we are supposed to do today. Within an hour, I am on the phone with Len Gengel, Britney's dad, in Massachusetts.

It all happens very naturally, in a way that feels meant to be. Junior and I make our way to a nearby relief operation asking for directions to "Be Like Brit." Lex Edmé, one of the main point people for the project, is there and Len Gengel happens to call him on his Blackberry while we are chatting. In no time, I am having a heartfelt conversation with Britney's dad. The points of connection are clear. Len answers one of the questions I have quietly wondered about: Why Grand Goave? The choice has offered one more point of resonance. This is the region of Haiti where I worked so closely when I was part of the human rights mission. "Brit and the Journey of Hope were supposed to go to Grand Goave the next day," Len tells me. "So we just wanted to find a way to help her continue her journey."

As I have been talking with Len, Britney's cousin Ross, who is on summer vacation from Florida, helping to oversee the construction of the orphanage, has arrived as if on cue. He offers to drive Junior and me up to the site where "Be Like Brit" is coming to life. We get halfway up the steep hillside and then ditch the car to walk the remaining stretch. Ross, twenty-four, is friendly and open-spirited. As I spoke with Len by phone, I watched as he became entangled in a group of children, gently cradling a boy as he practiced his new Creole words with the giggling crowd. Ross tells me the foundation for the orphanage was just poured on Saturday—in the shape of the letter "B" in memory of Britney. It's a beautiful, peaceful site on a hill overlooking the sea. Len said the family took care to choose a spot with the same gorgeous views that Britney would have enjoyed from the Montana.

I stand near the mango tree that will mark the entrance to the orphanage and look to Junior, wondering what this cosmic detour means to him. He looks to a little boy carrying an empty plastic bottle who has been following us up the hill. "He looks hungry," Junior says concerned. That is one of the dualities of life in the Haitian countryside. There is abundance and a lulling quality of life, but it has not been matched with economic opportunity. Hunger is a constant presence. I remember a human rights victim in Petit Goave who once told me how his family had survived for months solely on the multiple varieties of mangoes that flourished like free offerings from the trees. "They are just getting started," I tell Junior. "They will help many people here." I feel our being here is a reminder to focus on the "now" and to look to the future. When the orphanage opens, slated for the three-year anniversary of the earthquake, this home, built to seismic standards modeled after San Francisco, will provide shelter for thirty-three boys and thirty-three girls—a figure chosen to represent the number of days that Britney was missing at the Montana site. In many ways, the past few days of my trip have been about this same lesson: Be here now.

c———≻———o

When I first arrived on Saturday, Junior and I immediately set out to visit his new home. He took possession of the house on Father's Day weekend. But already he told me by phone that he wasn't yet living in the house full time. The news had caught me by surprise. For months, I had been working toward this goal and held onto the idea that getting him out of the tent camp and into a permanent home would be an instant panacea that would set his life in motion. Of course, life in Haiti is never so simple. What little

I could glean by phone from Arizona on a scratchy connection was that there had been a powerful aftershock that had especially rocked Petionville, sending people scurrying from the quarter's new prominent high rises. Shaken, he returned to his tent, which he had not yet fully vacated, after just a few nights in the house.

As we approach Monoquil, the same neighborhood where Junior's one-room home was crushed to the ground, I wonder what we will discover. In the sixteen months since I have made a concerted effort to make a meaningful difference in Junior's life following the earthquake, I have come to understand that figuring out how to help Junior is a metaphor for how to best help Haiti. Under the "old" model of international tutelage, aid is given in "in-kind" donations—high-paid foreign technocrats, 50-pound sacks of rice, water treatment kits, and plastic tarps—and direct financial aid is avoided at all costs. Under this model, I never would have given Junior money. Instead I would have found a way to pay the landlord directly for the US$1,200 six-month rent, as it would be the only way I could know with certainty if Junior had really used the funds for this purpose. But I trust Junior and I want him to learn the lesson of becoming an adult and owning his decisions. I wire transferred him two payments of US$600 via Western Union—separate from the stipends I have been sending him for living expenses and his education—knowing full well he might find other uses for the money. If he decided that he preferred to stay in his tent and hold on to the $1,200 as a nest egg, that was okay, too. I just wanted him to be honest with me.

As we approach the home I anticipate this will be the moment of truth. Junior's former one-room home was located deep in the maze-like labyrinth of this working class neighborhood. The house he is now showing me is just a short walk from the main road.

It appears suddenly and unexpectedly, wedged between two other buildings and a tree in a rather permit-free and haphazard way. But it has an inviting and uniquely Caribbean appearance. It's a two-story, pistachio green building with newly lacquered wooden doors. Junior leads me to the downstairs unit. It's a light-filled space with tile floors and amber-colored walls. There is a sitting room, a bedroom, and a modern kitchen and bathroom. It's a modest home but it has warmth and a cozy feel to it. And it is a world apart from the dank, dirt floor hovel with the imposing metal bars that Junior had presented to me on my last trip, when we agreed to continue looking for something more stable. I'm very pleased with his choice—I'm just not convinced it's really his home. The place is completely empty. There is not a single personal item I can trace back to Junior. Knowing how much he treasures his clothing collection, I expected to see his logo t-shirts and Puma tennis shoes hanging in the closet or tossed in a corner on the floor.

"Junior, there is nothing here. I don't understand," I say. It's more of a statement than a question. I don't expect to solve this riddle on the spot.

Junior had mentioned that the house had a sweeping view from the rooftop and that he looked forward to working on his painting and drawing from that vantage point. I ask if we can go upstairs. The view is indeed soothing, looking out to where his best friend and brother, Fritznel, lays buried and beyond to the sea. On a neighboring rooftop below, I watch as three young boys play a game of kickball. I can see how this space would make for a nice artistic retreat. I look around perplexed, wondering what to believe. That's when I spot a man lying on his belly, hard at work on the ledge of the roof. "That's the owner," Junior tells me. We go over to say hello. The owner has a warm and genuine presence.

He strikes me as a member of Haiti's elusive, true middle class, a narrow sliver of the populace that does not form part of the elite, but who have made it above working class through their ingenuity and determination. The owner tells me he owns one other building in Monoquil and he is proud that both withstood the earthquake. He tells me he is working hard to get the three units in this building move-in ready.

"So, the units are all empty?" I ask.

"No, two are already vacated," he tells me. "Junior's is all his, but he hasn't moved in yet."

There has been no wink-wink. I believe him—and Junior. But I am no less perplexed. Standing on the rooftop, I offer my best guess to Junior.

"Is it like a *zwazo* who has always been free and he is afraid to go back into the cage?" I ask.

"No, San. Not exactly," he says. The outer corner of his lips curve into a small smile and together we both laugh.

Next we head out to see Jenny. When I first asked Junior how she was doing after I arrived he had offered an unexpected response: "She is not there. They are on vacation."

"Vacation? Junior, refugees don't go on vacation." I said, chiding him. But I was also concerned. What could have happened to them?

Junior tells me that when he went this week to tell Jenny, her grandmother, and aunts that I was returning, he was surprised to see that all the tents had disappeared from the once crowded lot abutting the ravine.

"Remember the man with the infected leg that we helped last time? He is better now. He remembered me and told me that Jenny and her family had gone on vacation."

We know the family has a connection to the southern coastal town of Jacmel, the gem of a town in southern Haiti that is a center for arts and culture. Perhaps they have managed to leave and visit relatives there.

Beyond yearning to see Jenny again, I have another reason for wanting to visit the family. Each time I have seen them, I have swooped in and out so quickly. Now that I have a few more days, I want to ask them a simple question: What do you need and how can I help? If I can find a way to get two families out of tents, that will be what I can do to help Haiti right now.

Although Junior has told me that there are no more tents at the camp where Jenny has been living, I am not prepared for the violence of the landscape that awaits us. Plastic tarps and remnants of tents have been razed to the ground in a wasteland peppered with fragments of corrugated metal sheeting and random cinderblocks. Black soot stains the ground and pools of charcoal-colored water litter the open field. The ever-present scavenger pigs patrol the remnants of the human settlement, doing clean up duty. I am not fully comprehending what I am seeing. "Where are the people?" I ask Junior. A bystander hovering under a partially completed cement structure on the fringe of the field has stepped forward with a response. City workers from the Petionville City Hall arrived last week and tore down the tents. The camp dwellers that lived here were squatting on private land, and it was time for the field to revert to its former existence as a charcoal factory. I have just one thought. Where is Jenny? "She is there," the bystander says, pointing to the unfinished cement structure.

Junior and I walk toward the building, which appears to be a kind of silo for the swollen bags of homemade charcoal briquettes, which are both the country's primary fuel source and cause of its endemic deforestation. It's only at that moment that I notice the menacing looking men stationed on the steps leading up to the second floor. I don't feel safe crossing their path, and my heart aches at the thought that they have Jenny in their clutches.

This camp, from the moment Junior and I were first drawn into its hardship, has been the most hardened, the Pigalle of refugee camps. Now, it has moved deeper into the abyss, hurtling a five-year-old girl further into despair.

"There are people smoking," Junior says loudly and disapprovingly in Creole as we approach the steps. An acrid smell permeates the air and I hold my breath as Junior charges past the sullen men standing on the stairs. I realize it is not a good idea for us to become separated, but I don't see how to avoid it. I can't bear the thought of a child living in these conditions. I feel as if Jenny is trapped in a burning building and we have to get her out.

Finally, after what feels like every grain in an hourglass falling individually, one at a time, I see Jenny's bobbing head, framed in tiny corn-row braids, coming down the steps. But she is not the same exuberant child with the golden complexion and chubby cheeks that I recall from my first visit. Her face is expressionless and she appears numb. Junior and her adoptive mother, Josette, come down the steps behind her. I am working with a driver for the day and we walk briskly to find him on the street outside, eager to escape this underworld.

Once in the car, we decide our first course of action will be to get a hot meal somewhere for Jenny and Josette, where we can sit together and talk and try to find a solution to their predicament.

As we drive, I notice that Jenny does not retreat from her expressionless daze, and it occurs to me that she might have imbued some of the drugs that have been consumed in her presence.

We sit down to a lunch of grilled chicken, rice and beans, and fried plantain, but Jenny only half-heartedly picks at her food. I want so badly to reach out to her and help her to feel safe. Instinctively, I pull out a fresh notebook from my bag and I offer it to her with a green felt-tipped pen. I see the glimmerings of a spark of life as she begins to carefully concentrate on making a page of green circles.

Junior has been talking with Josette and slowly I am piecing together more of her story. As I listen in, I feel as if I am slipping even deeper into the quicksand. Josette is not Jenny's adoptive mother. She is, in fact, her biological mother. At the time of the earthquake, Josette, twenty-four, was squatting with her boyfriend in the Delmas region of the capital, and she became separated from Jenny and her grandmother. Jenny has been separated from her biological father for four years. He lives in the National Penitentiary, following his arrest on drug dealing charges—although Josette says he has never been brought before a judge. Following the earthquake, Jenny's dad did manage to escape from prison, but police came looking for him and he was soon locked up again. Jenny's grandmother and aunt are from her father's side of the family—and they hail from the cultural heartland of Jacmel. Josette was born in the southwestern town of Jeremie, one of the most isolated corners of the country. An uncle brought her to Port-au-Prince at the age of nine, after her father died and her mother could no longer protect her. She has not returned to her hometown or seen her mother and six siblings since. Before the earthquake, Josette sold carrots and onions to support herself and Jenny.

Following the earthquake, she began selling *clairin,* or moonshine. The dealer who supplies the clairin to a network of vendors—in what appears to be part pyramid scheme, part cooperative—is now her boyfriend. Josette is beholden to her dealer boyfriend, required to pay him 125 gourdes, the equivalent of US$3.10, each day. She earns the money by manning a small stand at the refugee-camp-turned-charcoal-factory, with Jenny and her mother-in-law at her side late into the night. I understand now why I have seen Jenny yawn so repeatedly during our lunch.

Junior has been watching Jenny draw her circles and he asks her now if she knows how to make flowers. He has a nurturing and spirited manner with children—it's the same way he greets my son, Alexander, when we talk by phone from Arizona—and Jenny lights up in response to his warmth. Soon he is teaching her to create beauty on the page, handing her the first tools to her survival.

Still, there is more difficult news to come. Josette tells me she had an infant son, Macken, fathered by her dealer boyfriend, who died recently at the age of eighteen months in the same camp where Jenny now languishes. Little Macken woke up sick one Sunday morning. He was dead by 4:00 p.m. that afternoon. Josette has no other way to explain the senseless death other than to ascribe it to mysticism, the unknowable. "A *loup garou,* a were-wolf ate him," she says simply.

After lunch, we set out to find a small motel or inn that can provide Jenny and Josette temporary shelter until we can find a new home. We pull up at the first hotel and Junior slips in to inquire about the price. As we sit in the car, I notice a man with flashy jewelry and an overly made-up escort stepping from the hotel. Junior steps back into the car and reports that the rate is

US$80 per day. "Is this a safe place for a child?" I ask Junior quizzically. He shakes his head. "All of these little hotels are going to be like this. It's safer than where they are now." We agree the price is too steep and continue on our quest. The next inn, located in the clogged streets surrounding the Petionville marché, yields no better results. We consider more options. "What about your house?" I ask Junior. He does not hesitate. "Sure, they can have it." He says this as if he is offering them a T-shirt or a spare blanket he has lying around. I am more confused than ever about why Junior is not living in his newly rented home. But we focus on the challenge at hand. There are logistical circumstances to consider. The house is completely barren—obviously better than the charcoal factory and its unsavory characters. But at the very least, we will have to figure out how to get some basic bedding.

Junior and I quietly confer about a deeper concern. We are worried the dealer boyfriend will become a permanent fixture in Junior's new home. It is starting to feel as if Jenny is buried below multiple layers of rubble, and we have to work quickly and creatively to bring her back to life.

The first shades of grey are filling the sky, and I know we will have to make a decision soon, before it grows dark. That's when I have my light bulb moment. I have two beds in my room at the Villa Creole. I think I have found the perfect solution. "Josette, you and Jenny will stay at my hotel tonight—until we can find a safe place for you to stay." I am stunned by her response. She wants to return to the charcoal factory, wants to get back to her boyfriend. "You can take Jenny," she says. I resist. Plead. I ask her to at least accompany us to the hotel to help make Jenny comfortable and give her a bath. Josette's eyes are distant. She's already gone. "San, let her go," Junior says. I can hear Haiti's enthralling voice goading me. "Now what? What are you going to do? Are you going to walk away—or will you cross the line?" She offers no easy choices.

I make a snap decision to bring Jenny back to my hotel. She looks so worn out, tired, and forlorn in her sooty clothes. And she has a deep hacking cough that concerns me. I can't imagine sending her back into the wasteland where we found her today. I just want her to have a good night's sleep. It would be her first night sleeping in a real bed in at least seventeen months since the earthquake. If she is anything like Alexander when he gets really tired, I imagine she will fall asleep as soon as her head touches the pillow.

Before heading to the Villa Creole we stop to buy some new clothes for Jenny. "I'll take you where I buy clothes for Christopher," Junior tells me. He directs the driver to a nearby cavernous outdoor market covered by plastic sheeting that specializes in brand new children's clothing. Jenny gently holds each of our hands as we weave through the vendors and find a stall that specializes in girls clothing. We pick out an assortment of dresses and pajamas for her. This marketplace is nearly hidden from street view, only visible to those who know it's there. Has it always been here, I wonder? It's located across the street from my old apartment, mere steps away from where I first met Junior. I take this as a sign that we are doing the right thing.

Once at the hotel, I get settled with Jenny on the cool yellow tile floor outside my room. We are surrounded by verdant green plants in the courtyard and birds are squawking in the dusk. I want her to feel comfortable, safe, and free—not cooped up in a room. I have pulled out some of the children's toys that I packed for Christopher and his cousin, Nahomie's daughter. We are coloring together in an oversized Curious George coloring book with jumbo-sized crayons. Jenny carefully colors Curious George in blue. Once our artwork is complete, she picks up the soft cloth Dora the Explorer doll that I have placed next to the crayons. "M' vle peny cheve'l," she says sweetly. *I want to brush her hair.* I locate a wide-toothed hairbrush from my toiletry bag and deliver it to her. Jenny sits on the cool tile, Dora in her lap, and repeatedly strokes the doll's hair, the peaceful quiet punctuated at moments by her deep hacking cough. The brushing motion is self-soothing and Jenny cradles the doll for a long time. Then, as if coming out of a dream state, she looks up and asks, "Eske ou pral benyn'm?" *Are you going to give me a bath?* When I told Junior that I had felt nervous about giving Jenny a bath he had admonished me. "San, you are a mother. You must take care of her." I remember those words now and go draw her a bath. Jenny wears a thick, dirty hooded sweatshirt and pants I had mistaken for leggings. Now I realize that this child, just shy of her fifth birthday, is wearing a pair of 2T toddler pants that are cutting off her circulation. It is one more affront to Jenny's wellbeing that chisels an impercep-tible stress line through my heart. Once the bath is a comfortable temperature, I wash her hands and feet and then I sit back and let Jenny frolic in the water. She splashes and giggles, just like a child. A few minutes later, I look up when I hear her exclaim: "Cheve sal." *Dirty hair.* A pool of murky soot fills the tub as she places her head under the faucet. The traces of life in a charcoal factory have permeated her hair and lungs.

Following her bath, Jenny slips into her new pajamas and settles on her bed with Dora. I turn on the television and find some cartoons, hoping it will help her fall asleep. The cartoons don't hold her interest. Instead, she gravitates to a stack of Junior's drawings that he has proudly dropped off to show me his progress. He's been working as an understudy with a group of local artists for the past six months, and his artistic development is vividly apparent. Jenny delights in the richly colored world of spirits, serpents, butterflies, and beings intertwined with birds that Junior has created. There are elements of good and evil seamlessly coexisting in Junior's images, but the overriding feeling of the work is a sense of joy at the mystery of life. It makes sense that Junior would create a universe that would intrinsically appeal to a child—and a young survivor.

By 8:00 p.m., my fantasy world has turned into a pumpkin. Jenny sits on the bed, tired and unable to fall asleep, crying for her mother. I feel terrible, conflicted, and afraid. I wonder how I will explain this child's presence in my custody—and I briefly wonder if I will end up in the National Penitentiary together with Jenny's father. I immediately call Junior, but he is charging his phone and a recorded message tells me the line is unavailable. Next I call the driver who worked with us today imploring him to please take Jenny "home." "What's wrong? She doesn't want to stay?" he asks. It's as if he has been expecting my call.

Jenny and I walk out to the front of the hotel. I have packed up her new clothes and toys in a sack, and she is happy and smiling knowing that she is on her way back to *manman*. We sit outside in the cool night air until the driver arrives. He is a father of two and he puts Jenny at ease with his gentle nature. She sits in the front seat with her belongings, happy at the thought of her impending reunion. I tell the driver I will wait outside until he comes back and confirms he has delivered Jenny to her mother. The operation takes less than thirty minutes. When he returns, the driver, who is himself homeless and living in a camp together with his wife and children ages nine and fourteen, shakes his head sadly and tells me that where Jenny is living " is no place for a child." He released Jenny to her mom and grandmother at their little *clairin* alcohol stand. "If you want my advice," he tells me, "get the family into a home and give the mom some money so she can start a new business."

The next morning, I awake to find my hands are inexplicably swollen and stiff. I can barely fold my hands. Did an insect bite my hands overnight, I wonder? I have never experienced this before. I stop to reflect on what could have triggered this flare-up. Perhaps this is the result of lugging the world's heaviest backpack through three airports. For his twenty-fifth birthday in May, Junior asked if I could bring him a good French-English dictionary. He has continued his language studies at a new institute and he is highly motivated. He has told me that there are people "smaller than me who ask me questions and I don't know the answers. They all have their own dictionaries. But they are very kind. They always share with me." To help him find the answers he is seeking, I packed a library of illustrated dictionaries, French-English textbooks, and a verb conjugation guide the size of a small phone book. The books had tipped my suitcase—already chockfull of art supplies and children's clothing and toys—over the weight limit, so I found myself cramming them into my stuffed backpack upon my departure. And like many travelers from the developed world, I have also packed some unwelcome baggage on my trip—workplace stress. I had about four hours of work from my editing job in Phoenix that I couldn't get to before leaving, and it has been hovering and hanging over me like an unwelcome guest. The backpack and the work angst have probably contributed to the leaden state of my hands. But I sense that the real trigger is the helplessness I feel knowing that Jenny is in such a dangerous and predatory environment—and I don't know how to help her. My hands are literally tied, or at least swollen tight.

Today is the day we had originally planned to go to Junior's hometown of Camp Perrin. Sunday would have been a great day for an excursion to the countryside. With almost no traffic, we would have avoided the rush-hour snarls and smog and we would have made excellent timing to the south, enjoying a leisurely drive through verdant pastures. But last night, when Jenny ended up in my care, I had called Pierre—the experienced guide, driver, and cameraman who had first helped me find Junior after the earthquake—to let him know I needed to cancel the trip to deal with the urgency at hand. Our initial plan had been to leave at 5:30 a.m. and to go first to Leogane where we would stay for Mass and meet with Pere Marat Guerand. More than a year has passed since I had sat with him on the recovered church pew next to his vanished temple and listened to his anguish. I am eager to learn if his situation and that of his community has improved since the earthquake.

Junior arrives at the hotel and we agree to make the best of the day and go to Leogane. Jenny has slipped from our grasp and we will need more time to devise a plan to try to help her. It's too late to make it out to Camp Perrin—and we probably won't even make it in time for Mass. But I'm hoping a trip to Leogane will help soothe my soul.

Pierre had said he would come by the hotel this morning just in case I still need to work with him. Junior and I find him sitting in his parked car when we arrive. It's 9:00 a.m. and the roads are clear. Driving into downtown we see families dressed in their

Sunday finery. There are bright colors, satins, freshly polished shoes, and little girls who look like they are on their way to a wedding.

As we approach the National Palace, I see that the Marassa Twins have not been able to intercede on my behalf. A bulldozer and three heavy hauling trucks are out front. Two of the three cupcake-shaped cupolas that once adorned the sugary, wedding cake–like architectural confection are now gone. I have the sensation of watching history disappear before my eyes. The dreamscapes posted here for the one-year anniversary of the earthquake have been removed. This is now a tear-down project. Junior and I are standing in front of the green palace gates, staring in silence. I am wondering if this is the last time I will see this broken beauty when a voice approaches from behind. "We call that Devil's House," the voice says in English. Junior and I turn around to find a man in his early thirties peddling scrolled art canvases. "I live right there," he says, pointing to the tent city directly in front of the palace. He introduces himself as Ronadin. He hails from the northern city of Gonaives, where Haiti's independence from France was first declared in 1804. Ronadin is part philosopher, part camp spokesman. "There are 2,800 of us who live there," he continues. "Young girls of just ten-years-old have to sell their bodies to eat. People are dying, au fur et à mesure," *in great measure.* "That's why we call this the Devil's House." Before the quake, Ronadin worked as a clerk in the government tax office where he was tasked with making identification cards. He lost his mother, father, and eight-year-old daughter, Sophia, in the earthquake. As he stumbles on this painful shard, his voice quivers. It's as if the memory of his lost daughter has awakened him to the oppression of young survivors in the camp. "Many of the girls who live there lost their mothers. Now they must prostitute themselves in order to survive."

As we continue on our way, Junior and I are engaged in an age-old habit. I am writing in my journal and he is drawing in a small sketchbook. He periodically passes me his book to show me a sketch. Following our chat with Ronadin, Junior has composed an image of spirit-like beings intertwined with snakes.

The drive to Leogane is comforting and familiar. I am looking out the window, watching scenes of a Sunday morning. I see a man in perfectly pressed magenta-colored pants and a silk magenta shirt with gleaming white loafers nimbly scale a gaping puddle and climb into the back cabin of a colorfully painted tap-tap.

At the coastal enclave of Mariani, I spot a vintage Mercedes Benz sedan evoking the retro seventies excesses of the Duvaliers and I am reminded of prodigal son Jean-Claude's return to Haiti. I am curious to hear Pierre's take on this quixotic turn of events.

"He came here a 'tonton.' He wanted to come home. He did not come to stir up trouble or enter politics," Pierre says. "Twenty-five years in exile, that is not a *jouet*," a plaything, he adds. It's a curious observation. The word tonton in this case refers to an elderly uncle, while at the same time recalling Haiti's most feared political death squads, the Tonton Macoutes militia initiated by his father, Francois "Papa Doc," Duvalier.

Pierre's perspective is oddly sympathetic given that the Duvalier family pillaged an estimated $300 million from state coffers and executed and tortured thousands of political opponents. And yet, his viewpoint is widely shared in Haiti. It can only be understood from the prism that Haitians have suffered so much from their politics that they have come to expect neglect—and fear persecution—from their leaders, and have no means to hold them accountable. And Jean-Claude, a.k.a "Baby Doc," is widely regarded as a dullard who was born into an outlandish and repressive neverland he didn't have the capacity to mastermind. History has also been kind to the Duvaliers: Most Haitians recall their rule as the last time the country had twenty-four-hour electricity and well-paved roads.

Another phantom also has emerged from the shadows.

"And what about Titid?" I ask, referring to Aristide by his nickname.

The question sparks impassioned discussion in the car. There is skepticism about his true motives, fears he has come to try to instigate a political comeback and that he will send the signal to armed street gangs and unleash political violence. Ultimately, there appears to be a collective shrugging of the shoulders in response to both Duvalier and Aristide's return. The earthquake shook the foundation of the Haitian state, destroying Devil's House and creating a space for two vermin to crawl out of their hiding places from France and South Africa. While both polarizing figures were away, it was like Haiti had a wound that could not scab. Now back on Haitian soil, both camps have a channel to enter the body politic, instead of remaining on the chimerical margins. Given a magic wand, it would be ideal to see both men put on the witness stand, if not to face criminal prosecution, at the very least to set the historical record and allow a collective dialogue, like South Africa's Truth and Reconciliation Commission.

"Tous les deux ont fait des crimes," Pierre says in French. *They both committed crimes.*

Arriving in Leogane, it appears as if the town has suffered from cancer or a plague. On my last visit, most of the historic structures were destroyed, but still standing. Now that much of the rubble has been cleared, Leogane looks like a cardboard village. We find a creative construct standing on the foundation of the St. Rose de Lima Catholic Church. Simple wooden posts are wrapped in plastic sheeting, providing a shelter for the original altar and mosaic tile floor. The A-frame temporary structure artfully evokes the region's buried past. Inside the sanctuary, the roof is branded with USAID plastic sheeting and paper cut-out birds strung from the altar offer words of strength. Force, intelligence, science, *sagesse, crainte de dieu, piété,* read the bellies of the messenger doves, offering a mix of science, fear of God, wisdom, and piety among their prescription for healing. This will be our message for the day. As anticipated, we have not arrived in time for the early-bird Mass. And Pere Marat Guerand has retreated to his family home in the crowded Port-au-Prince suburb of Carrefour for the remainder of the day. It will be a few days before I am able to return and join him in conversation. When I do, he tells me he is overwhelmed by the prospect of rebuilding his church, which he estimates will cost $800,000. With the Sunday collection basket yielding an average of $50 in donations, it will take him at least thirty-three years to start anew. "Everyone makes promises and sometimes they make liars out of me," Pere Guerand says dejectedly. Two months ago, a surprise visitor stepped out of a motorcade at his shambled parish. It was Jean-Claude Duvalier. It was as if the heavens had parted. Jean-Claude offered to personally finance the rebuilding of the church and to build 500 new homes for the victims of Leogane. Pere Guerand joyously shared the news with his congregation. "There have been many promises," he says, "but so far there are no fruits."

Back in Port-au-Prince, the city is electrified at the impending soccer match between Brazil and Venezuela that is part of the Copa America tournament. Brazil is Haiti's defacto national team—and Pierre and Junior remark on how if Haiti ever plays Brazil, Haitian fans are unyielding in their support of their iconic Brazilian sports heroes, cheering against the home team. Junior is eager to go and watch the game and I'm planning to spend the afternoon catching up on my editing work, which continues to shadow me. But my fingers remain swollen and my body feels crushed. Once at the hotel, I lay down to rest and I cannot fight off the feeling of inertia. Eventually, I make myself get up for dinner. Sitting outside in the half light by the pool, I give myself a serious talking to.

"What is wrong with you?" I ask.

The answer that comes back: Jenny.

Now I know for sure what is causing this lethargy and paralysis to invade my body. In my twenties, when I first arrived in Haiti, I was thrown into a complex situation and I didn't really know how to help Junior. Now as a mother, and presumably with greater life experience, I still don't have any deeper insights into how I can help Jenny. I feel as if I am up against so many forces: government, community, family, and the insidious cycle of alcohol addiction and drug dealing. The City Hall razed Jenny's camp to the ground; she's now living in a charcoal factory populated by hardened drug dealers; her mother is beholden to a moonshine dealer; and her father has been jailed for years on drug charges. It's not like I can show up at a child protection office and ask to speak with a case worker, at least not as far as I'm aware. And I know of no nongovernmental organization that offers direct assistance to victims—earthquake or otherwise. I sit quietly at dinner wondering who I can turn to for help, sorting through the alphabet soup of NGOs in my mind. One suddenly rises to the surface. The name says it all. Save the Children. I have my laptop with me and I go straight to their website. Their country page is plain-spoken and to the point:

"Still reeling from the devastating earthquake of January 2010, Haiti is a dangerous place for children. With 500,000 children living in camps and many others living in slums, all lacking the protection of social and police services, children are under continued threat of exploitation and abuse."

I feel an instant connection and sense of hope. I go next to a description of the organization's values, and the principal of "creativity" immediately waves at me from the screen. "We are open to new ideas, embrace change, and take disciplined risks to develop sustainable solutions for and with children." Disciplined risks. That's what I undertook when Jenny's mom walked away and left a sick and tired quake survivor in my care. If anyone will understand what Jenny is facing, I believe it is this organization.

Today is July 4th and it's been hard being away from home on a holiday. The sadness I've been feeling over Jenny is fueling my homesickness, and I especially miss Alexander today, wishing I could hold him during the nighttime firework display. When I called home earlier he told me in his exuberant voice: "Mommy, I woke up from my nap and I cried for you." I know he needs me and I can't wait to get home to him. Coming back to Haiti three times since the earthquake has been hard on him. And yet I know it has enriched him as well. Alexander is aware of this bright and colorful place called Haiti. He has learned a few words in Creole. And most important, he feels a genuine connection to Junior and Christopher and he has a growing curiosity for the world. I have asked Tom to send me some photos from their outing tonight. I expect to find images in my e-mail inbox, but instead, Tom has sent a picture in words:

> *So, we rode the bike to the Hyatt, wheeled right past the security posted on the driveway and ended up with a front row seat in their garden for the fireworks. I bought Alexander a glow-in-the-dark necklace and he danced on the lawn with a little friend. We rode home along the dark path with heat lightning in the sky. Got home and he was asleep in 10 minutes . . . I forgot to mention that our storm the other day blew both umbrellas and the chaise into the pool. Pretty wild.*
> *Ok. It's late. Talk tomorrow.*
>
> *love, t*

The next morning, Junior and I set out for the "Save the Children" office. I don't recall ever seeing it before, but Junior says he knows where it's located and together he and the driver negotiate the address. When the car starts driving up the hill toward the Hotel Montana, I register an inquisitive look. This is the way, Junior assures me. The hotel appears to be open, and I suggest a quick detour on our way. The devastation was so staggering on my last visit, it's hard to believe it has re-opened for business. When we reach the summit, Junior and I get out of the car and survey the surroundings. Gone is the mountain of neatly compressed rubble and the buildings scattered helter-skelter in a path of capricious annihilation. The new hotel is being carved in the low-lying "anti-seismic" architectural style cropping up from the ruins around the country. The revamped outdoor restaurant—which has a free-flowing, gauzy, St. Tropez meets Miami vibe, with outdoor sculptures, pendant lights, and a retractable tented sail ceiling—is the new hub of energy and activity. Even as construction crews hammer away, hard at work on a new conference center and additional rooms, the Montana has risen from the ashes with the most sophisticated modern design of any hotel in Haiti's capital. There are some familiar echoes, as well. The 300-year-old mahogany tree continues to stand sentry at the entrance to the hotel and I recognize recovered furniture from the former lobby. The sight of the carved wooden lounge chairs with the brightly colored pillows at first takes my breath away. Did some of those who lost their lives here spend their final resting moments in these seats? And then my perspective shifts. I see the carved wooden pieces as relics honoring the presence of everyone who passed through here before; all of us who came here to make a difference. In the swimming pool, a woman is doing laps and a middle-aged man wearing glasses reads a report on a lounge chair. Haiti's humanitarian soldiers continue to report for duty—and enjoy a refreshing dip in the clarifying water.

Arriving at the office of Save the Children, I brace myself to be turned away. I don't have an appointment, and I'm not even sure how to characterize the reason for my visit. Luckily, an astute Haitian program officer overhears me as I try to make my case and offers to find an appropriate counterpart who can help me. Ultimately, I plead my case to three staffers, including an American who oversees the child protection team. All listen carefully. They study my photos of Jenny "before" and "after." And most important, I can see the compassion and concern in their eyes. A Haitian staff member on the protection team sits down with me to review options. He explains that all interventions regarding child safety are channeled through the Ministry of Social Affairs. He shares three precise contacts at the ministry, complete with ranking and cell-phone number, and he sends me with laser-like precision on my way.

The scene at the ministry's satellite office tasked with child protection is like one of the nine circles of suffering in Dante's Inferno. Parents carrying malnourished and bandaged children are snaked outside in long lines that don't appear to be attended by anyone. Junior and I step into an office to find a civil servant at his desk, a floor fan dousing him with a cool breeze, as he casually sits reading a book. He looks up from his text in disdain, perturbed by the interruption, and vaguely points us to another wing of the building. In the next room, we encounter a woman who walks with a limp. She appears to be the hardest working person in the ministry. She is on her cell phone, taking down an account of a young girl who was just raped in her hospital bed. Finally, we make it to a small office at the back of the building. Here we find the contact whom I've been told offers our best hope of getting Jenny out of the inferno. The official, in his mid-thirties, is attentive and well-spoken. He listens carefully to my account. He explains that the first order of business will be to dispatch a team to conduct an assessment of Jenny's situation. If the team deems she is in life-threatening danger, they will take custody of her on the spot—but the government policy is to avoid family separations. We agree that removing Jenny from her mother's care would be too traumatic for her. I know I have managed to get this official's attention for a finite moment, and the demands and pressures facing his office are overwhelming. And yet, I feel an uneasy sense of relief that I have cast a low-watt spotlight on Jenny's plight, and I have made the government aware of her precarious existence. "I can't promise I will be able to find her a new home, but I will send a team tomorrow morning," the official says. "At the very least, we will be able to provide her medical care and counseling." He asks me to e-mail him a full report with all the information. I do—but I won't hear back.

Although I'm hopeful some form of help is on the way to Jenny, I don't want to delay getting her treatment for her deep, hacking cough. Junior and I return to the refugee camp turned charcoal factory to find Jenny and her mother, although this time I wait behind in the car. I tell myself I don't want to stir up too much attention in the camp—attention that can turn into jealousy and create resentment against Jenny. But I'm also afraid. The people we saw there were so hardened and the camp's location is so isolated, tucked down an alley off the main street, that I fear I would be doomed if a scuffle broke out. Junior returns to the car with just Jenny. Where is Josette? I ask confused. "She was smoking," Junior says, widening his eyes to convey disapproval. I can tell he doesn't want to alarm Jenny. This is not ideal.

I don't want to end up in the same situation as last time, but we focus on the task at hand: Jenny needs to see a doctor.

We take her to the office of an established Petionville pediatrician. But we soon run into trouble when we can hardly answer any of the receptionist's questions for a basic medical file. Date of birth? Mother's maiden name? Home address? I stay with Jenny in the waiting room while Junior hops back in the car with the driver to go make a plea to Josette to come join us. Eventually they return. Josette, eyes glazed over, fills in the receptionist on the needed personal information. She and I both accompany Jenny into the exam room. Jenny happily eyes the photos of children assembled on the wall in a large collage of the doctor's past patients. The children in the photos offer a glimpse into another world: They are well-cared for, playing happily, dressed up for special occasions, and held in the loving embrace of their parent's arms. The doctor diagnoses Jenny with asthma, which he ascribes to her living conditions. We buy Jenny's medications and go have one last meal together. Then we take Jenny and Josette back to the camp. I am returning to Arizona in a couple of days and I have accepted that I will not be able to transform Jenny's situation right away. Junior will be following up to see if the government intervenes on her behalf. If it does not, he will begin searching for a small home for Jenny and Josette near his own new home. But for now, I will have to release Jenny back to the dreaded den of drugs and soot. I can think of nothing else I can do for her right now except to walk upstairs with her to face the reality of her conditions and stand there with her in the fire.

⚬━━◆━━⚬

Today was the day of our attempted outing to Camp Perrin. After the car broke down, the driver managed to improvise a repair, but we couldn't use the air-conditioning on the return trip, and we were seared by the intense heat and doused with dust and pollution as we re-entered the perimeter of the capital. The circuitous journey left Junior and I both reeling and in need of some time to recover. He returned to his tent to work on his painting and I wrote in my journal back at the hotel. Now, as the late afternoon sun begins to drop, we have one more very important mission to accomplish before I return home tomorrow. We need to visit Christopher.

We ascend the now familiar path up to Fanfan's family cave in the Stenyo Vincent neighborhood of cinder-block homes stacked high into the hillside above Petionville. Stepping into the dimly lit dwelling, I sense the lingering tension between Junior and his former in-laws. Fanfan's mother, her hair swept up in a bright red satin scarf indicating she may be inviting the presence of the spirit Erzulie Danto—embodied as a fierce and hard-working country woman described as a "single mother with a knife," vigilantly protecting her supplicants and her children—rebukes Junior for not coming to visit Christopher. Junior has told me it has been a few weeks since he has visited Christopher, but I can tell from his expression now that it has been longer. He's hardly seen his son in three months.

I am shocked and saddened by this revelation, but I do my best not to intervene. Later, Junior will confide that Christopher's custody situation makes him feel powerless, like he has no rights. During these past few months, as he has flourished in a linguistic and artistic renaissance, he has avoided the stressful confrontations with Fanfan's family—and he has avoided Christopher in the process. Now, he again regresses into a defensive and combative demeanor. Both Nahomie and Fanfan have emerged from the shadows and I hear Junior shout, "You need to respect me." I do my best to distract Christopher, who looks like one of the little spirit beings from Junior's drawings, albeit with a confused expression etched on his face. Removing two Matchbox cars from a bag with provisions I have brought, I show Christopher how the small cars roll on the hard-packed dirt floor. Despite the tensions, I am glad to see both sisters on my impromptu visit. They greet me warmly and I also share some gifts with them. I have brought a printed fabric headband for Fanfan, a nod to her aspiration of becoming a hairdresser, and for Nahomie I have an embossed card set stamped with the words "Thank-you."

Junior and I return to the Villa Creole to have dinner and to sit and talk. Unlike the heated exchange following our visit to

Nahomie's house on my last visit, this time Junior listens openly. I explain that we don't necessarily *"renmen,"* or like everyone around Jenny—but we try to understand them. And we don't let those feelings stop us from seeing Jenny because we know she needs our protection. "It's the same thing with Christopher," I say. I can tell he gets it.

"True respect can only come from you, Junior," I continue. "Once you respect yourself, others will respect you, too. That will come from working to your full potential and connecting it to the world around you."

Next, I ask Junior to help take me on a visual journey to his hometown. "What would I have seen today in Camp Perrin?" I ask. He begins by describing the trees. The first thing I would notice, he tells me, would be the coconut, coffee, banana, and mango trees. Then he would take me to see the house where he was born. "My aunt Marise is still there. You would have seen her, too," Junior tells me. I'm bowled over by this information. It hadn't occurred to me that the oppressor who tortured Junior as a child, launching him on his flight, might still remain in his hometown. I thought she now lived in Canada with most of Junior's blood relatives. "She's still there," Junior assures me. "But she can no longer talk. She's in her eighties now. Still, her daughter would have told you some things."

I am suddenly filled with self-doubt, wondering if we might have missed the intended meaning of our outing. "I'm so sorry, Junior," I say, full of chagrin. "You know we would have made it to Camp Perrin if it hadn't been for Jenny."

The clarity and maturity of Junior's response startles me.

"If you abandon a person who is living in conditions that are not human, it is as if you abandon 'tèt pa'ou,' *your own head,*" he says. "We were right to stay and help take care of Jenny."

Junior demonstrates a powerful protective instinct toward Jenny that fills me with happiness. "You made an effort for me that no one had ever done before. And nobody told you to do it. You gave me hope," he says. "I will do this now for Jenny."

I have my laptop at the table and I have shown Junior the website for the Be Like Brit orphanage. Together we look at the images of Britney during her final days in Haiti. Surrounded by Haiti's children, she looked radiant and alive. "We found what we were looking for today, San," Junior says.

Still, I am curious to know what Junior has come to understand about his mother and the mystery of her disappearance and painful absence from his life. I ask him about that now.

"My mother didn't really die. I just can't see her. No one has ever really given me an idea of what happened. I just have to live. All of that is destin, *destiny*. I just give *Bondye* thanks that I am alive. Even if I don't see her, life continues. I have forgiven my mother because she made me."

I had wanted to help Junior continue his heroes journey. Like Gilgamesh, the oldest story in the world, which unfolds in a landscape of dream, Junior's story is also about a man's quest to become fully human and free. Like Gilgamesh, Junior has learned to rule himself, guided by wisdom, temperance, and grace. Embedded in the story is a powerful bond of friendship and recognition about the duality of life. The clay tablets on which the story was originally inscribed in cuneiform characters lay buried in rubble for over 2,000 years until the first fragments were recovered amid ruins in what is now Mosul, Iraq in 1850. Mankind's oldest story—an art form older than both Homer and the Bible—emerged from rubble.

I know it is really not a coincidence that Junior and I crossed paths. My life has been quite different from his—and yet we share a certain life experience. My family tree has some branches gnarled by the disease of mental illness and at times when I was growing up, I feared that a close loved one might harm me. Junior had lived with this fear as well. It's what sent him running and onto the street at the age of five. I know now that Junior never needed me to "save" him. He has done that beautifully on his own—and he continues to. He and Haiti have taught me so much about love and survival.

I turn my attention next to the riddle of why Junior is not yet living in his new house. It comes down to this: Fear. Junior is a survivor. The recent aftershock that registered 4.7 on the Richter scale jolted Junior back to the day of the earthquake. In his quest to find a new home, he had hoped to find a wood house—as those structures overwhelmingly survived the earthquake. But he accidently mistook the price for the only wood house he found. It turned out to be a villa priced at US$1,200 a month—versus his US$1,200 for six months.

There is a secondary reason as well, an element of Haitian formality at play.

Like a newlywed embarking on a new life, Junior the home-dweller senses that his life needs to be substantively different. He doesn't want to live in a home in the same manner as if it were a tent. It's important to get the nuances just right. He tells me he still needs to get "a bed, table with chairs, and flat screen TV." And he knows these things will take a bit more time.

For our goodbye, Junior has brought some parting gifts of painted rubble—a new medium he is keenly perfecting. He removes three pieces from his backpack: one depicts an earthquake, another a bird, and the third a human face.

"Please remember to give the one with the bird to Alexander," he tells me. "It will make him happy. And it will make him curious.

He will see that there is always life. When you see a bird, it is a reminder that there is always life."

I can see that Junior is coming into his own as an artist. He is motivated and full of purpose. Out of this growth, a new healthy self-confidence and a calmness is emerging, rooted in working to his full potential and seeing hope for his future.

Junior hands me the triangular-shaped piece of rubble with the human face painted on it. It's a compelling piece. "This is for Paige," he tells me. "She did not forget me, and I will never forget her." And then he breaks out into a laugh. "Oh-oh, Elio is going to get jealous! I didn't have time to make one for him. Elio is the best. He used to always help me pay for my schooling, even though he always thought I used the money for something else," he says chuckling. "And Javier. Javier helped me so much. If someone helps you, you don't need to hide it. But I don't want people to always have to give me things. I want to make my life, too."

"Thanks, San, for finding such a unique way to help me," he adds. I know that one of the reasons he is working so hard to learn English is that he wants to read these pages.

At the airport the next morning, I realize there is something I still need to say. I apologize. During the last few days we went back to my old apartment. I wanted to get a close look at the space underneath the stairwell. It is now fenced, giving it the appearance of a cage, and it was strewn with garbage. Junior was good-natured about it and made a joke about coming back to his "home." The old guardian was there and together they posed for some photos, smiling. But inside, I felt broken. I could not imagine Alexander ever sleeping in such conditions. I felt sadness and I felt remorse.

"M'konnai, San," *I understand,* Junior tells me simply.

Junior hops back into the car. Inspired. He is on his way to pick up Christopher and Jenny to take them back to his house. He is excited to give them their first art lessons. "I need to do this today because I have classes all weekend," he says.

Inside the terminal, I watch closely to make sure the immigration official puts the stamp in my passport. And that's when I see the date. July 6. I remember that it's Marcelo's birthday. I quickly do the math and realize it would be his forty-first birthday. We first met at passport control at this airport. I know that Marcelo is here with me—he has joined me on this journey.

Going through the X-ray machine, my backpack gets pulled aside for extra scrutiny. I am sure it is the laptop I forget to take out. But the security screener reaches deep into my bag and pulls out something else. It is the piece of rubble with the bird painted on it, the symbol Junior has chosen to convey to Alexander about the continuity of life. He examines it carefully, as if he might be holding a piece of rare patrimony of mysterious origin in his hands. And then he leans in closely and asks earnestly, "Are you an archeologist?"

It's an intriguing question, poetically summing up what I have been doing since the earthquake jolted me awake, excavating memory and engaging in time travel in search for meaning and fleeting beauty. The airport screener is holding a fallen piece of UN headquarters, one of the shards the Indian peacekeepers invited Junior to collect on the day of the earthquake anniversary, now transformed into a catalyst of self-transformation.

"No," I say, by way of a smile. "It's art."

ACKNOWLEDGMENTS

I believe that, through the act of living,
the discovery of one-self is made concurrently
with the discovery of the world around us . . .
—HENRI CARTIER-BRESSON

I want to thank everyone who joined me on this path of discovery. I am grateful to all those named in this book, and I am very mindful that some people never planned to step into my story. I have tried to be judicious, never revealing more than needed to be told and never holding back in the service of emotional honesty.

I have tried to take that same approach in writing about Haiti and her people, looking beyond the accepted narrative of violence, chaos, misery, and tragedy—and instead looking deeply into Haiti's mirror image to source our common humanity.

I am forever grateful to my colleagues from the International Civilian Mission in Haiti (MICIVIH), a true family that lives on despite the boundaries of time and place. With love and appreciation to Elio Tamburi, Ettore Di Benedetto, Farah Brelvi, Paige Jennings, Paula Hacopian, and Vivian Brates—and to Wendy Cue, for the shared books and conversations that have inspired and sustained me. To Colin Granderson, with respect and admiration, for guiding us so ably with such integrity and warmth.

I thank Dr. Marco Percque for trusting me with his story and for revealing the true grace that comes from survival.

My deep appreciation to Alice Martell, without whose wisdom and belief this book would not have been published, and to Lara Asher, who provided a safe place where my story could come to life, and in the process became my dear friend.

In many ways, the writing of this story has been a search for family. My family includes my longtime friends Richard Toscano and Mark Jerusalem, whom I thank for their intuitive presence and pure acceptance. I am grateful to my cousin Mercelena Vasquez for her embrace of literature and deep compassion, and I am guided by the love and brio of my uncle, Enrique Vasquez, and my aunt, Inès Marquez. I thank my parents, Juan and Luz Elena Marquez, for the gifts of language and travel and for always giving from their hearts. I am grateful to my brother, Santiago, for sharing his innate curiosity for history and culture. To my sisters, Maria and Christina, I offer love.

And I thank Tom, for our spirited son, and for asking the question that gave shape to my quest and for making me laugh, always.

Sandra Marquez Stathis has worked as a staff writer for *People* magazine, *The Miami Herald,* the Associated Press, and as a correspondent for Reuters. She lived in Haiti for four years as a human rights observer and press officer for a United Nations mission. She lives in Scottsdale, Arizona.